FREEMASONS

FREEMASONS

A History and Exploration of the World's Oldest Secret Society

H. PAUL JEFFERS

CITADEL PRESS
Kensington Publishing Corp.
www.kensingtonbooks.com

CITADEL PRESS BOOKS are published by

Kensington Publishing Corp.
850 Third Avenue
New York, NY 10022

All Kensington titles, imprints, and distributed lines are available at special
quantity discounts for bulk purchases for sales promotions, premiums, fund-
raising, educational, or institutional use. Special book excerpts or customized
printings can also be created to fit specific needs. For details, write or phone the
office of the Kensington special sales manager: Kensington Publishing Corp.,
850 Third Avenue, New York, NY 10022, attn: Special Sales Department; phone
1-800-221-2647.

First printing: March 2005

20 19 18

Printed in the United States of America

Library of Congress Control Number: 2004113764

ISBN 0-8065-2662-9

For Hy Turner

Contents

Introduction: The Mysterious Masons

THE PURPOSE OF THIS BOOK IS TO EXAMINE FREEMASONRY by exploring its complex and often controversial history, delving into its rituals and rites, and drawing back a shroud of mystery and suspicion that has enveloped it for centuries. In the interest of full disclosure, I'm not and never have been a Freemason. Because I meet basic rules for membership, I could have been. I believe in God, I'm over the age of twenty-one, and I have no criminal record. I am not among the Freemasonic fellowship, or other groups, such as Kiwanis, Rotary, Odd Fellows, Elks, and so on, for two reasons. I've not been invited to join, and, except for professional societies, a few labor unions in which membership was a condition of employment, and a peculiar group dedicated to keeping green the memory and the spirit of Sherlock Holmes, known as the Baker Street Irregulars, I've never been a joiner. Consequently, when I was asked if I would be interested in writing a book on the Masons, I knew almost nothing about them. I was aware of "Shriners" wearing quaint, colorful outfits consisting of flowing capes and a tasseled cap called a fez as they march in the annual Tournament of Roses and other parades, that the motion picture Academy Awards are handed out at the Shrine Auditorium in Los Angeles, and that the Shriners run several hospitals for children. I've passed by the Masonic lodge in my hometown and others in cities in the United States and elsewhere. I've known men who wore Masonic rings and other emblems that seemed to me to be no more significant than the class rings adorning high school and college graduates and the pins on sweaters of members of college fraternities.

Deciding to launch a quick exploration of the subject before committing myself to the project, I learned that Freemasonry is an international fraternity, although some lodges admit women. Membership is open to adults who believe in a Supreme Divine Being and immortality of the soul. While Freemasonry does not claim to be a religion, its beliefs have been heavily influenced by eighteenth- and nineteenth-century Universalism and Deism. Its critics find in it influences of occultism, anti-Christianity, and even Satanism. While its members must swear a belief in a Divine Being, Masonry is open to people of all religions and races. Although Freemasonry is found all over the world, it is not a monolithic organization with a central authority figure, such as the Catholic Church's papacy, an "international president" or "secretary-general," board of directors, or other overarching global authority. The governing body in a country is called the Grand Lodge. In the United States, there is one for each state in which Masonry exists

The oldest secret society in the world, Freemasons engage in rituals and rites that are said to date to the building of Solomon's Temple and the murder of its chief architect, Hiram Abiff. Common ancient tools used in construction that are employed in Masonic ceremonies—trowel, plumb, level, and compass—have symbolic meanings that are related to developing morality and the advancement of the members to the understanding of "Universal Light." Although Freemasons engage in secrecy regarding these rituals, they dispute a popular belief that Masonry is a sinister organization. They also dismiss allegations of a Masonic conspiracy to control the United States and the world. Masons answer that they are simply idealists who have banded together to study and celebrate common moral beliefs and individual improvement.

What is not in dispute is an astonishing number of significant individuals throughout the history of Europe and the United States in all fields of human endeavor who were Freemasons, from kings, presidents, and politicians to tycoons of industry, writers, composers, educators, generals, doctors, journalists, and other cultural, social, and civic leaders. The provocative question that has persisted since the rise of Freemasonry is whether these men were engaged in a conspiracy to impose the tenets of Freemasonry in a "new world order." Some critics have gone so far as to allege that Freemasons already run everything.

The origins of the fraternity are debated by Masons themselves. Some accounts trace it back to the building of Solomon's Temple and even earlier to Greece and Egypt. What is known is that in 1717 several Masons met in London to form the first United Grand Lodge of England as a governing force over groups of stonemasons in Britain. As the British Empire extended into the American colonies, Freemasonry followed. Many of the founding fathers were Masons. Some students of Freemasonry contend that it was at the heart of the American Revolution and that it became the cornerstone of the U.S. government. Since George Washington, numerous presidents have belonged, as well as members of Congress and other government officials. Although the U.S. Treasury Department denies that the one-dollar note contains Masonic symbols, and some historians dispute that the plan for Washington, D.C., was laid out according to Masonic beliefs, there is a great deal of compelling evidence to bolster belief in a Masonic link.

That Freemasonry is shrouded in closely held rites and rituals, including an oath of secrecy taken by its members, has created a mystique and a widely held belief that Masons are a group with sinister objectives and that they are anti-Christians. This belief has resulted in an opposition to Freemasonry by the Roman Catholic Church, which bans the faithful from joining.

Masons counter a belief that it is the prototype of antidemocratic secret societies by noting that there is no overall veil of secrecy. One Masonic group states, quite correctly, that the degree of secrecy varies widely around the world. It notes, "In English-speaking countries, most Masons are completely public with their affiliation, Masonic buildings are clearly marked, and meeting times are generally a matter of public record."

While this is true, central aspects of Freemasonry *are* kept hidden. Meetings are closed to the public. Members are sworn to silence on what goes on and why. They also have a system of signs of recognition, including a secret handshake. Because of this, Masons have been suspected of showing favoritism to other Masons, as in France recently, when the chief prosecutor accused some judges and lawyers of stalling cases involving Masons. In the 1990s in Great Britain, the Labour Party government tried to enact a law requiring all public officials who were Masons to make their affiliation public.

In this examination of the history of Freemasonry, these and other aspects of the group will be explored, including organization of Masonic lodges, rites and rituals, symbolism, the role of women, black Masons (Prince Hall Masonry), Masonic literature, membership requirements, how one joins, involvement of Freemasons in social and charitable causes, and Masonic terms that have made their way into everyday language, such as "hoodwink" and someone being "on the square." Other topics include the role of Freemasonry in the Crusades, an exploration of the hostility to Freemasonry by the Roman Catholic Church, links to Mormonism, the possible role of Freemasonry in the death of Wolfgang Amadeus Mozart, a controversial theory that Freemasons were connected to history's first serial killer (Jack the Ripper), and a nineteenth-century mysterious disappearance and murder of a critic of Masonry that resulted in the formation of America's first "third party."

Although Freemasonry has been vehemently opposed and feared as a sinister conspiracy, it has been vigorously defended as essentially a religiously rooted philosophic system expressed in dramatic ceremonies intended to answer the questions posed by every thoughtful human: Who am I? Why am I here? What's the purpose of life? According to one of Freemasonry's eminent historians, W. L. Wilmshurst, it "supplies a need to those who are earnestly enquiring into the purpose and destiny of human life."

With symbolism "its soul," Freemasonry has been described as a means by which all "good men" can unite to cultivate "freedom, friendship, and character." Recognizing that other groups exist for these purposes, Wilmshurst notes in his book *The Meaning of Masonry*, "It is absurd to think that a vast organization like Masonry was ordained merely to teach grown-up men of the world the symbolic meaning of a few simple builders' tools" or to teach its members elementary virtues of temperance, justice, brotherly love, charity, and morality that can be found in the "fountain of truth and instruction" of the Bible.

Because participants in "the Craft," as Freemasons call it, assert that it has some larger end in view than merely inculcating the practice of common social values, this book explores not only Freemasonry's origins and development, its numerous controversies, suspicions as to its intent, rituals, rites, symbols, and signs, but also its religious and philosophical influence throughout the rise of Western civilization and the extent of its influence today.

FREEMASONS

CHAPTER 1

CORNERSTONES

I
F THE STORY OF A MURDER COMMITTED 3,000 YEARS AGO IN Jerusalem that represents one of the cornerstones of Freemasonry ritual is true, the victim was no ordinary man.

The tale begins in the first verse of the third chapter of Second Chronicles in the Holy Bible. It records that the building of "the house of the Lord," on the order of King Solomon at Jerusalem, in Mount Moriah, commenced on the second day of the second month in the fourth year of his reign. To construct the temple, Solomon assembled "three score and ten thousand men to bear burdens, and fourscore thousand to hew the mountain, and three thousand and six hundred to oversee them." Needing a master artisan to properly adorn the holy edifice, he asked his friend, the king of Tyre, to lend him the services of a man "cunning to work in gold, and in silver, and in brass, and in iron, and in purple, and crimson, and that can skill to grave with the cunning men that are with me."

The king despatched Hiram. To this "cunning man, endued with understanding," in all of the artistic fields that Solomon had requested, as well as "in stone," tradition has added the name "Abiff." Although little more is noted about him in the Bible beyond recording that he worked with precious metals and made most of the gold and silver adornments of the temple, including a pair of columns named Jachin and Boaz, it is assumed that he was placed in command of all aspects of temple construction along specifications revealed to Solomon by God. According to first-century historian Flavius Josephus, in *Antiquities of the Jews*, the foundations of the temple were set "very deep" in the ground. They were "very strong stones," said Josephus, that would "unite themselves with the earth" and be "a basis and a sure foundation" for the superstructure that was to be erected over it that would "resist the force of time."

As the supervising figure with authority for assigning jobs to achieve this perfection in cutting and fitting enormous stones, Hiram would have also decided when a man was qualified to learn certain "mysteries" necessary for elevation to more challenging tasks in a workforce that was divided into three ranks: apprentice, fellow craftsman, and grand master.

According to Freemasonry tradition, as the temple neared completion there were fifteen fellow craftsmen who conspired to coerce Hiram into promoting them by threatening to pass for grand masters in other countries to earn higher wages. While twelve of these men eventually abandoned the scheme, Jubela, Jubelo, and Jubelum were determined to go ahead. Knowing that it was Hiram's custom to enter the temple's sanctum sanctorum to pray at noon each day, they placed themselves at the three entrances (west, south, and east) and waited. As Hiram left through the east door, Jubela demanded to be named master. Hiram replied that he could not receive the "mysteries" without the approval of Solomon and the king of Tyre.

Infuriated at being told to wait, Jubela slashed Hiram's throat with a twenty-four-inch measuring gauge. As Hiram tried to escape through the south door, he was attacked by Jubelo with a blow to the chest with an architect's square. Reeling to the west door, he was slammed on the head by Jubelum wielding a common gavel or setting maul that killed him. The three then carried his body through the west door and hid it in a heap of rubbish. Returning at midnight, they dug a grave that measured six feet east, six feet west, and six feet deep. With Hiram buried, they fled from Jerusalem for the town of Joppa on the coast of the Mediterranean Sea. The next day, King Solomon noticed Hiram's absence and began an inquiry. When the twelve craftsmen who had backed out of the plan went to see Solomon to inform him of the plot and incriminate Jubela, Jubelo, and Jubelum, they appeared before the king wearing white aprons and gloves as tokens of innocence. Solomon sent search parties in all directions of the compass.

As the men going west to the Mediterranean Sea arrived at Joppa, one of the searchers sat on a rock to rest and heard Jubela wail from nearby, "O that I had my throat cut across, and my tongue torn out by the root, and buried in the sands of the sea at low water a cable length from the shore, where the tide doth regularly ebb and flow twice in the course of the twenty-four hours, than that I had been concerned in the death of our master Hiram."

A moment later, Jubelo blurted, "Oh! that I had my heart torn from under my naked left breast, and given to the vultures of the air as a prey, rather than I had been concerned in the death of so good a master."

Jubelum exclaimed, "But oh! I struck him harder than you both, for I killed him. Oh! that I had had my body severed in two, one part carried to the south, and the other to the north, my bowels burnt to ashes and scattered before the four winds of the earth, rather than I had been concerned in the death of our master Hiram."

Seized and taken back to Jerusalem, they confessed to Solomon, described how they had killed Hiram, and declared no desire to live. Solomon answered, "They have signed their own deaths, and let it be upon them as they have said."

With that, Jubela was taken out and had his throat cut across and his tongue torn out by the root. He was buried in the sands of the sea at low water, a cable length from the shore, where "the tide doth regularly ebb and flow twice in the course of the twenty-four hours."

Jubelo's heart and "vitals" were torn from his naked left breast and "thrown over the left shoulder" to be consumed by vultures.

Jubelum's body was cut in half, with one part carried to the north and the other to the south. His bowels were burned to ashes and cast to "the four winds."

Although we know of the existence and the work of Hiram in the building of Solomon's temple from the Bible and Josephus's history of the Jews, there is no record outside the rites and rituals of Freemasonry as to whether Hiram Abiff was the supervising architect of the temple, the manner of his death, nor if Jubela, Jubelo, and Jubelum were actual persons who were so impatient in their ambition to rise to the supreme rank of grand master that they murdered him and suffered ghastly deaths. Consequently, no one can state with certainty that Freemasonry is as old as the first temple built by Jews. Whatever evidence might have existed within Solomon's temple to provide credence to the story of Hiram Abiff, and whether a trio of strivers killed him, was lost in the destruction of the temple. Despite the description by Josephus that the stones of the temple were strong enough "to resist the force of time," they were dismantled by invading and pillaging Babylonian troops in 597 B.C.

How and why Solomon's Temple and the death of Hiram Abiff are central to Freemasonry was explained and interpreted by W. L. Wilmshurst in one of a series of papers for "members of the Masonic Order, constituted under the United Grand Lodge of England." In the collection *The Meaning of Masonry*, he asserts that Solomon's Temple was meant to represent "the temple of the collective body of humanity itself." Describing Hiram Abiff, Solomon, and the king of Tyre as a "triad" corresponding to Christianity's Holy Trinity, he writes, "The tragedy of Hiram Abiff, then, is not the record of a vulgar, brutal murder of an individual man. It is a parable of cosmic and universal loss; an allegory of the breakdown of a divine scheme. We are dealing with no calamity that occurred during the erection of a building in an eastern city, but with a moral disaster to universal humanity."

With the slaying of Hiram, Wilmshurst contends, "the faculty of enlightened wisdom has been cut off from us." As a result, the temple of human nature remains unfinished:

> Hiram Abiff is slain. The light and wisdom to guide and enlighten humanity are wanting in us. The full blaze of light and perfect knowledge that were to be ours are vanished from the race, but in the Divine Providence there still remains to us a glimmering light in the East. In a dark world, from which the sun has disappeared, we still have our five senses and our rational faculties to work with, and these provide us with substituted secrets that must distinguish us before we regain the genuine ones.

Freemasonry is defined as a system of religious philosophy that provides "a doctrine of the universe and of our place in it," by which we may understand that mankind has fallen away from "a high and holy" center. Those who desire to regain it must look within themselves.

"The regenerated man, the man who not merely in ceremonial form but in vital experience, has passed through the phases of which Masonic degrees are the faint symbol," Wilmshurst writes, "is alone worthy of the title of Master-Mason in the building of the Temple that is not made with hands but that is being built invisibly out of the souls of just men made perfect."

This explanation of Solomon's Temple as a metaphoric foundation of Freemasonry was also provided in a speech in 1858 by Albert Pike, published with other addresses under the title *The Meaning of Masonry*. Esteemed as "master genius of Masonry, both as scholar and artist," and regarded as the most significant figure in American Freemasonry during the 19th century, Pike was born in Boston in 1809. Among his relatives were Nicholas Pike, the author of the first book on arithmetic in the United States, and the explorer Zebulon (Pike's Peak) Pike. (The controversial life of Albert Pike as a poet, journalist, Confederate soldier, jurist, and orator and his influence on Freemasonry in the United States will be discussed in detail in chapter 11.) Settling in Arkansas in 1850, at the age of forty-one, he became intensely interested in Masonic symbols. As he studied them, he found that Freemasonry began to shape itself into "something imposing and majestic, solemnly mysterious and grand," along with "dim intimations, half-revealed and half-concealed," and of "the repository of the highest wisdom of the ancient world."

Noting that in all periods of the world's history secret orders and societies had formed outside "official churches" to impart "to suitable and prepared minds certain truths of human life" and instructions about "divine things," Pike asserted that Freemasonry offered a "synthesis, a concordat, for men of every race, of every creed, of every sect," with "foundation principles being common to them all." These principles are that after mankind's separation from God as the result of the rebelliousness of Adam and Eve in the Garden of Eden (known as "the Fall"), God provided a means by which individuals could find their way back to Him. To assist men in this quest, God provided guidance through human intermediaries. Imbued with "the light of the divine truth," they have appeared through history as sages, prophets, teachers, philosophers, the leaders of moral movements, and the founders of great religions. One of these "illuminated" men, St. Paul, called such leaders "stewards of the Mysteries." Although these enlightened men differed in accordance with the cultures, societal structures, and religions of the civilizations of their eras, they sought to share their knowledge of human nature, purpose of life, and steps by which mankind could pursue reconciliation and ultimate unity with the Deity. They found eager followers among people who'd become dissatisfied with formal rituals of official religions that consisted principally of appealing to a god or gods on behalf of a city-state or tribe. Individuals seeking a route to personal salvation and immortality hoped to find it within cults. They met in secret and practiced elaborate initiations, rites of purification, veneration of objects; took part in sacred dramas; and advanced by steps to full knowledge and mastery of the Mysteries.

By the fifth century B.C. in Greece, these cults had become an integral part of the fabric of life. With the conquest of the Hellenistic empire by Rome, the Mysteries became even more widespread and so entrenched that the cult was recognized as a public institution. It remained a central element of Roman society until the fall of the empire and the advent of Christianity and its adoption as the state religion by Emperor Constantine. The final blow fell in A.D. 399 when Emperor Theodosius decreed, "Whatever privileges were conceded by the ancient laws to the priests, ministers, prefects, hierophants of sacred things, or by whatsoever name they may be designated are to be abolished henceforth, and let them not think that they are protected by a granted privilege when their religious confession is known to have been condemned by the law."

While the Mysteries are primarily associated with ancient Greece and Rome, their origins are attributed to earlier cults that flourished in Crete and Egypt. Freemasonry historian, student of the occult, and self-proclaimed clairvoyant C. W. Leadbeater contends in *Freemasonry and Its Ancient Mystic Rites* that the Mysteries and the "great doctrine of the 'Inner Light'" had been introduced to the Egyptians around 40,000 B.C. At that time, a "World-Teacher" came forth from the "White Lodge" to reveal that a universal "Light," which was God, "dwelt in the heart of every man."

Having learned from the World-Teacher, the priests passed on the teachings and "secret instructions, which they enshrined in their Mysteries,
and students came from all nations to learn the Wisdom of the Egyptians,
and the fame of the Schools of Egypt went abroad to all lands." Among
those who learned the Egyptian Mysteries and carried them to another
place was a former prince named Moses. Described by the historian Philo
as "skilled in music, geometry, arithmetic, hieroglyphics, and the whole
circle of arts and scientists," he was inspired by God to lead Hebrews out
of bondage toward "a land of milk and honey," where, as Leadbeater
writes, the Mysteries were "faithfully handed down from generation to
generation from the days of Moses until King Solomon came to the
throne of his father David" and built the temple that would be the center-
piece of Judaism and eventually stand as a symbol of the path to mankind's
reunion with God that is at the heart of Freemasonry.

While Masons may claim to be, in Leadbeater's words, "lineal descendants of the kings and prophets of old who have been the bearers of the
Hidden Light to men through countless generations," they have more
tangible and recent connections to builders of the great cathedrals of Europe
during the Middle Ages and their artistic and spiritual heirs in eighteenth-
century Britain.

CHAPTER 2

WITH STONE SO STRONG

I N *A HISTORY OF FREEMASONRY*, AN EXPLORATION OF VARIOUS hypotheses on biblical and even more ancient foundations of Freemasonry, H. L. Haywood writes:

> From time immemorial Freemasonry has exercised the right to ask of each of its votaries whence he came and whither he was traveling. The answer to neither part of the question can be conclusive. If memory could go back to Masonry's beginning, it would be a misuse of words to describe its past as immemorial. The best account of its remote history is that it had not one origin but many origins. Modern Freemasonry is in the truest sense a reservoir into which the cult lore and social experiences of countless eons of human experience have poured their treasures. Into this mighty lake streams have trickled from the remotest mountain tops; it is fed from innumerable founts. It signifies little how the life-giving waters have found their way into its bosom, by what channels they have come, across what continents they have flowed.

That each of these theories of Masonry's ancient roots should find ready acceptance is not surprising, Haywood explains, because human beings are incurably romantic. "Make a tale brave enough," he writes, "uniform it with noble trappings, embroider it with glamour and utter it in the cadences of minstrelsy, and it is characteristic of human nature that willing believers will accept it without troubling to inquire too closely into the substance of their faith."

While Haywood is dubious about tracing the origins of Masonry to Solomon and his energetic architect, Hiram Abiff, and even earlier, he finds sounder footing in "that long period when Gothic builders were dotting Europe with God's cathedrals." Defined by historians as "the Middle Ages," this epoch of construction of magnificent Christian edifices began after Emperor Constantine converted to Christianity in 312 and decreed it the official religion of the Roman Empire. By his order in 325, construction commenced on the Church of the Lateran in Rome and another was dedicated to St. Paul. Architects for these edifices were members of the Collegium Fabrorum (Roman College) and, therefore, initiates into the Mysteries. While the plans they drew for the Christian churches ordained by Constantine were laid out in the form of a cross, the design was not only inspired by the symbol of Christ's crucifixion, but also by the ground plan of Solomon's Temple in Jerusalem. Revered as a masterpiece of architecture and the first building erected and dedicated to one God, the temple's cross shape also represented the unity and trinity of the Christian faith.

For the masses of illiterate faithful, the cathedrals were a means of religious instruction through symbolism. The three long aisles extending from the entrance, which represented the earth as the habitation of the church, were called the nave. Located above the cross-space that formed the parallel beam of a cross and represented penitence and judgment, the choir had a screen that permitted worshipers only glimpses of the mysterious events taking place beyond it. The choir stood for a mystical world of angels and departed souls. The sanctuary was the representation of heaven. The altar, containing the blessed sacrament, was the abode of divinity (Christ).

Among the cathedrals built in England were those at Canterbury (its foundation was laid in 600), Rochester (602), and London's St. Paul's (605). Three hundred years later, every large town in Britain had a group of Freemasons engaged in construction of cathedrals, churches, and other works, including fortifications, walls, and bridges. Known as Gothic architecture, the style was intended to lift the devotion of the masses by using soaring lines, ascending curves, and a graceful design to glorify God and, coincidentally, extol the skills and artistry of the builders.

In Britain, these men were classified as those who handled hard stone ("hard hewers" or "rough masons") and more highly skilled cutters of softer, chalky rock (known as "free stone"), giving these craftsmen the name "free stonemasons," eventually shortened to "freemasons." The word "maszun" (of French origin, meaning "stone craftsman") was noted in an English glossary that was compiled around 1217. A document at Exeter Cathedral, compiled in 1396, used the term "freemasons." By 1292, English masons were accustomed to speak of a hut near the construction site where they stored their tools and had a midday meal as a "lodge."

While in many instances work was provided to masons by the monarch, primarily in the building of forts and palaces, most opportunities for employment came either from bishops and deans of congregations with a desire to have a splendid sacred edifice in their town or from groups of employers called trade guilds. As early as 1220, Freemasonry in London was controlled by the Masons' Livery Company. In addition to establishing the top wage rate for masons (there was no minimum wage), and regulating the number of and type of workers on a project, trade guilds laid out rules of conduct. Known as "Charges," they demanded fealty to God, the Catholic Church, the king, the employer, and the master mason. In terms of personal morality, the Charges imposed a duty to keep the master's secrets and refrain from "any disobedient argument," fornication and adultery, carousing in inns and brothels, staying out after 8 P.M., and playing cards, except for the period of the twelve days of Christmas.

A consequence of the strictures on the maximum hourly wage that a mason could earn was widespread disobedience. Because masons were in short supply and demand for them was great, they found themselves in a strong position to make demands for better wages. They did so by forming trade unions. Because these groups were illegal, they had to meet in secret.

The oldest known Masonic document is a manuscript poem, found in the 1830s in the King's Library of the British Museum and published in 1840 by James O. Halliwell, who was not a Mason. Scholars have assigned various dates to it, but it is probably not much older than 1390 and not much younger than 1445. Known both as the Halliwell manuscript and the Regius poem, it consists of 794 lines of rhymed English verse, with the Latin title *Hic incipiunt constitutiones artis gemetrioe secundum Euclydum* (Here begin the constitutions of geometry according to Euclid.) The first eighty-six lines present a legend of the foundation of Masonry in Egypt by the mathematician Euclid, and its introduction into England by King Athelstan (924). This is followed by an account of a great assembly of "the Craft" under the patronage of Prince Edwin. Certain regulations for "the governance of the society" were divided into fifteen articles and fifteen points, followed by an ordinance regarding "further assemblies." After this come forty-eight lines recording a legend of "Four Crowned Martyrs" who refused to obey the Roman emperor and deny their Christianity. For this defiance, they were put in lead coffins and thrown into a river alive. This story is followed by a version of the origin of Masonry, tracing its history from the Great Flood (Noah) and the Tower of Babel. Dated from its adoption in 926 by a Masonic convention at York, the poem is known as the "Gothic Constitutions."

One of the greatest achievements of the Freemasons in thirteenth-century England was Westminster Abbey. Completed in 1272, it was erected under the supervision of Grand Master Giffard, the archbishop of York. A nonreligious masterpiece was London Bridge. Constructed of stone to replace a wooden span over the Thames that was torn down in 1176, it was completed in 1209. As it was being built, Londoners serenaded the workers with the song "London Bridge Is Falling Down," which included the lines "Build it up with stone so strong / That 'twill last for ages long." The bridge stood for 623 years. It was demolished in 1832 when its supports were deemed too narrow for increasingly larger merchant ships and those of the British navy to pass under it.

While Westminster Abbey was under construction, an event unfolded in France that was to have a significant influence on the evolution of Freemasonry, give it one of its most revered figures, and provide another link to Solomon's Temple.

CHAPTER 3

FREEMASONRY AND THE KNIGHTS TEMPLAR

SINCE THE DESTRUCTION OF SOLOMON'S TEMPLE BY THE Babylonians in 486 B.C., the city of Jerusalem had been conquered and ruled by the Persians, Greeks, Romans, and the Christian Byzantine Empire until A.D. 638. In that year, a new power swept through the gates of the holy city to take it over in the name of a new religion that had already claimed Arabia for its God, Allah. Led by Caliph Omar, the forces of Islam had defeated troops of Emperor Heraclius in a battle at Yarmuk on August 20, 636, and marched on to lay siege to the city until it surrendered without a fight in February 638. Because Mohammed, the founding prophet of Islam, had been miraculously taken into Heaven from the city and returned to Earth to promulgate the faith, the city was regarded as holy by Muslims. To venerate the prophet's journey, they built two sacred structures, the Dome of the Rock and the Al-Aqsa Mosque, on the site of Solomon's Temple and its successor that had been restored by King Herod and destroyed by Rome in A.D. 70.

During two centuries of Islamic rule, relations between Muslims and Christians proved to be amiable. But this mutual toleration between the two religions changed after the crowning of Charles, later called Charlemagne ("Charles the Great"), as king of the Franks by Pope Leo III in 800. When the head of an empire that was now called "Holy Roman" was invited by the ruler of the Muslims, Caliph al-Harun al-Rashid, to build a hospice in Jerusalem, it marked the start of a Christian revival that increasingly alarmed Muslims. Two centuries later, it was the Christians who found cause for concern as reports flowed out of Jerusalem to the capitals of Europe that Christian pilgrims and holy places were suffering at the hands of Muslims.

Disturbed by these accounts, and also concerned about a growing threat to the Byzantine Empire by the westward spread of Islam, Pope Urban II, in a speech at the Council of Clermont in the spring of 1096, called on European powers to set aide their internal disputes and unite in a holy war to liberate the holy city from the "infidels." The reward for those who took up arms in the name of Christ would be absolution and remission of sins.

He declared, *"Deus Vult"* (God wills it).

The day after this exhortation, the council granted the privileges and protections that he promised. Those who took up arms to liberate Jerusalem adopted a red cross as their emblem and garnered the name "Crusaders." Setting out for the Holy Land, 60,000 soldiers and hordes of noncombatant peasants and pilgrims, with wives and children, were followed in the fall of 1096 by five more armies. After a year of arduous marching, the Crusaders were at Jerusalem's gates. When they took the city and thronged to the Church of the Holy Sepulchre (the traditional site of the Crucifixion and Resurrection), one of the leaders, Raymond of Agiles, saw a scene that would be "famous in all future ages, for it turned our labors and sorrows into joy and exultation." It was to him and his Crusader comrades a day of "justification of all Christianity, the humiliation of paganism, the renewal of faith."

Between 1096 and 1250, there would be seven Crusades. As they continued and many thousands of Christians made their way to and from Jerusalem, the pilgrimages were frequently attacked by Muslims. To provide protection for them, an order of warrior monks was founded in 1118 in France by Hugues de Payens, a knight of Burgundy, and Godefroid de St. Omer, a knight of southern France. They took a vow of poverty and the name "Poor Knights of Christ and of the Temple of Solomon." Given sanction by the church in 1128 at the Council of Troyes, and with the support of St. Bernard of Clairvaux, who was commissioned to write their "Rule," the Templars became renowned for their ferocity in battle. Welcomed to the holy city after the First Crusade by Baldwin I, the self-proclaimed king of Jerusalem, they were provided living space near the site of Solomon's Temple, hence the name "Templars."

Writing between 1170 and 1174, Archbishop William of Tyre noted that "certain noble men of knightly rank, religious men, devoted to God and fearing him, bound themselves to Christ's service in the hands of the Lord Patriarch [of Jerusalem]" and promised to live "without possessions, under vows of chastity and obedience." Because they had no church

> nor any fixed abode, the king gave them for a time a dwelling place in the south wing of the palace, near the Lord's Temple. The canons of the Lord's Temple gave them, under certain conditions, a square near the palace which the canons possessed. This the knights used as a drill field. The Lord King and his noblemen and also the Lord Patriarch and the prelates of the church gave them benefices from their domains, some for a limited time and some in perpetuity. These were to provide the knights with food and clothing. Their primary duty, one which was enjoined upon them by the Lord Patriarch and the other bishops for the remission of sins, was that of protecting the roads and routes against the attacks of robbers and brigands. This they did especially in order to safe-guard pilgrims.

For nine years after their founding, the Templars wore donated secular clothing. But at a council in France in 1125 they were assigned a white habit. At this time, there were nine knights, but Archbishop William recorded that "their numbers began to grow and their possessions began to multiply." By 1174, their roster had swelled so much, he wrote, "that there are in this Order today about 300 knights who wear white mantles."

The order also amassed wealth. William recorded:

> They are said to have immense possessions both here and overseas, so that there is now not a province in the Christian world which has not bestowed upon the aforesaid brothers a portion of its goods. It is said today that their wealth is equal to the treasures of kings. Because they have a headquarters in the royal palace next to the Temple of the Lord, they are called the Brothers of the Militia of the Temple.

Although they maintained their establishment honorably for a long time and fulfilled their vocation with sufficient prudence, later, because of the neglect of humility (which is known as the guardian of all virtues and which, since it sits in the lowest place, cannot fall), they withdrew from the Patriarch of Jerusalem, by whom their Order was founded and from whom they [had] received their first benefices and to whom they denied the obedience which their predecessors rendered. They have also taken away tithes and first fruits from God's churches, have disturbed their possessions, and have made themselves exceedingly troublesome.

Nine centuries after Crusaders ventured into the Holy Land in the name of Christ, the fact that they had accumulated enormous wealth became the basis of the plot of what is arguably the finest detective novel by an American. In Dashiell Hammett's *The Maltese Falcon*, fat, greedy, and treacherous Caspar Gutman summarizes the history of a lost, fabulous, jewel-encrusted statuette of "a black bird" that had been made as a gift for King Charles of Spain by the Crusader Order of the Order of the Hospital of St. John of Jerusalem. Noting that the knights "were rolling in wealth" acquired as spoils of their expeditions, he continues, "We all know that the Holy Wars to them, as to the Templars, was a matter of loot."

Following the retaking of Jerusalem by Islam in 1239, the Templars obtained the island of Cyprus as the headquarters of the order and used their accumulation of enormous wealth to establish themselves in France as international financiers and bankers. With the "Paris Temple" becoming the heart of the mid-thirteenth-century world money market, the formerly "Poor Knights of Christ" were richer than any government on the continent and owned 9,000 manors and castles. Between 15,000 and 20,000 knights and clergy were attended by thousands of squires, servants, and vassals.

While history attests that many Crusaders were more interested in profit than making the Holy Land safe for Christianity, there is no evidence that a young Templar named Jacques de Molay was motivated to join the order by anything but piety. Born around 1244 in Vitrey, France, he entered the Knights Templar in 1265 at age twenty-one. After rising quickly through the ranks, he spent a great deal of time in Great Britain. Eventually appointed as visitor general and grand preceptor of all England, he was made head of the order following the death of its twenty-second grand master, Theobald Gaudin. He then moved from England to Cyprus. It was there in the autumn of 1307 that he found himself called back to France by order of King Philip IV, known as "the Fair," and Pope Clement V. It is believed that the summons was the result of kingly and papal fear and envy of the power and wealth of the Templars. Another explanation is that Philip was so deep in debt to the Templars that he decided the only way to eradicate it was by eliminating the order.

On Friday, October 13, 1307, royal bailiffs entered Templar headquarters in Paris and arrested the knights. Imprisoned and tortured, they were forced to confess to heresies, among them devil worship and sexual perversions. They were offered a choice of recantation or death. While de Molay gave a confession under torture, he soon renounced it. Condemned along with another Templar, he was taken to an island in the Seine in the shadow of Notre Dame Cathedral and set ablaze in 1312. A legend holds that as the flames raged around him, he prophesied that the king and the pope would die within a year. The prophecy came true, but before his death the pope dissolved the order and warned that anyone even thinking of joining the Templars would be excommunicated and charged as a heretic.

Among many stories, legends, and myths that grew up around the Templars is a claim that they possessed mystical knowledge. An ancient artifact called the Rubant document recorded that the knights had "secret knowledge" that they had obtained "from books." This "complete and absolute knowledge" of a secret wisdom was revealed only to "the initiated." Raoul de Presle, a lawyer of the period, said that there was a strict secret held within the order, the nature of which was so sensational that men would prefer to have their heads cut off rather than divulge it. De Molay reportedly had told his inquisitors before his death that he would have liked to tell them "certain things," but they were not authorized to hear them.

Concerning this mystical aspect of the Knights Templar, the Masonic historian C. W. Leadbeater writes that the order was "one of the repositories of the Hidden Wisdom of Europe in the twelfth and thirteenth centuries, although the full secrets were give only to the few."

Exactly what became of the Templars after de Molay's execution and the papal decree abolishing the order is a question that has been disputed by Masonic historians. The favored view is that remaining Templars made their way to Scotland to protect its warrior king, Robert Bruce. Fighting the English and having no significant force of his own, he declared that all Templars would be welcome to join him. When the Scots fought the English on June 24, 1314, at Bannockburn, they comprised an army of foot soldiers who were armed with ineffective pikes and bowmen. As the battle raged throughout the day, the Scots appeared to be losing, but late in the day a force of Templars appeared. Believing them to be a fresh army of Scots, the English panicked and fled. Following the triumph, the Templars found refuge on islands off the west coast of Scotland for about eighty years. Moving to the east coast at the end of the fourteenth century, they settled in Aberdeen and called themselves Freemasons.

The explanation for this transformation from warrior knights defending the Holy Land pilgrims to Masons has been attributed to a mingling over time of Templar precepts with those of more ancient Celtic mystery cults. This merger eventually resulted in the formation of one of the most significant branches of Freemasonry: the Royal Order of Scotland. Known as the Scottish Rite, it would flourish in parts of Europe and eventually take root and thrive in America.

Another view of the ultimate fate of the Knights Templar following de Molay's execution and the papal outlawing of the order casts doubt on the claim that Templars were the genuine ancestors of Freemasonry. Historian Jasper Ridley surmises that some Freemasons simply chose to believe that it was more romantic for Freemasonry to be descended from a persecuted religious order of chivalry than from trade unions of English stone cutters.

CHAPTER 4

FREEMASONRY AND THE PROTESTANT
REFORMATION

T WO CENTURIES AFTER CHRISTIANITY WAS NAMED THE
official religion of the Roman Empire in a decree by Emperor
Constantine, cults of the ancient Mysteries that had become public
institutions were abruptly prohibited by Emperor Justinian I. His purpose
was to strengthen the religion of the empire and to establish himself as
the supreme authority over the church in matters of organization and
dogma. (The term for this was "casesaropapism.") Toward this end, he issued a declaration of faith (544) and convened an ecumenical council at
Constantinople (553). The resulting *Corpus Juris* made paganism and
apostasy punishable by death. There was no toleration of dissent. He decreed, "Let no place be afforded to heretics for the conduct of their ceremonies, and let no occasion be offered for them to display the insanity of
their obstinate minds. Let all persons know that if any privilege has been
fraudulently obtained by means of any rescript whatsoever, by persons of
this kind, it will not be valid. Let all bodies of heretics be prevented from
holding unlawful assemblies."

Because the emperor was declared both king and supreme authority on
Earth in matters ecclesiastical, Justinian placed himself in conflict with
the claim of the Catholic Church that the pope was the true worldly representative of Jesus. As a result, the *Catholic Encyclopedia* states that a present-
day Roman Catholic "cannot applaud the great emperor's ecclesiastical
polity." While recognizing Justinian's effort to promote peace and union
within the empire, the entry notes that it was "a matter of course that this
union was to be that of the 'most holy Catholic and Apostolic Church.'"

History records that after the decline of the Roman Empire, it was indeed the church and papacy that emerged as supreme arbiters of the Christian faith. It would remain so for nearly a thousand years.

The judgment of history is that the effects of Justinian's reign were so crucial in every aspect of the development of post-Roman European civilization that the Middle Ages would never have happened had it not been for him. An ill-conceived military venture meant to unify the western and eastern parts of the empire, the abandonment of the Latin language as the official language of government and administrations, and a weakened eastern empire, which encouraged and strengthened the Persians, set the stage for a devastating war and made possible a westward spread of Islam. By overthrowing western Germanic governments that were committed to saving as much of the Roman imperial civilization as possible, Justinian was indirectly responsible for the rise of the medieval church and the papacy to a position of unchallenged power in the European nations that replaced the Roman Empire.

In addition to his significant role in the emergence of Christianity as the religion of Europe following the decline of the Roman Empire, Justinian provided impetus to the arts in the style of design and construction known as Byzantine architecture. As a prodigious promoter of building, he saw his empire come to be strewn with superb monuments and buildings that were to be models for all later architecture in the East (Islamic style) and in the West (Gothic).

While this change of style that spread quickly over a great part of Europe was the result of advances in construction technology, consisting of revolutionary innovations in the form of the vaulted ceiling and the pointed arch, its enthusiastic acceptance was rooted in the birth of a new national consciousness that sparked a rivalry between cities and church officials who were eager to elevate their status with imposing cathedrals and public buildings.

It was a time, writes art historian H. B. Cotterill in the multivolume *History of Art*, when the Romanesque style of building "suddenly gave way to that of a new, popular, and civic architecture" in which "Christendom cast aside its outworn attire and put on a fresh white robe of new-built Churches."

The Gothic style in religious edifices was meant to raise the devotion of the illiterate masses to a greater height represented by the soaring, majestic cathedrals than was ever possible in the flat, stolid lines of Romanesque structures. In this era of fresh Christian fervor, known as the Middle Ages, every stone was carved to glorify God by men who found in the craft of masonry a means for the expression of their own faith. Possessing not only religious feelings, but also skills with which to express them in stone, they went from job to job and place to place. They called themselves "free masons," but they were always under the domain of those who employed them. Whether its was a monarch, a civic corporation, or a prince of the church who commissioned a building, the masons found every aspect of their work and lives strictly regulated. The result of strictures in the matter of limits on wages was the formation of trade unions that were necessarily steeped in secrecy. Employers who chose not to engage in clandestine dealings with the masons sought to stifle the practice. In 1360, a law banned secret agreements among masons and carpenters and prohibited all oaths of secrecy. In 1425, English masons were forbidden to hold assemblies. A code of laws drafted by the duke of Bedford, acting as regent for three-year-old King Henry VI, noted that a common bond united separate units or working lodges and declared them illegal. In less than two years, the law was being so widely ignored that attempts to enforce it were dropped.

While free masons were exhibiting economic strength in Great Britain, their counterparts in France and masons in Germany had also benefitted from the premium placed on their skills during the period of cathedral building. The French organization of masons called *compagnons* also held secret meetings that ran into governmental resistance and restrictive laws. In Germany, masons were called Steinmetzen (stonemasons). Among their masterpieces were cathedrals at Strasbourg and Cologne. Both became schools where masons of other countries were received in masonic lodges with symbolic ceremonies. But it was the consequences of an event at a far less imposing church in Germany that would alter the course of Western civilization and change the direction of Freemasonry from a fraternity of men bound by their unique craft with a desire to be respected for it, and paid accordingly, to a broader society of gentlemen from all walks of life.

The incident that triggered the chain of events that would transform

Freemasonry took place in the university city of Wittenberge, Germany, on the front steps of a church. Part of a castle erected between 1490 and 1499 for Frederic the Wise and called Castle Church (Scholsskirche), it had a sturdy wooden front door that was frequently used by city and university officials and faculty and students for the posting of messages, notes, and notices, but never with an impact of a document nailed to it on October 31, 1517, by a thirty-four-year-old monk named Martin Luther.

A university graduate with a doctorate in theology who was serving as Augustinian Vicar of Meissen and Thuringia, he had been ordained a priest in 1507. Described by a biographer as "temperamental, peevish, egomaniacal and argumentative," he had come to the conclusion that there was no place for intermediaries between man and God in the form of church priests and in the church institution of buying remission of sins through "indulgences." Believing that the only requirement for the soul's salvation was faith, he wrote a document attacking the system, titled "Ninety-five Theses," nailed it to the Castle Church door, and began the Protestant Reformation.

Although there had been a strong strain of anticlericalism in England, Freemasons had remained loyal to the Catholic Church. When King Henry VII led a procession to a ceremony for the laying of the cornerstone of a chapel at Westminster in 1502, Freemasons participated. The Freemasons could be rightly accused of flaunting laws intended to curtail and punish them for their secret dealings on the rate of wages, notes Jasper Ridley in a history of Freemasonry, but however "wicked" they were in forming illegal trade unions, "they were perfectly law-abiding as far as religion was concerned."

When Henry VIII's personal wishes collided with the supremacy of the pope on the issue of his demand that his marriage to Catherine of Aragon be dissolved so that Henry could wed his mistress, Anne Boleyn, Henry found it expedient, profitable, and popular to promulgate the Act of Supremacy in 1534, putting him at the head of the Church in England. Between 1535 and 1540, a policy decreeing dissolution of the monasteries stripped the church of huge tracts of land and placed them in the hands of the Crown and ultimately those of the nobility and gentry. Because this resulted in an end to the building of churches, Freemasonry entered a period of decline that resulted in a change in the character of membership and from "operative," meaning those who had actually worked in stone, to "speculative," in which the tools of masonry were employed as symbols in the contemplation of the mysteries of life and its meaning.

At precisely what period the lodges started admitting non-Masons is unknown. The practice was noted in 1646 when a lodge was recorded as having admitted Elias Ashmole and Colonel Henry Mainwaring. "There was nothing in the circumstance," notes H. L. Haywood, "to indicate that this was a new thing."

This shift in the purpose of Masonry from workers' guild to philosophical society was regarded at the time as so much of an innovation that secretaries of some of the operative lodges burned their records because they feared that with admission of non-Masons the secrets of the fraternity would become public. Comparing this feeling of the necessity for secrecy among the speculative Freemasons to ancient cults, Haywood explains that steps had always been taken to preserve some precious and secret knowledge or magic. Such societies, when they attained to a real or fancied revelation of truth, sought to perpetuate their lore and to secure to themselves exclusive enjoyment of the power or dignity it conferred.

As later secret societies developed, they also masked their discoveries in allegorical terms, legends, and symbolical dramas. To protect themselves from intrusion, they emulated the early cults that had veiled their rituals in impenetrable mystery and had bound their members by oaths. To ensure propagation of their work by competent successors, they invented ordeals of initiation and submission by which candidates for admission proved their fortitude and zeal in ceremonies consisting of successive phases that sometimes took years to complete. These secret societies invested their symbols and ceremonials with significance that was suitable to the understanding of novices and led step by step to those that could be comprehended only by the most advanced.

Describing the passed-on secrets of Freemasonry as "heirlooms," Haywood writes, "It is true they do not prove the continuous existence of the Fraternity from before the Flood [Noah] to the institution of the first Grand Lodge. They do not establish connection between it and any particular band, society, group or cult in existence before the Dark Ages. But they do reveal the kinship of Freemasonry with the religious and philosophical societies of previous ages."

This connection was known as the "Old Charges." Also called "Ancient Manuscripts," "Ancient Constitutions," "Legend of the Craft," and "Gothic Manuscripts," they dated from the fourteenth century and incorporated traditional history, legends, and rules and regulations of the Craft. Sometimes found in the form of handwritten paper or parchment rolls that were either sewn or pasted together in book form, these traditions and legends were the cement of Masonry until the period of religious, political, and social upheaval, tumult, and civil warfare that started with the defiance of the Catholic Church by Henry VIII and ended with the solidification of Protestantism in England by William of Orange.

Near the end of this tempestuous era, London suffered two back-to-back calamities. In 1665, the Great Plague of London consumed thousands of lives. The next year, the Great Fire destroyed 40,000 homes and 86 churches. Because local masons were insufficient in number to meet the demands of rebuilding the ruined city, help was imported from all over the British Isles. They united in a lodge under the authority of England's greatest architect, Sir Christopher Wren, who furnished plans for the rebuilding, including St. Paul's Cathedral. When he was buried in its crypt, his tomb bore the Latin inscription *"Si monumentum requris circumspice"* (If you would see his monument, look around).

Except for the flourish of building following the Great Fire of 1666, new ecclesiastical construction ground to a halt, resulting in a decline of Masonic lodges. Those that remained had lost almost all trace of the ancient rituals and their symbolism. The annual feasts were neglected and the four remaining lodges in London were deserted. In *A Dictionary of Freemasonry*, Robert Macoy writes, "Notwithstanding the zeal displayed by Grand Master Wren, the number of Masons was continually diminishing." By 1700, England had only six lodges.

Masonic historian C. W. Leadbeater writes of this period that the decay of the lodges had a disastrous effect on the ancient ritual that had been handed down orally from the days of the Roman Collegia. He notes that the oral tradition had become corrupted and that although the ancient rituals were still remembered, the words accompanying them had degenerated into mere verbal jargon, often quite unintelligible to those who received it.

The Craft was also the object of a wave of anti-Mason sentiment. Emblematic of this was a leaflet circulated in London in 1698. Signed by a "Mr. Winter," it warned "all godly people" of the "Mischiefs and Evils practised in the sight of God by those called Freed Masons." The tract went on, "For this devilish Sect of Men are Meeters in secret and swear against all without their Following. They are the Anti Christ which is to come, leading Men from fear of God."

Facing a crisis that threatened the future of Freemasonry, members of four London lodges decided to create a "Grand Lodge" that would have authority over all lodges in England. Those that came together for this purpose in February 1717 were Lodge No. 1, which met at the Goose and Gridiron alehouse near St. Paul's; No. 2, meeting at the Crown alehouse in Parker's Lane, near Drury Lane; No. 3, convening at the Apple Tree tavern, Covent Garden; and No. 4, meeting at Rummer and Grapes tavern, Channel Row, Westminster. The largest was No. 4, with about seventy members. The meeting to organize the Grand Lodge was held in the Apple Tree. Convened again four months later on June 24, 1717 (the day of one of the patron saints of Masonry, St. John the Baptist), at the Goose and Gridiron, they elected "a gentleman of Lodge No. 3," Anthony Sayer, as their grand master.

After choosing a "commoner " as grand master for each year between 1717 and 1721, they bestowed the honor on a member of the nobility. They elected John Montagu, the second duke of Montagu. He had been high constable at the coronation of George I, held the rank of colonel in the Horse Guards, and as a boy had been present at the famous siege of Menin under Lord Marlborough. Reputed to be the richest man in England, he later wed the war hero's youngest daughter, Lady Mary Churchill, and became an ancestor of Winston Churchill. Following his election as grand master, the exalted position was bestowed on a member of the nobility or a member of the royal family for the next 278 years.

Having obtained the protection of the aristocracy, the Freemasons of Britain felt free to proclaim their fundamental, guiding principles. To digest the Old Gothic Constitution and codify it for eighteenth-century Freemasonry, they turned to a scholar and clergyman from Scotland.

CHAPTER 5

DR. JAMES ANDERSON'S CONSTITUTIONS

BORN IN EDINBURGH, SCOTLAND, PROBABLY ON AUGUST 5, 1662, Doctor of Divinity James Anderson had become a hero of Scottish nationalism by publishing "An Essay Showing That the Crown of Scotland Is Imperial and Independent." In what year he became a Freemason is not known, as is almost everything about his life before he was called on to write a new code of Freemasonry. In *A New Encyclopaedia of Freemasonry* composed by Arthur Edward Waite, he is described "as a son of Aberdeen" who may have earned his doctorate in that city, then served "somewhere" as a Presbyterian minister, and "ultimately drifted to London prior to 1710." Civic records show that he purchased the lease of a Huguenot chapel in Swallow Street. The press of the period described him as "a dissenting minister." Except for several sermons in the years after he was chosen for the task that has enshrined him in the lore of the Craft as "the father of Masonic history," little is recorded regarding the remainder of his life. He died on June 1, 1739, and was buried with Masonic funerary honors.

His legacy is "The CONSTITUTION, History, Laws, Charges, Orders, Regulations, and Usages, of the Right Worshipful FRATERNITY of AC-CEPTED FREE MASONS; collected from their general RECORDS, and their faithful TRADITIONS of many Ages." Much of what is known about how it was written is from Anderson's own account. He noted that he was ordered on September 29, 1721, to digest the Old Gothic Constitutions in a new and better method and that on December 27 his work was examined by "fourteen learned brothers," given approval, and ordered "published and recommended to the Craft."

A contrary version of this story holds that "the true state of the case appears to be that Anderson undertook to write the work as a private venture of his own" and that it was sanctioned by the Grand Lodge because "it was desirable that the Regulations at least be published" and that this was done "without any very careful examination of his text." The result of haste was the inclusion in the constitutions of "unwarrantable liberties" that Anderson had taken with the traditional Old Charges.

In constructing the document, Anderson followed the pattern of several versions of the Old Charges. In a historical section, Anderson traced Masonry from Noah to Solomon, then jumped to France, and finally to the establishment of the Craft in England. He traced the art of architecture from Cain, who had built a city and had been instructed in geometry by Adam. The narrative stated that Noah and his sons were Masons, that Moses had been a grand master, and that Hiram Abiff was the grand master in the building of Solomon's Temple.

In the section named "Six Charges," claimed to have been extracted from the ancient records of lodges "beyond the sea," and of those in England, Scotland, and Ireland, Anderson did away with the old invocation of the Christian Trinity and whatever else there may have been of statements of religious and Christian belief in the practice of the lodges by a vague statement on a Masonic obligation to "that religion in which all men agree." In asserting a general Deism, the document referred not to God, but to the "Great Architect of the Universe."

Although religious tolerance had been the rule of the Craft, the Grand Lodge of 1723 was not prepared for so sudden a shift from its historic adherence to Christianity. But in the removal from the literature of the Craft of all definite religious allusions, Anderson introduced a tenet of nondenominationalism that has been the basis of Freemasonry ever since:

> A Mason is oblig'd by his Tenure, to obey the moral law; and if he
> rightly understands the Art, he will never be a stupid Atheist nor an

irreligious Libertine. But though in ancient Times Masons were charg'd in every Country to be of the Religion of that Country or Nation, whatever it was, yet 'tis now thought more expedient only to oblige them to that Religion in which all Men agree, leaving their particular Opinions to themselves; that is, to be good Men and true, or Men of Honor and Honesty, by whatever Denominations or Persuasions they may be distinguish'd; whereby Masonry becomes the Centre of Union, and the Means of consolidating true Friendship among Persons that must have remain'd at perpetual Distance.

Concerning civil authority:

A Mason is a peaceable Subject to the Civil Powers, wherever he resides or works, and is never to be concern'd in Plots and Conspiracies against the Peace and Welfare of the Nation, nor to behave himself undutifully to inferior Magistrates; for as Masonry hath been always injured by War, Bloodshed, and Confusion, so ancient Kings and Princes have been much dispos'd to encourage the Craftsmen, because of their Peaceableness and Loyalty, whereby they practically answer'd the Cavils of their Adversaries, and promoted the Honor of the Fraternity, who ever flourish'd in Time of Peace. So that if a Brother should be a Rebel against the State he is not to be countenanced in his Rebellion, however he may be pitied as any unhappy Man; and, if convicted of no other Crime though the Loyal Brotherhood must and ought to disown his Rebellion, and give no Umbrage or Ground of political Jealousy to the Government for the time being, they cannot expel him from the Lodge, and his Relation to it remains indefeasible.

Concerning the lodge:

A Lodge is a place where Masons assemble and work; Hence that Assembly, or duly organized Society of Masons, is call'd a Lodge, and every Brother ought to belong to one, and to be subject to its By-

Laws and the General Regulations. It is either particular or general, and will be best understood by attending it, and by the Regulations of the General or Grand Lodge hereunto annex'd. In ancient Times, no Master or Fellow could be absent from it especially when warned to appear at it, without incurring a sever Censure, until it appear'd to the Master and Wardens that pure Necessity hinder'd him. The persons admitted Members of a Lodge must be good and true Men, free-born, and of mature and discreet Age, no Bondmen, no Women, no immoral or scandalous men, but of good Report.

Of masters, wardens, fellows, and apprentices:

All preferment among Masons is grounded upon real Worth and personal Merit only; that so the Lords may be well served, the Brethren not put to Shame, nor the Royal Craft despis'd: Therefore no Master or Warden is chosen by Seniority, but for his Merit. It is impossible to describe these things in Writing, and every Brother must attend in his Place, and learn them in a Way peculiar to this Fraternity.

Freemasons at work:

All Masons shall work honestly on Working Days, that they may live creditably on Holy Days; and the time appointed by the Law of the Land or confirm'd by Custom shall be observ'd. The most expert of the Fellow-Craftsmen shall be chosen or appointed the Master or Overseer of the Lord's Work; who is to be call'd Master by those that work under him. The Craftsmen are to avoid all ill Language, and to call each other by no disobliging Name, but Brother or Fellow; and to behave themselves courteously within and without the Lodge. The Master, knowing himself to be able of Cunning, shall undertake the Lord's Work as reasonably as possible, and truly dispense his Goods as if they were his own; nor to give more Wages to any Brother or Apprentice than he really may deserve. Both the Master and the Masons receiving their Wages justly, shall be faithful to the Lord and honestly finish their Work, whether Task or journey; nor put the work to Task that hath been accustomed to Journey. None shall discover Envy at the Prosperity of a Brother, nor supplant him, or put him out of his Work, if he be capable to finish the same; for no man can finish another's Work so much to the Lord's Profit.

On personal behavior in the lodge:

You are not to hold private Committees, or separate Conversation without Leave from the Master, nor to talk of anything impertinent or unseemly, nor interrupt the Master or Wardens, or any Brother speaking to the Master: Nor behave yourself ludicrously or jestingly while the Lodge is engaged in what is serious and solemn; nor use any unbecoming Language upon any Pretense whatsoever; but to pay due Reverence to your Master, Wardens, and Fellows, and put them to Worship. If any Complaint be brought, the Brother found guilty shall stand to the Award and Determination of the Lodge, who are the proper and competent Judges of all such Controversies (unless you carry it by Appeal to the Grand Lodge), and to whom they ought to be referr'd, unless a Lord's Work be hinder'd the meanwhile, in which Case a particular Reference may be made; but you must never go to Law about what concerns Masonry, without an absolute necessity apparent to the Lodge.

Behavior after the meeting of the lodge:

You may enjoy yourself with innocent Mirth, treating one another according to Ability, but avoiding all Excess, or forcing any Brother to eat or drink beyond his Inclination, or hindering him from going when his Occasions call him, or doing or saying anything offensive, or that may forbid an easy and free Conversation, for that would blast our Harmony, and defeat our laudable Purposes. Therefore no private Piques or Quarrels must be brought within the Door of the Lodge, far less any Quarrels about Religion, or Nations, or State

Policy, we being only, as Masons, of the Catholic Religion above mention'd, we are also of all Nations, Tongues, Kindreds, and Languages, and are resolv'd against all Politics, as what never yet conduct'd to the Welfare of the Lodge, nor ever will.

Behavior if brethren meet when a lodge is not formed:

You are to salute one another in a courteous Manner, as you will be instructed, calling each other Brother, freely giving mutual instruction as shall be thought expedient, without being ever seen or overheard, and without encroaching upon each other, or derogating from that Respect which is due to any Brother, were he not Mason: For though all Masons are as Brethren upon the same Level, yet Masonry takes no Honor from a man that he had before; nay, rather it adds to his Honor, especially if he has deserve well of the Brotherhood, who must give Honor to whom it is due, and avoid ill Manners.

Behavior between Freemasons when not in a formed Lodge: Behavior in the presence of non-Masons:

You shall be cautious in your Words and Carriage, that the most penetrating Stranger shall not be able to discover or find out what is not proper to be intimated, and sometimes you shall divert a Discourse, and manage it prudently for the Honor of the worshipful Fraternity.

Behavior at home and in one's neighborhood:

You are to act as becomes a moral and wise Man; particularly not to let your Family, Friends and Neighbors know the Concern of the Lodge, &c., but wisely to consult your own Honour, and that of the ancient Brotherhood, for reasons not to be mention'd here You must also consult your Health, by not continuing together too late, or too long from Home, after Lodge Hours are past; and by avoiding of Gluttony or Drunkenness, that your Families be not neglected or injured, nor you disabled from working.

Behavior toward a stranger brother-Mason:

You are cautiously to examine him, in such a Method as Prudence shall direct you, that you may not be impos'd upon by an ignorant, false Pretender, whom you are to reject with contempt and Derision, and beware of giving him any Hints of Knowledge. But if you discover him to be a true and genuine Brother, you are to respect him accordingly; and if he is in Want, you must relieve him if you can, or else direct him how he may be relieved; you must employ him some days, or else recommend him to be employ'd. But you are not charged to do beyond your ability, only to prefer a poor Brother, that is a good Man and true before any other poor People in the same Circumstance.

Summation:

Finally, all these Charges you are to observe, and also those that shall be recommended to you in another Way; cultivating Brotherly Love, the Foundation and Cap-stone, the Cement and Glory of this Ancient Fraternity, avoiding all wrangling and quarreling, all Slander and Backbiting, nor permitting others to slander any honest Brother, but defending his Character, and doing him all good Offices, as far as is consistent with your Honor and Safety, and no farther. And if any of them do you Injury you must apply to your own or his Lodge, and from thence you may appeal to the Grand Lodge, at the Quarterly Communication and from thence to the annual Grand Lodge, as has been the ancient laudable Conduct but when the Case cannot be otherwise decided, and patiently listening to the honest and friendly Advice of Master and Fellows when they would prevent your going to Law with Strangers, or would excite you to put a speedy Period to all Lawsuits, so that you may mind the Affair of Masonry with the more Alacrity and Success; but with respect to Brothers or Fellows at Law, the Master and Brethren should kindly offer their Mediation, which ought to be thankfully submitted to by the contending Brethren; and if that submission is impracticable, they must, however, carry on their

Process, or Lawsuit, without Wrath and Rancor (not In the common way) saying or doing nothing which may hinder Brotherly Love, and good Offices to be renew'd and continu'd; that all may see the benign Influence of Masonry, as all true Masons have done from the beginning of the World, and will do to the End of Time.

In a critical analysis of the Anderson Constitutions, H. L. Haywood notes that "save in the hands of the most expert Masonic antiquarian," the document provided "little dependable historical facts" as to why it should be accepted as "a bona fide history of the Craft." He feels that Anderson's history belongs "in the realm of fable for the most part, and has never been accepted as anything else by knowing ones."

Providing his own summation of the history of Masonic documents, Haywood notes that in 1757 King George II had presented to the British Museum a collection of 12,000 volumes, the nucleus of which had been laid by King Henry VII and which came to be known as the Royal Library. Among these books was a manuscript written by hand on sixty-four pages of vellum, about four by five inches in size. Titled "A Poem of Moral Duties," it was discovered in the 1830s by James O. Halliwell and came to be called both the Halliwell manuscript and the Regius poem. Following this find, Halliwell presented a paper on the manuscript before the Society of Antiquaries in 1839. David Casley, a specialist in manuscripts, dates the Regius to the fourteenth century. Another expert dates it to the middle of the fifteenth century and a German specialist places it between 1427 and 1445. The majority of experts agree on 1390 as the most probable date. Written in meter, possibly by a priest, and providing a picture of the regulations of the Craft at that time and referred to things "written in old books," Haywood notes, it was a book *about* Masonry, rather than a document *of* Masonry.

The second to the Regius as the oldest manuscript was published by R. Spencer in 1861 and edited by Matthew Cooke. Dated around 1450, it was probably compiled and written in the southeastern portion of the western Midlands of England, perhaps Gloucestershire or Oxfordshire. According to Haywood, it was most certainly in the hands of George

Payne, in 1720, when he compiled "General Regulations," which Anderson includes in his own version of the Constitutions three years later.

For these reasons, writes Haywood, Anderson's historical pages are to be read "with extreme caution" because the Constitution "itself, or that part dealing with the principles and regulations of the Craft, is most certainly a compilation made of extracts of other versions of the Old Charges pretty much mixed with the Doctor's own ideas."

Yet, for all of Anderson's "faults as a historian," Haywood admits, "Anderson is a great figure in our annals" who had produced a document that was "the groundwork" of a symbolic, philosophically speculative Masonry with no sectarian character as to religion or politics.

With the adoption and publication of Anderson's Constitutions, William Cowper, clerk of the Parliaments, was appointed secretary to the Grand Lodge to keep minutes of its meetings. By 1730, the Grand Lodge had over 100 lodges in England and Wales under its authority and had begun to spread Freemasonry abroad, warranting lodges to meet in Madrid and Calcutta. For historical reasons, separate Grand Lodges were formed in Ireland (1725) and Scotland (1736).

As the premier Grand Lodge of England continued developing in the 1730s and 1740s without any opposition, its meetings were advertised and reported in newspapers that exhibited an interest in the Masonic ceremonies. Enterprising journalists and pamphleteers were eager to produce exposures of what they believed were the "secrets" of Freemasonry. Publicity increased interest and a growing number of aristocrats, landed gentry, and professional men began to seek admission. In 1737, the first Royal Freemason was Frederick Lewis, the prince of Wales, and son of King George II.

Grand Lodges also spread Freemasonry around the globe. From the 1730s, lodges were established in Europe, the West Indies, and India. As the British Empire expanded in the late eighteenth and into the nineteenth centuries, English Freemasonry was carried into the Middle and Far East, Australia, Africa, and South America. When colonies eventually achieved nation status in the second half of the twentieth century, many of them saw formation of independent local Grand Lodges, while others remained with the parent Grand Lodge, resulting in the United Grand Lodge of England having some 750 lodges overseas, principally in Commonwealth countries.

But it was in Britain's colonies in North America that Freemasonry would not only take root and thrive, but also contribute significantly to history's first successful anticolonialist war and the birth of the United States of America.

CHAPTER 6

FREEMASONRY TAKES ROOT IN AMERICA

THE FIRST KNOWN FREEMASON TO SETTLE IN AMERICA WAS John Skene. The son of Alexander Skene and Lilias Gillespie of Newtyle, England, he was born around 1649. He arrived in the New World via the Delaware River with his family aboard the *Golden Lion* in 1682 and settled at Mount Holly, New Jersey, on a plantation that he named Peachland. He went on to be deputy colonial governor of West Jersey. He died 1690.

The first Freemason *born* in America was Andrew Belcher. The son of Jonathan Belcher, a former governor of Massachusetts and New Hampshire who had been made a Mason in 1704, Andrew was admitted in 1733. Three years earlier (June 1730), the grand master of England had appointed Daniel Coxe of New Jersey as the first grand master of the New World, but Coxe was evidently not interested in vigorously promoting the brotherhood in the colonies. The entry for New Jersey in the "General History of Freemasonry" portion of Robert Macoy's authoritative *Dictionary of Freemasonry* states, "That Bro. Coxe exercised any of the powers delegated to him we are not informed, nor has any evidence of action on his part been discovered." Macoy also notes, "The first authentic information that we have is that a convention of Masons in the State was held at the city of New Brunswick, Dec. 18, 1786."

When Masonic lodges were established in New Jersey, New York, and Pennsylvania, they were "irregular," meaning that they had not been chartered by the Grand Lodge of England. The first to be given a grant of "warrant" from England's grand master (Lord Montague) was in Boston,

Massachusetts. It was presented to Henry Price on July 30, 1733. At a meeting on that day in the Bunch of Grapes tavern, he and several now formally recognized "brethren" claimed the title "first Lodge in Boston" and named it "St. John's Grand Lodge." None of the members of the Boston lodge had ever been employed in the craft of stone working. They were attracted to Freemasonry by its intellectual, philosophical, and religious aspects and by the opportunities membership afforded for convivial social intercourse. But these sentiments of Masonic fraternity among the members of St. John's Lodge would be tested in 1752 in the form of a rival lodge that was sanctioned by the Grand Lodge of Scotland.

"The prayer of the petitioners being granted," notes Macoy's general history, "they received a dispensation, dated Nov. 30, 1752, from Sholto Charles Douglas, Lord Aberdour, then Grand Master, constituting them a regular Lodge under the title of 'St. Andrew's Lodge, No. 82,' to be holden in the province of Massachusetts Bay." Installed as grand master of the new lodge was a renowned military figure, Joseph Warren. Among the members were Boston silversmith Paul Revere and attorney at law John Hancock.

Outraged by this competing lodge, the St. John's Lodge membership "imagined their jurisdiction infringed" and refused any communications or visits from members of St. Andrew's. This state of affairs continued for years. The rivalry was exacerbated by the creation in 1769 of a "Massachusetts Grand Lodge," with the assistance of three Masonic lodges within the ranks of the British army stationed in Boston. At a "festival" held on May 30, 1769, a commission from the earl of Dalhousie in his role of grand master of Masons in Scotland was given to Warren, appointing him grand master of Masons in Boston and within 100 miles of the city. The situation worsened on August 28, 1769, when St. Andrew's conferred a new Masonic degree that recalled and honored the Knights Templar. Describing the competing lodges in *The Temple and the Lodge*, historians Michael Baigent and Richard Leigh observe, "Not surprisingly, things became acrimonious, tempers flared, a 'them against us' situation developed and a miniaturized civil war of Free-masonic insult ensued. St. John's looked askance at St. Andrew's and, with vindictive passion, repeatedly 'passed resolutions against it.' Whatever they entailed, these resolutions produced no effect and St. John's proceeded to sulk, petulantly forbidding its members to visit St. Andrew's."

Three years before the establishment of the St. John's Lodge in Boston, the flourishing of Freemasonry in the colonies was noted in a Philadelphia newspaper. On December 8, 1730, the *Pennsylvania Gazette* referred to "several Lodges of FREE MASONS erected in this Province." The owner, editor, and printer of the *Gazette* was a former Bostonian, Benjamin Franklin. Born in 1706, he was the tenth son of a soap and candlemaker. Mostly self-taught, he served an apprenticeship to his father between the ages of ten and twelve, then went to work for his half brother, James. A printer, James founded the *New England Courant,* the fourth newspaper in the colonies, to which Benjamin contributed fourteen essays. Because of brotherly dissension, he left New England for Philadelphia in 1723 and obtained employment as a printer. After a year, he sailed to London. Returning to Philadelphia two years later, he rose rapidly in the printing trade and took over the *Pennsylvania Gazette* from its founder. His most successful literary venture was the annual *Poor Richard's Almanac.* Begun in 1733, it won immediate popularity in the colonies (second only to the Bible) and gained such a following in Europe that its author was wildly famous. During this period, he had a common-law wife, Deborah Read, who bore him a son and daughter (he is also believed to have had children with another woman out of wedlock). By 1748, he was financially independent and recognized for his philanthropy and the stimulus he gave to such civic causes as libraries, educational institutions, and hospitals.

Franklin also found time to pursue an interest in science and politics. He served as clerk (1736–1751) and member (1751–1764) of the legislature, deputy postmaster of Philadelphia (1737–1753), and deputy postmaster general of the colonies (1753–1774). Representing Pennsylvania at the Albany Congress (1754), called to unite the colonies during the French and Indian War, he won approval of his "Plan of Union." It envisioned a national government, but was rejected by colonial assemblies because it encroached on their powers.

In the years 1757–1762 and 1764–1775, Franklin lived in England, originally in the capacity of agent for Pennsylvania and later for Georgia,

New Jersey, and Massachusetts. During this period of growing political unrest at home, he eventually defended American rights and cautioned the government of King George III against the imposition of an act requiring a royal stamp on all colonial documents. When he returned to Philadelphia in May 1775, he became a member of the Continental Congress. Thirteen months later, he served on the committee created to draft the Declaration of Independence. Less than a year and a half after his return to America, he returned to Europe as one of three American commissioners to France who negotiated treaties of alliance and commerce.

Not a Mason when the Masonry articles appeared in the *Pennsylvania Gazette* in 1730, Franklin seemed interested in Freemasonry enough to use the power of the press to advance what appears to have been a desire to join the fraternity. Some historians say that he used the articles to advertise himself to Philadelphia's St. John's Lodge so that when he applied he would not be regarded as a stranger. Two months after the first printed notice of Freemasonry in America, he became a member of the St. John Lodge. Less than six months later, on St. John the Baptist's Day (June 24, 1732), he was named junior warden of the Pennsylvania Grand Lodge. Two years later, he was chosen grand master.

Eleven months after the formation of the first warranted lodge in America, and six years after Anderson's Constitutions was first published in England, Franklin's *Pennsylvania Gazette* in issues from May 6 to 16 announced the pending publication for sale as a pamphlet of "THE CONSTITUTIONS OF THE FREEMASON; Containing the History, Charges, Regulations, etc., of that most ancient and Right Worshipful Fraternity, London Printed, Reprinted, by B. Franklin, in the year of Masonry 5734." The Masonic calendar was based on a calculation by a clergyman that God had created the world in 4004 B.C., but to make counting the years easier the date was pushed back four years on the calendar so that Masonic years began with a millennium year (4000 B.C.). Despite Franklin's advertisement of imminent publication of the constitution, it did not appear until August. Seventy copies of the "Masons' Book" were sent to St. John's Lodge in Boston, others to a lodge in Charleston, and still later more to Boston.

On November 28, 1734, Franklin wrote to the Boston lodge in reply to a letter from its Grand Master Henry Price. After noting that Price had "so happily recovered" from an illness and wishing well to him and "the prosperity of your whole lodge," he turned to the legal status of the lodge in Philadelphia. Noting that he had read "in the Boston prints an article of news from London" that Price's "power was extended over all America," he appealed to Price to "give the proceedings and determinations of our Lodge their due weight."

Asking for the granting of "a Deputation or Charter," he continued:

> This, if it seems good and reasonable to you to grant, will not only be extremely agreeable to us, but will also, we are confident, conduce much to the welfare, establishment and reputation of Masonry in these parts. We therefore submit it for your consideration, and, as we hope our request will be complied with, we desire that it may be done as soon as possible, and also accompanied with a copy of the R.W. Grand Master's first Deputation, and of the instrument by which it appears to be enlarged as above-mentioned, witnessed by your Wardens, and signed by the secretary; for which favours this Lodge doubts not of being able to behave as not to be thought ungrateful.
>
> We are, Right Worshipful Grand Master and Most Worthy Brethren, Your affectionate Brethren and obliged humble servants, Signed at the request of the Lodge, B. Franklin, G.M. Philadelphia, Nov. 28, 1734.

Franklin's lodge's meetings were held in Tun's Tavern. Between 1769 and 1790, they were also held occasionally in a building in Videll's Alley off Second Street below Chestnut Street. It was there that the Grand Lodge of Free and Accepted Masons of Pennsylvania declared its independence from the Grand Lodge of England on September 25, 1786. From 1790 to 1799, the lodge met at the Free Quaker Meeting House. In 1800, it convened on the second floor of the Pennsylvania State House (Independence Hall). After Freemasons Hall was dedicated in December 1802, Philadelphia Freemasonry would have its own building at various sites until the opening of the present Masonic Temple in 1873. The original meeting place, Tun's Tavern, would gain another historical distinction in 1775. When the Continental Congress authorized raising two battalions of a "United States Marine Corps," the first volunteers were enlisted in the tavern.

Four years after publication of the U.S. Constitution, Franklin and Philadelphia Masonry found themselves in the middle of a scandal involving a practical joke that resulted in the death of a young man. When apothecary Evan Jones learned that his apprentice, Daniel Rees, wanted to become a Freemason, he and other apprentices decided to pretend to be members and stage a mock initiation ceremony by dressing up like devils. Informed of the plan, Franklin treated it as a good joke, but quickly changed his mind. He sought to alert Rees, but was unable to find him. During the fake ceremony, Jones required Rees to swear obedience to the devil and seal the oath by kissing the behinds of the other apprentices. In the culmination of the initiation, Jones poured hot brandy on Rees. The resulting burns proved so severe that they became infected and Rees died. Convicted of manslaughter at a trial in which Franklin was a prosecution witness, Jones was punished by having his hand branded.

In a published statement, Franklin denied that Jones and the others were Freemasons, but the incident served to fuel suspicions that Masonry was a sinister organization. The incident was also exploited by a Franklin rival, William Bradford. The publisher of the *American Weekly Mercury*, he used Rees's death as a pretext to launch attacks on Franklin's affiliation with the Freemasons. The incident also alarmed Franklin's mother over his membership in the order. To allay the fears, he wrote his father on April 13, 1738:

> As to the Freemasons, I know of no way of giving my mother a better account of them than she seems to have at present, since it is not allowed that women should be admitted into that secret society. She has, I must confess on that account some reason to be displeased with it; but for anything else, I must entreat her to suspend her judgment till she is better informed, unless she will believe me, when I assure her that they are in general a very harmless sort of people, and have

no principles or practices that are inconsistent with religion and good manners.

In 1743, Franklin held "fraternal communion" with his brethren in the First (St. John's) Lodge of Boston. Six years later, he was named provincial grand master, an appointment that lasted one year. In 1755, he was present for the quarterly communication of the Grand Lodge of Massachusetts and prominent in the anniversary and dedication of the Freemason's Lodge in Philadelphia, the first Masonic building in America. Two years later, he went to London in the interest of Pennsylvania and stayed five years. He befriended leading intellectuals in England and Scotland, including political and economic theorist Adam Smith, and contacted English Freemasons. After returning to Philadelphia for two years, he was back in Britain in 1764. As a negotiator on behalf of the thirteen colonies concerning increasing tensions between them and King George III's government on the issue of taxation, he remained in London ten years. But on January 29, 1774, he found himself summoned before the king's privy council. Denounced as a thief and a man without honor, he was called on to answer for an event that had occurred in Boston harbor six weeks earlier.

On the night of December 16, 1773, a small group of men disguised as Mohawk Indians boarded the British East India Company's merchant ship *Dartmouth* to protest a tax on tea by dumping its cargo of 342 tea chests, valued at 10,000 pounds, into the harbor. Immediately named the "Boston Tea Party" and enshrined in U.S. history as a landmark on the road to the American Revolution, the act of defiance has also been proudly claimed by Freemasonry as the work of members of the St. Andrew Lodge. The claim rests on a story that the tea party was planned in the "Long Room" of Freemason's Hall (formerly the Green Dragon tavern), a facility that was also used by groups dedicated to resisting "taxation without representation." Although historic records are clear that the tea party was planned and carried out by the non-Masonic "Sons of Liberty," twelve St. Andrew Lodge members were among the tea-dumping raiders and a dozen of the participants became members soon after the tea party.

The day after the raid, it was St. Andrew Lodge member Paul Revere who mounted a horse to carry the news to New York. On the night of April 18, 1775, he would be in the saddle again to sound the alarm to "every Middlesex village and farm" that British troops were marching from Boston to seize caches of weapons at Concord. When the smoke of battles at Lexington and Concord cleared and British soldiers were back in Boston, the stage was set for Freemasonry to claim its first American hero in the person of St. Andrew's grand master, Dr. Joseph Warren.

Born in Roxbury, Massachusetts, in 1740, he graduated from Harvard and was made a Mason in the St. Andrew Lodge on September 10, 1761. He received the second degree on September 2, 1761, but it was not until November 28, 1765, that he was made master Mason. Described as "somewhat impetuous in his nature, but brave to a fault," he spoke to a large crowd at Boston's Old South Church on the anniversary of the Boston Massacre (March 3, 1770) with the knowledge that English army officers usually attended such gatherings in order to heckle the speaker. Describing that day, a Masonic biographer of Warren writes:

It required a cool head and steady nerves, and Grand Master Joseph Warren had both. The crowd at the church was immense; the aisles, the pulpit stairs, and the pulpit itself was filled with officers and soldiers of the garrison, always there to intimidate the speaker. Warren was equal to the task but entered the church through a pulpit window in the rear, knowing he might have been barred from entering through the front. In the midst of his most impassioned speech, an English officer seated on the pulpit stairs and in full view of Warren, held several pistol bullets in his open hand. The act was significant; while the moment was one of peril and required the exercise of both courage and prudence, to falter and allow a single nerve or muscle to tremble would have meant failure—even ruin to Warren and others. Everyone present knew the intent of the officer but Warren having caught the act of the officer and without the least discomposure or pause in his discourse, simply approached the officer and dropped a white handkerchief into the officer's hand! The act was so cleverly

and courteously performed that the officer was compelled to acknowledge it by letting the orator to continue in peace.

On June 14, 1775, Warren was elected major general by the Provincial
Congress of Massachusetts. With no military education or experience, he
was placed in command of the rebel force on Breed's Hill (later called
Bunker Hill) as the "Red Coats"crossed the bay from Boston to lift a siege
on the city that had been established after Lexington-Concord. Against
the protests of Generals Artemis Ward and Israel Putnam, Warren shoul-
dered a musket to join his men behind barricades on the hill.

The shooting on June 17, 1775, lasted less than one hour, with the
Americans running out of ammunition. Fatally shot in the back of the head,
Warren's body was thrown in a ditch by a British officer and buried with
several other bodies. After the mass grave was discovered months later,
Warren's body was identified by Paul Revere by a false tooth he had made
for Warren. The remains were eventually placed in the Warren family vault
at Forest Hill Cemetery. On April 8, 1777, Congress ordered a marker for
the grave, but it was never installed. In 1794, King Solomon's Lodge of
Charlestown erected a monument on Bunker Hill on land donated by
Mason Benjamin Russell. The monument was an eighteen-foot pillar placed
on an eight-square-foot platform surrounded by a fence. In 1823, the
Bunker Hill Monument Association was formed for the purpose of erect-
ing "a more fitting and enduring monument to the memory of the brave
men who fell there in the cause of human liberty." The land was donated
by King Solomon's Lodge (1783) on the condition "that some trace" of
the former monument's existence be preserved in the new memorial. On
June 17, 1825, the Grand Lodge of Massachusetts formed a procession on
Boston Common and proceeded to Bunker Hill. In the presence of the
Marquis de Lafayette, who was visiting the United States for the first time
since he served with the Americans in the Revolutionary War, members
of lodges from every New England state except Rhode Island, along with
the Grand Lodge of New Jersey, took part in laying the cornerstone. The
completed memorial was dedicated on June 13, 1843. In 1976, it came
under the jurisdiction of the U.S. National Park Service.

One year, two weeks, and three days after Warren's death on Bunker Hill, Congress published the Declaration of Independence. Fifteen of the fifty-six signers (27 percent) were Freemasons or probable Freemasons. Known Masons were Benjamin Franklin, John Hancock, Joseph Hewes, William Hooper, Robert Treat Payne, Richard Stockton, George Walton, and William Whipple. Those for whom there is evidence of membership or affiliations were Elbridge Gerry, Lyman Hall, Thomas Jefferson, Thomas Nelson Jr., John Penn, George Read, and Roger Sherman.

While the declaration was being discussed in June 1776, Congress took time out to appoint a committee to prepare plans for treaties "of commerce and amity" with other countries. When it issued a report in September, Congress presented the task to three "commissioners." It named Silas Deane, who was already in Europe, Thomas Jefferson, and Benjamin Franklin.

As an envoy to France, Franklin formed affiliations with the country's Masonic lodges. In 1777, he was elected a member of the Lodge des Neuf Souers (Lodge of the Nine Sisters, or Nine Muses) of Paris, and in 1778 he assisted in Voltaire's initiation into the lodge. In 1782, he became a member of the Lodge de St. Jean de Jerusalem. In the following year, he was elected venerable d'honneur of that body. The same year he was made an honorary member of the Lodge des bons Amis (Good Friends), Rouen. These and other distinctions were honored in a sermon at St. Paul's Church, Philadelphia. On St. John's Day in December 1786, he was referred to as "An illustrious Brother whose distinguished merit among Masons entitles him to their highest veneration." One scholar of Franklin's contributions to Masonry writes that no catalog of his offices, services, dates, names, and places could adequately convey his importance and "facets of a many-sided jewel which best reflect the influence Freemasonry had upon him."

Enshrined in the literature of Freemasonry is this from Franklin:

> Freemasonry has tenets peculiar to itself. They serve as testimonials of character and qualifications, which are only conferred after due course of instruction and examination. These are of no small value; they speak a universal language, and act as a passport to the attentions and support of the initiated in all parts of the world. They cannot be

lost as long as memory retains its power. Let the possessor of them be expatriated, shipwrecked or imprisoned, let him be stripped of everything he has got in the world, still those credentials remain, and are available for use as circumstances require. The good effects they have produced are established by the most incontestable facts of history. They have stayed the uplifted hand of the destroyer; they have softened the asperities of the tyrant; they have mitigated the horrors of captivity; they have subdued the rancor of malevolence; and broken down the barriers of political animosity and sectarian alienation. On the field of battle, in the solitudes of the uncultivated forest, or in the busy haunts of the crowded city, they have made men of the most hostile feelings, the most distant regions, and diversified conditions, rush to the aid of each other, and feel a special joy and satisfaction that they have been able to afford relief to a Brother Mason.

Franklin also wrote of the Craft, "Masonic labor is purely a labor of love. He who seeks to draw Masonic wages in gold and silver will be disappointed. The wages of a Mason are earned and paid in their dealings with one another; sympathy that begets sympathy, kindness begets kindness, helpfulness begets helpfulness, and these are the wages of a Mason."

During the convention in Philadelphia that produced the U.S. Constitution, Franklin used language that Freemasons interpret as evidence of his Masonry:

The longer I live, the more convincing proofs I see of this truth, that God governs in the affairs of men. And if a sparrow cannot fall to the ground without his notice, is it probable that an empire can rise without His aid? We have been assured, Sir, in the Sacred Writings, that "except the Lord build the house, they labor in vain that build it." I firmly believe this; and I also believe, that, without His concurring aid, we shall succeed in this political building no better than the builders of [the Tower of] Babel.

A Masonic Franklin biographer writes, "It is not for us to say what he would have been had there been no Freemasonry in his life; it is for us only to revere the Franklin who was among the very greatest of any other nation, in all times; for us to congratulate ourselves and be thankful for our country, that this wise philosopher, this leader of men and of nations, had taken to his heart the immutable and eternal principles of the Ancient Craft."

The period of the American Revolution also saw the first American Indian initiated into Freemasonry. Named Thayendangea, he was the son of the chief of the Mohawks in the 1750s. He was brought up in the household of a prominent British administration official, Sir William Johnson, a Freemason, who gave him the name Joseph Brant. Having fought several battles with Johnson in the French and Indian War, he became Johnson's personal secretary, and by the time of Johnson's death in 1774, had become accepted by the British administration. When he went to England in 1775, he was made a Mason in a London Lodge. Returning to America to enlist the Mohawks in the fight against the American rebels, he fought under the command of Colonel John Butler in several attacks on and massacres of Americans. But when prisoners were turned over to the Mohawks to be tortured to death made Masonic signs, he released them. After the war, he became a member of St. John's Lodge of Friendship No. 2 in Canada, of which Butler had become master, before returning to the Mohawks in Ohio.

Although Franklin is a towering figure in American Freemasonry, in the lore and legend of American Freemasonry he stands in the shadow of George Washington. Born in Virginia on February 22, 1732, Washington became a Mason in the lodge at Fredericksburg, Virginia, on August 4, 1753, at the age of twenty-one. When a lodge in Alexandria was chartered in 1788, he was named charter master. As the first president of the United States, he wrote to a lodge in Rhode Island in 1790, "Being persuaded that a just application of the principles on which the Masonic Fraternity is founded must be a promotive of private virtue and public prosperity, I shall always be happy to advance the interest of the Society and to be considered by them as a deserving brother."

Masonic historians note that while Washington admired the principles and goals of Freemasonry, he was not especially familiar with them and did not attempt to learn more about the Craft. Although he wrote letters indicating that he was happy to be a Freemason, and never sought to resign or repudiate his Masonic membership, there is little or no evidence that he attended many Masonic lodge meetings after his initiation in 1753. Records indicate that he attended at most three meetings, and possibly fewer or none. He may have attended the dinners, but he seems not to have participated in meetings of the lodge of which he was the first master under its Virginia Charter that today is called Alexandria-Washington Lodge No. 22. While master of the lodge, he did not assist in the work of the lodge.

As commander in chief of the army, Washington was virtually surrounded by Masons. Half of his generals belonged to the Craft, including Lafayette and German army officer Baron von Steuben. While they battled regular English troops and Prussian mercenaries on land, John Paul Jones, a young seagoing Freemason who had been born in Scotland and had embraced the American cause, carried the fight to the high seas by attacking British ships and raiding English ports. Revered as the father of the U.S. Navy, he gave Americans one of their most stirring battle cries: "I have not yet begun to fight."

While Freemasons are justifiably proud of Masons who served gallantly in the War for Independence, one of its most brilliant and heroic generals proved to be an embarrassment. Early in the war, Benedict Arnold (initiated in Connecticut in 1763) distinguished himself by leading an assault on Quebec, Canada. Wounded in a leg in the bold attack that failed to take the city, he emerged as a hero. During later battles at Saratoga, New York, he proved to be a brilliant strategist who again exhibited heroics. But the commander, General Horatio Gates, a Mason, relieved him of his command, in part for insubordination and because Gates viewed Arnold as a "pompous little fellow."

This insult to Arnold was assuaged following British abandonment of Philadelphia when George Washington appointed him to the post of commandant of the city. But by this time he was an embittered figure with open disdain for his fellow officers and resentment toward Congress for not promoting him more quickly. He was also a widower who courted and married Margaret (Peggy) Shippen, described as "a talented young woman of good family." At nineteen, she was half Arnold's age and pro-British.

Plunging into the social life of America's largest and most sophisticated city by throwing lavish parties, he was soon deeply in debt. This extravagance drew him into dubious financial schemes that caused Congress to investigate his activities, resulting in a recommendation that he be brought before a court-martial. Arnold complained to Washington that having "become a cripple in the service of my country, I little expected to meet ungrateful returns." Confronted with personal and financial ruin, facing an uncertain future of promotion, and disgusted with the politicians in Congress, Arnold made a fateful and ultimately disastrous decision to wipe out his difficulties by offering his services to the British.

He began by writing to their commander, General Sir Henry Clinton, a Mason, and promising to deliver the garrison at West Point, with 3,000 defenders, in the belief that the surrender would bring about the collapse of the American cause. To put himself in a position to deliver, Arnold persuaded Washington to place the fort under his command. In September 1780, he was ready to execute his plan. To assist him in the plot, the British chose Major John André, a Mason, as the go-between. The two men shared more than the conspiracy to neutralize West Point. Before Arnold married Shippen, André had been her suitor.

Serving with the Fifty-fourth Foot as adjutant general to General Clinton, André was also in charge of British spy operations. To make it easier for the British to take over the fort, Arnold scattered his troops to weaken West Point's defenses. Following a meeting with Arnold on September 21, 1780, André set out for his own lines in civilian clothes and carrying identification papers in the name of "John Anderson." He was stopped by three suspicious Americans, taken to headquarters, searched, and exposed as a spy. Learning this, Arnold hastened to New York and the safety of his British allies.

When the British expressed a desire to gain André's release, Washington sent prominent political leader (and Mason) Aaron Ogden to inform General Clinton that he would release André only in exchange for Arnold. Clinton refused and André was hanged on October 2, 1780. He accommodated his executioner by placing the noose around his neck and tying his own handkerchief as a blindfold. His body was eventually disinterred and buried with much pomp as a hero in Westminster Abbey.

Arnold served the British in 1781 by leading devastating strikes on American supply depots. In Virginia, he looted Richmond and destroyed munitions and stores of grain intended for the American army opposing Lord Cornwallis. In his native Connecticut, he burned ships, warehouses, and much of the town of New London, which was a major port for American privateers. When the war ended with American independence secured, he settled in London and died there in obscurity in June 1801.

Shortly after Arnold became an American hero at the Battle of Saratoga in October 1777, the Continental Congress in Philadelphia concluded a year-long debate over the nature of the government of the "United States of America" that had been proclaimed in the Declaration of Independence. On November 15, 1777, representatives of the former colonies voted to adopt thirteen "Articles of Confederation" and sent them to the states for ratification. Because of Maryland's refusal to agree until states claiming western lands ceded them to the new nation, approval did not occur until March 1, 1781. With independence secured by the surrender of the British force under General Charles Cornwallis to Washington at Yorktown, Virginia, on August 19, 1782, Americans had won their independence, but as Masonic historian H. C. Clausen notes in *Masons Who Helped Shape Our Nation*, "Though free, we were not yet united. The loose Article of Confederation did not provide a strong national government, common currency or consistent judicial system. Men of vision realized that another step must be taken if the weak Confederation of American States was to become a strong, unified nation."

In the calling for a convention to devise a new structure of governance, and during the debate that resulted in the formation of the U.S. Constitution, Freemasons played a significant role. When the Constitutional Convention opened on May 25, 1787, in Philadelphia, with eighty-one-year-old Benjamin Franklin as a delegate and George Washington the unanimous choice of fifty-five representatives as presiding officer, Freemasonry was not only the single remaining pre-Revolution fraternal entity, but also the sole organization operating nationally, with lodges in every state. Of the five dominant and guiding men in the debate on the structure of the nation's new governmental structure, three were Freemasons: Washington, Franklin, and Edmund Randolph. The others, John Adams and Thomas

Jefferson, while not adherents of the Craft, held views that were similar. Twenty-eight of forty signers of the Constitution were Masons or possibly members. The known Freemasons were Franklin, Washington, Gunning Bedford Jr., John Blair, David Brearly, Jacob Broom, Daniel Carrol, John Dickinson, and Rufus King. Those for whom there is evidence of membership or affiliations were Alexander Hamilton, Abraham Baldwin, William Blount, Nicholas Gilman, James Madison, Roger Sherman, George Read, and Robert Morris. Those who later became Masons were Jonathan Dayton, James McHenry, and William Patterson.

After an addition of ten amendments (the Bill of Rights), the Constitution was declared ratified by the required number of states on September 13, 1788. When balloting by electors for the first president of the United States was held in the states on February 4, 1789, the unanimous choice was George Washington. Following certification of his election by Congress, he set out from his Virginia home for the nations's new capital, New York City, on April 16, and arrived one week later. On April 30 at Federal Hall at Wall and Broad Streets, the presidential oath of office was administered by Robert Livingston, grand master of the lodge.

Not present to witness the inauguration was Benjamin Franklin. He died thirteen days earlier. Half of Philadelphia's population had turned out for his funeral, but because of a rift in Freemasonry, the lodge that had embraced him as a member in 1730 denied him the rites of Masonic burial.

The rupture over the foundation, structure, and practices of Freemasonry, known as "the schism," would last for six decades and have a profound, lasting effect on the nature of Masonry in the United States.

BROTHERS DIVIDED

W HEN THE FOUR MASONIC LODGES OF LONDON CAME
together in 1717 to revive the Craft, the Premier Grand Lodge
of England assumed authority over all aspects of a Masonry that
were codified in 1723 in the Anderson Constitutions. By that time, the
number of lodges had increased to thirty. Gradually, lodges outside London came into the jurisdiction and the Grand Lodge chartered new organizations, including a Grand Lodge in Munster, Ireland, in 1725, the
Grand Lodge of Ireland in 1730, the Grand Lodge of Pennsylvania in
1731 (Benjamin Franklin's), and the Grand Lodge of Scotland in 1736.

The schism in English Freemasonry began in 1751 with the formation
of a new Grand Lodge under the name of Grand Lodge of England.
Created according to the Old Charges, it was composed of six lodges of
Irish Masons that had not affiliated with the original Grand Lodge of
England. The members called themselves "Antient York Masons," a reference to an assembly of Masons at York in 926. The word "Antient" was
intended to convey the new Grand Lodge's claim that only its ritual preserved the "ancient customs and usages" of Freemasonry. In an ironic re-
versal of meaning, the Antients called the older original Grand Lodge of
England "Modern" Masons. As one historian of Masonry observes, the
Antients proved to be "better propagandists" and more interested in promoting themselves than were the Moderns. This was largely because of
their grand secretary, Laurence Dermott. Author of the Book of Constitutions
for the Grand Lodge of Antients, titled *Ahiman Rezon* (Hebrew for "help
to a brother"), he was tireless in increasing the strength and importance of

the Grand Lodge, gaining recognition by the Grand Lodges of Ireland and Scotland, and starting lodges in other countries and also in the ranks of the army. It was these military lodges that lent impetus to the spreading of Freemasonry to the colonies.

While serving in the British army during the French and Indian War under the command of Lord Jeffrey Amherst, young Americans who learned the arts of war that would be of use to them in the Revolutionary War included Benedict Arnold, Israel Putnam, Ethan Allen, and Philip John Schuyler. This influx of British troops also resulted in their American cousins being introduced to Freemasonry known as the Scottish Rite.

Despite the name, it originated not in Scotland, but in France. It was introduced by Scots who had fled strife in the British Isles. Masonic historians say that the beginning of the Scottish Rite can be traced to the establishment of the Chapter of Clermont in 1754 outside of Paris, when Chevalier de Bonneville honored the duc de Clermont, grand master of the English Grand Lodge of France. Replaced by the Knights of the East and Emperors of the East and West, known in France as the Rite of Heredom (1750s), this rite organized the Rite of Perfection, comprised of twenty-five degrees, twenty-two of which were called the *haut grades*, or high degrees, with the three degrees of the symbolic lodge added. A document pertaining to the Rite of Perfection, known as the Secret Constitutions of 1761, designated officers as inspectors general of the thirty-third degree.

With the emergence of this document, a joint "patent" was issued from the Grand Lodge of France and the Emperors of the East and West to a merchant named Étienne (Stephen) Morin, for the purpose of establishing the Rite of Perfection in the Americas. It granted Morin the title of inspector general, with the authority to create other inspectors general and to establish lodges to work in "the perfect and sublime degrees." A year later, the Grand Constitutions of 1762 was adopted, providing for twenty-five degrees, including the three degrees of English Masonry. From Morin's original authority, patents were granted establishing the Rite of Perfection in the West Indies, Albany, New Orleans, Philadelphia, and Charleston. Morin added several more degrees, the highest being the sovereign grand inspector general, thirty-third degree.

The Grand Constitutions of 1786, adopted in Berlin on May 1, 1786, provided for a rite consisting of thirty-three degrees under the title "Ancient and Accepted Scottish Rite" and governed by a Supreme Council. It created the structure and governance of the Scottish Rite that would become the form of Freemasonry practiced in the United States today.

While the Scottish Rite was evolving in France, the Freemasonry of England that took root in the American colonies was being nurtured by lodges established within the ranks of King George III's army. Describing the Freemasonry that British soldiers brought to America as an "ambience, a mentality, a hierarchy of attitudes and values," historians Michael Baigent and Richard Leigh in *The Temple and the Lodge* observe that it was largely through military lodges "that 'ordinary' colonists learned of that lofty premise called 'the rights of man'[and] the concept of the perfectibility of society." A result of the introduction of the Scottish Rite to the Americans was the formation of St. Andrew's Lodge, with its leader Joseph Warren and other lodge members joining the Boston Tea Party; Paul Revere making his midnight ride; the Battle of Bunker Hill; and the formation of a revolutionary army with half its generals being Masonic brothers and commanded by a Mason named George Washington.

It was also a period in which the Freemasonry of the mother country remained torn by the schism. By the beginning of the nineteenth century in England, members of both the Antients and Moderns had begun to recognize the disadvantages of disunity and the desirability of forging harmony. In 1809, the Grand Lodge of the Moderns rescinded a rule forbidding admission of the Antient Masons in Modern Lodges. The next year, the Antients made similar concessions and committees were appointed to devise ways and means of further reconciliation. This movement gained impetus when the duke of Atholl resigned as grand master of the Antients to be succeeded by the duke of Kent, whose brother, the duke of Sussex, was a grand master of the Moderns. They were sons of George III. The final ratification of the union of the two bodies took place on December 27, 1813, at Freemasons Hall in London. The two Grand Lodges met in adjoining rooms and, after having opened in accordance with their own rites and ceremonies, marched into the main hall, headed by their respective grand masters. After the Grand Lodges marched in side by side, prayers were offered and the Act of Union was read.

It proclaimed the establishment of "The United Grand Lodge of Ancient Freemasons of England." In advance of this meeting, a "Lodge of Reconciliation" had devised a system of rites and ceremonies that was adopted as the universal system for the United Grand Lodge of England. The Articles of Union contained concessions by both groups that required giving up various points of ritualism and procedure that had divided them for more than three-quarters of a century. The most significant was a modification of the language of the Anderson Constitutions concerning "that Religion in which all Men agree." This was changed to allow "a man's religion or mode of worship be what it may," provided that "he believes in the glorious Architect of heaven and earth, and practices the sacred duties of morality." The result was the replacement of the Judaic-Christian foundation of the Freemasonry of the Old Institutions to unspecific Deism.

The schism of Moderns and Antients in England had a counterpart in America. Moderns predominated, except in Pennsylvania, where the Antients were in complete control. During the Revolutionary War, twenty-seven other lodges were warranted. Nine were in Pennsylvania (one in Philadelphia), two in New Jersey, three in Maryland, two in South Carolina, one in Virginia, two in Delaware, one as an English army lodge, and seven as American army lodges. Rivalry between Antients and Moderns in the colonies became evident over the issue of independence from England. Moderns were inclined to be Loyalists, while a large majority of the Antients backed a break with England. By the end of the war, because many of the Loyalists moved to England and Canada, Modern lodges had mostly disintegrated. During the "Quarterly Communication" meeting of the Grand Lodge of Pennsylvania on September 25, 1786, a unanimously adopted resolution declared that it was independent of the Grand Lodge of England with the declaration, "This Lodge acting by virtue of a Warrant from the Grand Lodge of England was closed forever."

Although Benjamin Franklin had been an ardent leader for political independence from England, he remained a Modern. Consequently, when he died, his now Antient lodge denied him the trappings of a Masonic funeral. With his death, the mantle of America's most famous Freemason prior to the Revolutionary War passed to the general who had led the Con-

tinental army to a victory that ensured the assertion in the Declaration of
Independence that "these colonies are of right ought to be free and independent states."

As George Washington recited the presidential oath of office as required by the Constitution, his right hand rested on a Bible opened to
Genesis, chapters 49 and 50, consisting of prophecies of Jacob concerning
his sons and his son Joseph's death. Printed by Mark Baskett, "Printer to
the King's Most Excellent Majesty," in London in 1767, its first page bore
a steel-engraved portrait of King George II. The second page was inscribed, "On this sacred volume, on the 30th day of April, A. L. 5789, in
the City of New York, was administered to George Washington, the first
president of the United States of America, the oath to support the Constitution of the United States. This important ceremony was performed
by the Most Worshipful Grand Master of Free and Accepted Masons of
the State of New York, the Honorable Robert R. Livingston, Chancellor
of the State." This was followed with:

> Fame stretched her wings and with her trumpet blew
> Great Washington is near. What praise is due?
> What title shall he have? She paused and said
> "Not one—his name alone strikes every title dead."

A King James version, complete with the Apocrypha and elaborately
supplemented with the historical, astronomical, and legal data of that period, this Bible contained numerous artistic steel engravings portraying
biblical narratives from designs and paintings by old masters and engraved by the celebrated English artist John Stuart. It had been presented
to the lodge by Jonathan Hampton on November 28, 1770.

This Bible was used at the inaugurations of Presidents Warren Harding
(1921), Dwight D. Eisenhower (1953), Jimmy Carter (1977), and George
H. W. Bush (1989). It was also to have been used for the inauguration of
George W. Bush in 2001, but rain prevented it. It has also been present at
numerous public and Masonic occasions. To list but a few, they include
Washington's funeral procession in New York, December 31, 1799; the
introduction of Croton water into New York City, October 14, 1840; the

dedication of the Masonic Temple in Boston, June 24, 1867, and in Philadelphia in 1869; the dedication of the Washington Monument, February
21, 1885 (and its rededication in 1998); and the laying of the cornerstone
of the Masonic Home in Utica, New York, on May 21, 1891. It was also
used at the opening of the present Masonic Hall in New York on September
18, 1909, when St. John's Lodge held the first meeting and conferred the
first third degree in the newly completed temple. It was displayed at the
1964 World's Fair in New York, at the Central Intelligence Agency headquarters in Langley, Virginia, and at the *Famous Fathers & Sons* exhibition
at the George H. W. Bush Memorial Library in Texas in 2001. When not
in use by St. John's Lodge or on tour, it is on permanent display in what is
now Federal Hall in New York, where Washington took the oath.

On September 25, 1793, Washington left New York for the laying of
the cornerstone of the Capitol building in a city that had been named for
him in the federal District of Columbia. He was to be the central figure in
what the *Columbian Mirror & Alexandria Gazette* called "one of the grand-
est MASONIC Processions" ever seen. The newspaper reported:

> About 10 o'clock, Lodge, No. 9, were visited by that Congregation,
> so graceful to the Craft, Lodge, No. 22, of Virginia, with all their
> Officers and Regalia, and directly afterwards appeared on the south-
> ern banks of the Grand River Potomack: one of the finest companies
> of Volunteer Artillery that has been lately seen, parading to receive
> the President of the United States, who shortly came in sight with his
> suite—to whom the Artillery paid their military honors, and his Ex-
> cellency and suite crossed the Potomack, and was received in
> Maryland, by the Officers and Brethren of No. 22, Virginia and No. 9,
> Maryland whom the President headed, and preceded by a bank of
> music; the rear brought up by the Alexandria Volunteer Artillery;
> with grand solemnity of march, proceeded to the President's square
> in the City of Washington: where they were met and saluted, by No.
> 15, of the City of Washington, in all their elegant regalia, headed by
> Brother Joseph Clark, Rt. W.G.M.—P.T. and conducted to a large
> Lodge, prepared for the purpose of their reception. After a short space
> of time, by the vigilance of Brother C. Worthy Stephenson, Grand

Marshall, P.T. the Brotherhood and other Bodies were disposed in a second order of procession, which took place amid a brilliant crowd of spectators of both sexes.

The assemblage consisted of the Surveying Department of the city of Washington; the mayor and officials of "George-Town"; the Virginia Artillery; the commissioners of the city of Washington and their attendants; stone cutters; mechanics; two sword bearers; Masons of the first, second, and third degree; bearers of "Bibles &c on the Grand Cushions"; stewards with wands; a band; Lodge No. 22, of Virginia, "disposed in their own order"; bearers of corn, wine, and oil; "Grand Master P.T. [Prince of the Tabernacle] George Washington, W.M. [Worshipful Master] No. 22, Virginia"; and a "Grand Sword Bearer."

The newspaper account continued:

The procession marched two a-breast, in the greatest solemn dignity, with music playing, drums beating, colors flying, and spectators rejoicing; from the President's Square to the Capitol, in the City of Washington; where the Grand Marshall called a halt, and directed each file in the procession, to incline two steps, one to the right, and one to the left, and face each other, which formed a hollow oblong square; through which the Grand Sword Bearer led the van; followed by the Grand Master P.T. on the left—the President of the United States in the Centre, and the Worshipful Master of Number 22, Virginia, on the right—all the other orders, that composed the procession advanced, in the reverse of their order of march from the President's Square, to the south-east corner of the Capitol; and the Artillery filed off to a defined ground to display their maneuvers and discharge their cannon: The President of the United States, the Grand Master, P.T. and the Worshipful M. of No. 22, taking their stand to the East of a huge stone; and all the Craft, forming a circle westward, stood a short time in silent awful order. The Artillery discharged a Volley. The Grand Marshall delivered the Commissioners, a large Silver Plate with an inscription thereon which the missioners orders to be read, and was as follows:

This South East corner Stone, of the Capitol of the United States
of America in the City of Washington, was laid on the 18th day of
September 1793, in the thirteenth year of American Independence,
in the first year of the second term of the Presidency of George
Washington, whose virtues in the civil administration of his country have been as conspicuous and beneficial, as his Military valor
and prudence have been useful in establishing her liberties, and in
the year of Masonry 5793, by the Grand Lodge of Maryland, several Lodges under its jurisdiction, and Lodge No. 22, from Alexandria,
Virginia. Thomas Johnson, David Steuart and Daniel Carroll, Commissioners, Joseph Clark, R.W.G.M. pro tem., James Hobam and
Stephen Hallate, Architects. Collin Williamson, Master Mason.

The Artillery discharged a volley. The Plate was then delivered to
the President, who, attended by the Grand Master pro tem., and three
Most worshipful Masters, descended to the cavazion trench and deposited the plate, and laid it on the corner-stone of the Capitol of the
United States of America, on which were deposited corn, wine, and
oil, when the whole congregation joined in reverential prayer, which
was succeeded by Masonic chanting honors, and a volley from the
Artillery.

The whole company retired to an extensive booth, where an ox of
five-hundred pounds weight was barbecued, of which the company
generally partook with every abundance of other recreation. The festival concluded with fifteen successive volleys from the Artillery....
Before dark the whole company departed with joyful hopes of the
production of their labor.

The earliest record of a formal and official Masonic ceremony is that of
the laying of the foundation stone of the New Royal Infirmary of Edinburgh
by the earl of Cromarty, grand master of Scottish Masons, on August 2,
1738. The description of the event was written sixty-six years later in
1804 by Alexander Lawrie in *History of Free Masonry*. He describes a simple, almost primitive ceremony:

When the company came to the ground, the Grand Master, and his brethren of the free and accepted Masons, surrounded the plan of the foundation hand in hand: and the Grand Master-Mason, along with the press [representatives] of the Managers of the Royal Infirmary, having come to the east corner of the foundation where the stone was to be laid, placed the same in its bed; and after the Right Honorable the Lord Provost had laid a medal under it each in their turns gave three strokes upon the stone with an iron mallet, which was succeeded by three clarions of the trumpet, three huzzas, and three claps of the hands.

James Anderson's Constitutions gave an account of a similarly simple ceremony that was held on March 19, 1721, although the Grand Lodge of England apparently was not involved. He recorded, "The Bishop of Salisbury went in an orderly Procession, duly attended, and having levell'd the first Stone, gave it two or three knocks with a Mallet, upon which the trumpets sounded, and a vast multitude made loud acclamations of joy; when his Lordship laid upon the stone a purse of 100 guineas as a present from his Majesty for the use of the Craftsmen."

The laying of the Capitol cornerstone occurred on a date between publication of the first edition of *Ilustrosions of Masonry* by William Preston in 1772 in London and the first edition of *The Freemason's Monitor* (a version of Preston adopted for American Freemasonry) by Thomas Smith Webb in 1797 in Albany, New York. Preston's publication was available to the Masons who planned the Capitol cornerstone laying. More familiar to the planners would have been John K. Read's *New Ahiman Rezon*, published in Richmond, Virginia, in 1791, two years before the Capitol event. It was published for the guidance of the Virginia lodges and dedicated to "George Washington, Esq. President of the United States of America."

The cornerstone ceremonies of Preston in 1772 and those of Webb in 1797 were simple. Preston limited attendance to the Grand Lodge. Webb welcomed members of private lodges. Webb's ritual included the introduction of corn, wine, and oil and tests of trueness of the stone with approbation by the grand master that the stone was "well formed, true, and trusty." Both Preston and Webb noted the generosity of the king toward the workmen and cited a voluntary collection taken for the workers. This may have been based on the description in Ezra 3:7 of preparations for the second temple in Jerusalem that said, "So they gave money to the masons and the carpenters, and food, drink, and oil to the Sidonians and the Tyrians to bring cedar trees from Lebanon to the sea, to Joppa, according to the grant they had from Cyrus, King of Persia."

Visual proof that Washington was a Freemason was provided in a portrait by William Williams in 1794. At the request of the Alexandria Lodge, he stood for the painting wearing his Masonic regalia. Documents show that on March 18, 1797, he "received" a delegation from the Alexandria Lodge, and on April 1, 1798, he attended a lodge banquet and proposed a toast.

Although Washington's last will and testament expressed his desire "that my Corpse may be Interred in a private manner, without parade, or funeral Oration," his lodge was permitted to prepare arrangements for the funeral procession. Mourners were instructed to arrive at Mount Vernon on Wednesday "at twelve o'clock, if fair, or on Thursday at the same hour." Early on Wednesday, December 18, the Masonic Lodge of Alexandria started for Mount Vernon and arrived about one o'clock. Two hours later the formal procession was formed, consisting of horse and foot soldiers, clergy, Washington's horse with an empty saddle, a military band, the bier, and dozens of mourners.

At a humble red brick tomb in a hillside below the mansion, Reverend Thomas Davis, rector of Christ Church, Alexandria, read the Episcopal Order of Burial. Next, Reverend James Muir, minister of the Alexandria Presbyterian Church, and Dr. Elisha Dick, both members of Washington's lodge, conducted the traditional Masonic funeral rites. The shroud was briefly withdrawn to allow a final viewing. A few days later, Muir wrote:

> In the long and lofty portico, where oft the hero walked in all his glory, now lay the shrouded corpse. The countenance, still composed and serene, seemed to depress the dignity of the spirit which lately dwelt in that lifeless form. There those who paid the last sad honors to the benefactor of his country took an impressive, a farewell view.

Three general discharges of infantry, the cavalry, and eleven pieces of artillery, which lined the banks of the Potomac, back of the vault, paid the last tribute to the entombed Commander-in-Chief of the Armies of the United States.

Henry "Light Horse" Lee, one of Washington's officers in the War of Independence, said of him, "First in war, first in peace, and first in the hearts of his countrymen, he was second to none." Thomas Jefferson would say, "On the whole, his character was, in its mass, perfect, in nothing bad, in few points indifferent, and it may be truly said that never did nature and fortune combine more perfectly to make a man great, and to place him in the same constellation with whatever worthies have merited from man an everlasting remembrance."

Masons everywhere mourned him in public ceremonies. Nearly half a century later, one in Pennsylvania was vividly recalled by Captain Samuel De Wees:

Immediately after the arrival of [the] sad news [of his death], a public meeting was held at the court-House in [the town of] Reading, and arrangements made for a funeral procession. The Free Masons met at their Lodge, and made arrangements to join in the procession. A bright and exemplary brother had gone from a mystic Lodge upon earth, to join in membership with that Grand Lodge of transplendent and unconceived of brilliancy, holiness and glory above, and now, that the last funeral tribute was about to be paid, they could not be idle. Two companies of volunteers, one commanded by Captain Keims, were ordered out. The procession formed in the following order: the military in front, then the coffin, then the order of Masons, then civil officers, and then the citizens. The procession was fully a mile in length. It moved to a large church in Reading where the military, Masons and many of the citizens entered. The military moved (proceeded by the music) and placed the coffin in an aisle in front of the pulpit. There were from twelve to twenty ministers of the gospel present on the occasion. A funeral oration was delivered, after which the procession moved through Philadelphia street and through some

others of the principal streets of Reading, and then to a grave yard
where the coffin carried in the procession, was deposited with military honors in the tomb, and with as much solemnity as though the
body of beloved Washington had been enshrined within it.

At the time of Washington's death, lodges in the thirteen states had become adherents of the Scottish Rite. Its earliest recording in America, at
Washington's lodge in Fredericksburg, is dated December 22, 1753. Two
years after his death, the "Mother Supreme Council of the World" was
formed in Charleston, South Carolina (May 31, 1801) and established the
thirty-third degree, in the words of C. W. Leadbeater in *Freemasonry and
Its Ancient Mystic Rites*, as "the most important and splendid of All Masonic
Obediences."

CHAPTER 8

THE FRENCH, THE POPE, AND PRINCE HALL

S WITH SO MUCH OF THE HISTORY OF FREEMASONRY, THERE is no certainty about its origin in France. One history records that English "gentlemen" went to France in the early eighteenth century and founded speculative lodges that welcomed French gentlemen. Between May and July 1728, all French lodges grouped themselves as the English Grand Lodge of France. Its grand master was the duke of Wharton, past grand master of the Grand Lodge of London. Another version is that the first lodges in France were imported from the United Kingdom by the Scottish and Irish Guards while they were in exile in St.-Germain-en-Laye.

The English Grand Lodge of France got its first French grand master in 1738. It was a doubly auspicious year. In an encyclical (bull) issued by the Vatican on April 28, Pope Clement XII asserted:

> Now it has come to Our ears, and common gossip has made clear, that certain Societies, Companies, Assemblies, Meetings, Congregations or Conventicles called in the popular tongue *Liberi Muratori* or *Francs Massons* or by other names according to the various languages, are spreading far and wide and daily growing in strength; and men of any Religion or sect, satisfied with the appearance of natural probity, are joined together, according to their laws and the statutes laid down for them, by a strict and unbreakable bond which obliges them, both by an oath upon the Holy Bible and by a host of grievous punishment, to

an inviolable silence about all that they do in secret together. But it is in the nature of crime to betray itself and to show itself by its attendant clamor. Thus these aforesaid Societies or Conventicles have caused in the minds of the faithful the greatest suspicion, and all prudent and upright men have passed the same judgment on them as being depraved and perverted. For if they were not doing evil they would not have so great a hatred of the light. Indeed, this rumor has grown to such proportions that in several countries these societies have been forbidden by the civil authorities as being against the public security, and for some time past have appeared to be prudently eliminated.

Born to nobility, Pope Clement XII (Lorenzo Corsini) studied law at the University of Pisa. He rose in the church hierarchy to become lawyer treasurer-general and governor of Castel Sant'Angelo in 1696, courtier to Pope Clement XI, and cardinal (May 17, 1706). Following the death of Clement XI, he was crowned pope (the 246th) in 1730. Nearly blind when he took the throne of St. Peter, he eventually became bedridden. Working to restore the finances of the Vatican, he forced corrupt ministers to return everything they had stolen under his predecessors. This brought in so much money that he embarked on numerous building and beautification plans around Rome, paving streets, supporting art galleries, and building a port at Ancona, Italy.

Citing "the great harm which is often caused by such Societies or Conventicles [as the Freemasons] not only to the peace of the temporal state but also to the well-being of souls, and realizing that they do not hold by either civil or canonical sanctions," he quoted Jesus' admonition on the duty of the "faithful servant and of the master of the Lord's household to watch day and night lest such men as these break into the household like thieves, and like foxes seek to destroy the vineyard."

To "prevent the hearts of the simple being perverted, and the innocent secretly wounded by their arrows, and to block that broad road which could be opened to the uncorrected commiission of sin and for the other just and reasonable motives," he continued:

We, therefore, having taken counsel of some of Our Venerable Brothers among the Cardinals of the Holy Roman Church, and also of Our own accord and with certain knowledge and mature deliberations, with the plenitude of the Apostolic power do hereby determine and have decreed that these same Societies, Companies, Assemblies, Meetings, Congregations, or Conventicles of *Liberi Muratori* or *Francs Massons*, or whatever other name they may go by, are to be condemned and prohibited, and by Our present Constitution, valid for ever, We do condemn and prohibit them.

A decree of excommunication notwithstanding, Freemasonry continued in France. In 1740, there were more than 200 lodges, with 22 in Paris. In 1754, a Scottish Rite chapter (the word "lodge" is not used in the Scottish Rite) was founded in Paris by the Chevalier de Bonneville, claiming that Freemasons were descendants of the Knights Templar. In 1756, the English Grand Lodge of France acquired complete autonomy, called itself the Grand Lodge of France, and declared adherence to the Scottish Rite. As in England and America, French Freemasonry was divided between Antients and Moderns. The result, writes Robert Macoy in *A Dictionary of Freemasonry*, was that masters governed lodges "according to their own caprice" and granted warrants to lodges that constituted "Chapters, Councils, Colleges, and Tribunals," creating so much confusion that "it was not known which was in reality the legitimate body." In 1772, the Grand Lodge changed its name to Grand Orient of France and adopted "The Statutes of the Royal Order of Freemasonry in France." Masons who disagreed with these alterations broke away and continued to use the name Grand Lodge of France. The groups contested each other's validity until the dispute was dramatically silenced in 1789 by the French Revolution. For the duration of the bloody struggle to end monarchy and install a republic, Masonry was suspended. The schism between Antients and Moderns would be closed on June 28, 1799, when an Act of Union absorbed the Grand Lodge into the Grand Orient. Unified, French Freemasonry would thrive so well under Emperor Napoléon Bonaparte that after his historic victory over Austrian and Russian armies at Austerlitz in 1805, a Brother

Brunet entertained at the traditional Masonic winter feast on St. John the Evangelist's Day (December 27) with a poem:

> *Tremble, for the gods carry Napoleon.*
> *Yield, or soon this noble war cry will penetrate into Albion's breast:*
> *Long live Napoleon!*

This exhortation during a Masonic ceremony is evidence that although the Grand Orient of France was Modern in that it embraced the 1723 Anderson Constitutions, the French Masons followed a laissez-faire policy concerning James Anderson's admonition that during lodge gatherings members were not to discuss politics. But the Grand Orient remained consistent with the Constitutions" requirement that a Mason "will never be a stupid Atheist nor an irreligious Libertine." The rule was that Masons follow "that Religion in which all Men agree" and leave "particular Opinions" to themselves. While no one could be excluded from the order on the basis of religious practice, every Mason was required to profess a belief in "the glorious Architect of heaven and earth."

A stricture that made it difficult for unorthodox believers to enter the Craft eventually contributed to a break between English and French Freemasonry. It occurred in the late 1870s when the Grand Orient of France began admitting atheists. It also created a modified ritual as an alternative for European jurisdictions that omitted direct reference to the "glorious Architect" and the terms "Supreme Being" and "Creative Principle." Preferring not to restrict themselves to a single rite, they offered French lodges what one Masonic historian calls a "menu of rites."

This difference would create tension between French Masonry of the United States as thousands of Americans flooded into France to join in World War I. Recalling the service of a Frenchman in the Revolutionary War, they exclaimed, "Lafayette, we are here." Because many of the "Doughboys" were Masons, the admission of atheists to French lodges was what would later be termed "culture shock"

As Masonic historian Paul M. Bessel (librarian of the George Washington Masonic National Memorial and secretary of the Masonic Library and

Museum Association) wryly notes in an essay on the history of relations between American and French Masonry, "Nothing seems to cause as much dispute among American Freemasons as the subject of recognition and regularity (with the possible exception of race and freemasonry)."

The history of blacks in American Masonry began one year before the Declaration of Independence when an American black man, Prince Hall, was initiated into the Irish Constitution Military Lodge along with fourteen other free black men.

Little is known of the life of Prince Hall. Even though no birth record has been found, he is believed to have been born in Barbados, West Indies, on September 12, 1748. He is also believed to have arrived in Boston from Africa in 1765 as a slave and been sold to a William Hall, who freed him in 1770.

During the Revolutionary War, he served in the Continental army and is believed to have fought at Bunker Hill. Initiated into military Lodge No. 441 with fourteen other black men, he and the other initiates were granted authority to meet as African Lodge No. 1. Other members were Cyrus Johnson, Bueston Slinger, Prince Rees, John Canton, Peter Freeman, Benjamin Tiler, Duff Ruform, Thomas Santerson, Prince Rayden, Cato Speain, Boston Smith, Peter Best, Forten Howard, and Richard Titley. After the war, Hall petitioned the Premier Grand Lodge of England for a warrant. It was delivered to Boston on April 29, 1787. A week later (May 6), African Lodge No. 459 was organized.

In an essay on Prince Hall Masonry written for members of present-day Texas Masonry, Robert E. Connors Jr. notes that because exclusive territorial jurisdiction was not a recognized doctrine of English Masonic custom at the time, the African Lodge of Boston was allowed to establish other lodges, making itself a mother lodge that gave Hall authority to issue warrants on the same basis as masters of lodges in Europe. African lodges were constituted in Pennsylvania, Rhode Island, and New York.

On June 24, 1791, the African Grand Lodge of North America was organized in Boston with Hall as grand master. This was one year before the organization of the United Grand Lodge of Massachusetts. In 1827, forty-five years after the Massachusetts Grand Lodge had done so, the

African Lodge of Boston declared itself independent of the Grand Lodge of England.

As a property owner and registered voter, Hall campaigned for the establishment of schools for Negro children in Boston, opened a school in his own home, and successfully petitioned the legislature to protect free Negroes from kidnaping and being sold into slavery. A biographer claims that he was a minister in the African Methodist Episcopal Church, but there is no record of this. In a legal deposition recorded in the Suffolk County, Massachusetts, Register of Deeds, in August 1807, a Prince Hall stated that he was a leather dresser by trade and that in November 1762 he had been received into the full communion of the Congregational Church.

Hall died on December 4, 1807. The next year, as a memorial to him, and by an act of the General Assembly of the Craft, the name of the lodge was changed from African Grand Lodge of North America to the Prince Hall Grand Lodge of Massachusetts. In 1869, fire destroyed the Massachusetts Grand Lodge headquarters. Kept in a metal tube in a chest, the charter escaped the flames. Charred by the intense heat, it was saved when Grand Master S. T. Kendall crawled into the burning building to rescue it and is now kept in a bank vault in Boston.

Throughout the world today, there are 44 Most Worshipful Prince Hall Grand Lodges, about 5,000 subordinate lodges, and more than 300,000 Prince Hall Masons. For many years, the black churches of America and Prince Hall lodges were the two strongest organizations in black communities. Masonic lodge halls were used as locations for church services and teaching blacks how to read and write. Prince Hall Masons used their resources to provide young black men and women scholarships to college, to conduct various forms of charity in their local communities, and to assist in many other programs in black communities.

Three years after the birth of the slave who would found black Masonry in the United States, another pope, Benedict XIV, reiterated Clement XII's condemnation of Freemasonry in a second papal bull. It was greeted in French lodges with the same indifference as the first. But elsewhere in Europe the edict fueled a wave of anti-Masonry by monarchs who saw Masonry's embrace of liberty, equality, and fraternity of the French Revolution and the democratic ideals of the American Revolution as a threat. A result of this fervor was a mystery that persists to this day concerning the death of a brilliant young Austrian Mason with a genius for music.

CHAPTER 9

THE MYSTERY OF "THE MAGIC FLUTE"

ITHIN WEEKS OF POPE BENEDICT XIV'S REMONSTRANCE,
Freemasonry was banned in Spain and the Kingdom of Naples
and under attack in the Austro-Hungarian empire by Empress
Maria Theresa, a devout Catholic. The first lodge in Austria had opened
in Vienna in 1742 under a warrant from the Grand Lodge of Germany,
only to be forced to close by pressure from the church. But twenty years
later (1762), several lodges were established in Vienna and Prague in defiance of the church. When lodges in Bohemia, Hungary, and Transylvania
declared their independence from the Grand Lodge of Berlin in 1784,
they created a Grand Lodge of Austria with its seat in Vienna.

Zur Wahren Eintracht, one of the city's smaller lodges, claimed as a
member the leading composer of the empire. Revered by the people as
"Papa," Franz Joseph Haydn had become a Mason at a time when the
Craft was gaining a following among musicians. The lodge of which he
was a member held the view that Freemasonry "serves mankind in all
parts of the world, under all kinds of governments, in public or in secret."

It is likely that Haydn and a young musical genius, Wolfgang Amadeus
Mozart, met in Vienna in 1781 at a gathering organized by Baron von
Swieten to hear the music of Johann Sebastian Bach. One historian writes
that Mozart found in Haydn "not only a composer whose achievements
were on a level with his own, but a warm and sympathetic friend in whom
he could confide." Haydn gave his advice and criticism to Mozart and
Mozart attached more importance to Haydn's opinion than to anyone
else, including his father, Leopold. The mentor and the student differed

in that Mozart had a frequently volatile impatience and Haydn was a relatively slow worker. Haydn thought his opera *Armida* was one of his best compositions, but after he heard several operas by Mozart, he recognized the superiority and lost the desire to write operas. After a performance of *Don Giovanni* (May 7,1788), he declared Mozart the greatest composer the world possessed.

According to Masonic lore, Mozart played a role in Haydn becoming a Mason. The story is that on February 12, 1784, Mozart gave a party in his flat in Vienna. Among those who attended were three Freemasons and Haydn, who had been considering joining a society to which many of his Viennese friends and acquaintances belonged. On December 29, 1784, Haydn officially asked to be allowed to join. He explained in a letter, "The advantageous opinion I formed about the Freemasons awakened in me, a long time ago, the sincere desire to join this Order with its humanitarianism and wise principles. I turn to you, Sir [the master of ceremonies of the lodge], in the hope that through your kind intervention at the Lodge of which you are an honoured member, you may be able to further my sincere wish."

The letter made Haydn a prospective candidate for the lodge Zur Wahren Eintracht, in which there were many musicians. Minutes of the lodge for January 1, 1785, record that it was decided "to circulate among the Lodges" names of the aspirants Franz Joseph Haydn and Baron Hallberg von Brussels. During the lodge on January 24, the date for Haydn's initiation was set for January 28. Mozart may have appeared to witness the ceremony and to congratulate him. Unfortunately, Haydn was unable to present himself because of an unexpected engagement to appear at Prince Nicolas Esterhazy's castle in Hungary. In his letter of apology for his nonappearance, he explained that "through the inefficiency of our Hussars, the letter of invitation didn't arrive punctually!"

Lodge minutes of Haydn's initiation note the presentation of "the foreign aspirant Joseph Haydn, son of Mathias, 51 years old, born 1 May, of Rom Cath. faith, of bourgeois parentage, born in Rohrau in Austria, at present Princely Esterhazy's Chapel Master, hitherto received in no known order and out of a sincere desire and will to become a member of the Ancient and Honourable Society of Knightly Freemasons, not driven to this by his own curiosity, nor seduced, driven or persuaded to this end by another." Haydn was "accepted into the Lodge of this Order of St John as Freemason, apprentice and brother."

A toast to Haydn's initiation, given by "Brother Joseph von Holzmeister, Chief Clerk to the War Ministry," proved lengthy, but acknowledged Haydn's contribution to the development of the symphony. "The purpose of music is emotional and pleasurable," he said, pointing out that the "Brother Initiate had created a new order in the orchestra" and continuing, "If every instrument did not consider the right and properties of other instruments, in addition to its own rights, if it did not often diminish its own volume in order not to do damage to the utterance of its companions, the end, which is beauty and harmony, would not be attained."

Bringing his remarks around to Freemasonry, he continued:

> I know of no more dignified, no more delightful concept than a society of upright men, each driven to drink from the spring of wisdom to find truth and share it with others for the common good—a Society where shining and enlightenment does not give rise to jealousy but is rather a source of emanation: where the manly handclasp is the sign of a heart expanded by much greatness, not the mask of false friendship: where man may open his heart to man without having to fear prejudice, hate or intrigue. A Society in which the meetings give joy to every member—an event to which each one looks forward with pleasure and leaves with deep satisfaction.
>
> Harmony can be, indeed must be, the characteristic of the order as a whole. It must be the center-point of each Lodge—the essential strength through which beauty is defined in the whole of nature: without it nature itself must fall, and the starry firmament must sink with the earth into chaos. You, newly elected Brother Apprentice, know especially well the design of the heavenly gift of harmony. To praise all her charms to you would be superfluous. I content myself if, in this brotherly talk, I have awakened in you the desire to remain steadfast to your Goddess (Harmony) in this circle, new my brother, to you.

Because his Catholicism often conflicted with practices of Masonry, Haydn's interest in the Craft was social. He would resign in 1787, leaving Mozart the preeminent composer in the Masonic brotherhood.

Born in Saltzburg, Austria, in 1756, Mozart had been quickly recognized as a musical prodigy. By the age of four, he exhibited such extraordinary powers of musical appreciation that his father, Leopold, a highly esteemed violinist and composer in his own right, enrolled him in harpsichord lessons. At the age of five, he was composing music, and by six he was a keyboard master. In 1762, his father took him and his sister, Maria Anna, on a tour of Munich and Vienna. A constant performer and composer, he became the darling of Austrian nobility, giving many concerts and recitals, including a performance at the Schonbrunn Palace for Empress Maria Theresa. By his teenage years, he was a master of the piano, harpsichord, and violin and was writing not only oratorios, but symphonies and operas. His first major opera, *Mitridate, Re di Ponto*, was presented in Milan in 1770. He was fourteen. A year later, he was installed as the concertmaster in the orchestra of Prince-Archbishop Siegismund, count of Schrafttenbach of Saltzburg. His relationship with the succeeding archbishop, Hieronymus Count Colloredo, although very successful in the early years, deteriorated, culminating in his resignation from the position against his father's wishes.

Little is known about Mozart's Masonic life. Initiated as an apprentice on December 7, 1785, in the lodge Zur Wahrent Eintrach (Lodge Beneficence), he then became a fellowcraft member of lodge Zur Neugekronte Hoffhnung (Lodge True Harmony) on April 1, 1785, along with his father. Five days later, Leopold was raised to the third degree.

Two years before entering Lodge Beneficence, Mozart had composed Adagio for Two Clarinets and Three Bassett Horns (1783). It is believed by some biographers to have been designed as part of a Masonic ritual procession because its length corresponds to the duration of a procession from the door of the lodge to the master's position. A cantata, *Dir, Seele des Weltalls* (1783), may have been commissioned for a Masonic celebration to which nonmembers were invited. Because he had not yet become a member of the order, it is surmised that whoever commissioned him

gave him some insight into the workings of Freemasonry and that this was
the impetus of his desire to join Freemasonry. Other scholars claim that
the system of dating Mozart's music is erroneous and that the Masonic
works were written in late 1784 or early 1785, when he was a member.

Gesellenreise (The Fellowcraft's Journey) is considered the first of his
truly Masonic works. The manuscript is dated March 26, 1785, and is assumed to have been dedicated to the occasion of his father being passed to
the second degree. The words were written by Mason Franz Joseph von
Ratschky. *Die Maurerfreude* (Masonic Joy), written in April 1785, was a
cantata in honor of Ignaz von Born, master of Lodge True Harmony, who
had recently been honored by Emperor Joseph II for discoveries in metal-
lurgy. An invitation to members of other lodges promised "a friendly and
joyous repast" for the purpose of "expressing their sentiments in convivi-
ality, through the arts of poetry and music."

Masonic Funeral Music was composed in November 1785 for the funeral
of two brother Masons, Duke Georg August of Mecklenburg-Strelitz and
Count Franz Eszterhazy von Galantha. While Mozart relied on commissions from writing music to earn his living, this piece was written without
any commission. Two other compositions, *Zerfliesset heut, geliebte Brüder*
(For the Opening of the Lodge) and *Ihr unsre neuen Leiter* (For the Closing
of the Lodge), were written in December 1785 for the newly formed
Lodge Newly Crowned Hope. This lodge was created after a decree by
Emperor Joseph II that the eight Viennese lodges be reduced to no more
than three and limiting membership of each to no more than 180. As a
consequence, two new lodges, Truth and Newly Crowned Hope, were
formed by merging the Lodge Beneficence, into which both Mozart and
his father had been initiated, and Lodge True Harmony. Joseph's order
also required the lodges to inform the police of names of members and
times and places of meetings.

A son of Maria Theresa, who was deceased but unmourned by Masons
because of her suppressive policy, Joseph II proved to be tolerant of Freemasonry, but declined an invitation to become the grand master. This acceptance of the Craft by the ruler of the empire lasted until Joseph's death
in February 1790. Inheriting the throne of the Holy Roman Empire as the
French Revolution in July 1789 sent a shock wave of fear through Europe's

capitals, and with evidence that it had been fomented by Freemasons, Joseph's brother, Leopold II, was advised by fellow kings, his chief of police, and the Roman Catholic Church to be wary of the Masons. A warning also came from his sister. The ill-fated Marie Antoinette, whose head would be chopped off on a guillotine, wrote pleadingly from Paris, "Take good care, over there, about any organization of Freemasons. You must already have been warned that it is by this road that all the monsters here hope to achieve the same ends in all countries."

Rather than plotting an uprising with the aim of deposing Leopold II even before he was to be formally crowned on September 6, 1791 (with an opera by Mozart written to celebrate the event), Mozart's librettist, Johann Emanuel Schikaneder, proposed that the opera be produced as Freemasonry propaganda. Mozart's relationship with Schikaneder is traced to around 1780. According to Masonic researcher Dr. Bernhard Beuer, Schikaneder's standing in Freemasonry was "altogether haphazard to say the least." He seems to have entered the Craft for "worldly reasons." His letter petitioning admission stated:

> Deeply revered gentlemen, Not curiosity or selfishness but the most sincere esteem of your exalted assembly motivates my most humble prayer for admission to your sanctuary from which, in spite of the greatest secrecy, radiates a glimmer of nobility, humanity and wisdom. Enlighten me by your wise teachings, make me in your image, and I will remain with warmest thanks,
>
> > Your most honoring and humble servant,
> > Johann Emanuel Schikaneder.

Dr. Beuer considers the letter "revealing" and showing his need for acceptance to a formal organization. It also shows his appreciation of the dramatic element and self-promotion.

Music historians note that Masonic opera was not a new idea in Mozart's time. The opera *Osiris*, written by Johann Gottlieb Naumann, had used ancient Egypt as its setting. The theme was in keeping with Freemasonry's views of the struggle between good and evil.

When Mozart expressed reluctance to undertake *The Magic Flute*,

Schikaneder appealed to his duty to the Craft. With Mozart's consent, both men went to work. The libretto had varied sources. Most research regarding the plot for *The Magic Flute* can be traced to Jakob August Liebeskind's *Lulu oder Die Zauberflote*, published in Christoph Martin Wieland's *Dschinnistan*. Containing "selected tales of fairies and spirits, partly newly invented, partly newly translated and revised," it inspired similar works, among them Benedict Schack's *Der Stein der Weisen*. Schikaneder would also have known of Phillip Hafner's 1763 play *Meagra.*

The story of *The Magic Flute* is that of Sarastro, the wise priest of Isis, who has taken Pamina to the temple for the humane purpose of releasing her from the influence of her mother, the Queen of the Night. The queen induces the young Prince Tamino to go in search of her daughter and free her from Sarastro's power. Tamino accomplishes this, but becomes the disciple of Sarastro, whose mildness and wisdom he has learned to admire. The prince and Pamina are united.

In act I, set in a "wood," Tamino is lost in the forest and pursued by a serpent. He cries ("Help! Help! for I am lost.") and then faints from fatigue. Three ladies, attendants of the queen, in black robes, appear and kill the serpent with their lances ("Die, monster, through our might."). They all fall in love with the prince and each plans to possess him.

Tamino recovers and sees before him Papageno, arrayed entirely in the plumage of birds. In a humorous aria, "Papageno," he sings, "I am the bird catcher." He explains to Tamino that the Queen of the Night is near and boasts that he himself has killed the serpent, but the three ladies punish his lie by placing a padlock over his mouth. They show to the prince a miniature of a young maiden. He gazes in ecstasy in the aria "This Picture Is Wondrously Beautiful."

The Queen of the Night now appears, demanding that Tamino free her daughter from the hands of Sarastro (recitative and aria: "To Misfortune Am I Born"). The ladies give Tamino a magic flute, remove the padlock from Papageno, and present him with a chime of bells. They set forth, guided by three boys, and escape all danger by the use of the magic instruments.

The next scene is a room in Sarastro's palace. Pamina is dragged in by Monostatos, a Moor who is persecuting her. Papageno arrives and announces to her that her mother has sent Tamino to her aid. Monostatos is terrified by Papageno's strange appearance and takes to flight.

In a grove and entrance to the temple, the three boys lead in the prince. When Tamino reaches the temple, he is denied entrance at two of the doors, but at the third a priest appears, who reveals to him the noble character of Sarastro. When Papageno appears with Pamina, all three boys are about to escape, but are prevented by Monostatos. Sarastro enters. Pamina falls at his feet and confesses that she was trying to escape because the Moor had demanded her love. This is received kindly by Sarastro, who tells her that he will not force her inclinations, but cannot give her freedom. He punishes the Moor for his insolence and leads Tamino and Papageno into the temple of Ordeal.

At the start of the second act in a grove of palms, the council of priests determine that Tamino shall possess Pamina if he succeeds in passing through the ordeal (they do not wish to return her to her mother, who has already infected the people with superstition). This is expressed in the aria and chorus "O Isis and Osiris." The scene changes to the courtyard of the temple of Ordeal. The first test is that Tamino and Papageno shall remain silent under temptation. The three ladies appear and tempt them to speak. Tamino and Papageno remain firm. Next, in a garden as Pamina sleeps, Monostatos approaches and gazes on her with rapture in the aria "All Feel the Joys of Love." When the Queen of the Night appears and gives Pamina a dagger with which to kill Sarastro (aria: "The Vengeance of Hell Is in My Heart"), Monostatos retires and listens. He tries to force Pamina's love by using the secret, but is prevented by Sarastro, who allays Pamina's alarm in the aria "In These Holy Halls."

The scene changes to a hall in the temple of Ordeal. Tamino and Papageno must again suffer the test of silence. Papageno can no longer hold his tongue, but Tamino remains firm, even when Pamina speaks to him. When he refuses to answer, she believes he loves her no longer. Pamina laments, "Ah, all is lost." In another change of scene (sometimes performed as act III) at the pyramids, the chorus sings "O Isis and Osiris, What Joy." Sarastro parts Pamina and Tamino. Papageno also desires to have a wife. At the first ordeal, an old woman had appeared to him and declared herself his bride. She now appears and changes herself into the young and pretty Papagena. In the next scene, in open country, the three boys prevent Pamina from taking her life because she believes Tamino is faithless. Papageno also wishes to kill himself, but he dances merrily after the boys advise him to use his magic bells to summon Papagena's image.

In a scene of rocks with water and a cavern of fire, men in armor lead in Tamino. When Pamina arrives, she is overcome with joy to find Tamino, who is now allowed to speak to her. Both pass unscathed through the final ordeal of fire and water with the help of the magic flute. The scene now changes to the entrance of the chief temple, where Sarastro bids the young lovers welcome and unites them and the opera ends.

Mozart clearly intended *The Magic Flute* to be seen by the widest possible audience. The theater was tax-exempt and located in a collection of tenements built around six courtyards outside Vienna. An opera historian notes that the importance of Mozart's varied audience cannot be overstated and that it "speaks volumes about the Enlightenment ideals that the opera itself exemplifies." Equality, as well as the ability of man to act compassionately, are at the center of Sarastro's character.

The nobility and wisdom associated with Sarastro has prompted much speculation about Mozart's relationship to Ignaz von Born, master of Masonic symbolism. The Queen of the Night, meant to suggest Maria Theresa, "litters the stage with the passion and coloratura that clearly states her opposition to Enlightenment ideals." Tamino's character has been equated with Joseph II, who saw equality between social classes, as well as unification and initiation between man and woman as depicted in the opera. This ideal comes to fruition when Tamino and Pamina complete their initiation together while the priests sing the chorus to Isis and Osiris.

The opera's debut performance occurred on September 30, 1790, in Vienna. Seated with Mozart was Antonio Salieri. A composer of operas who regarded himself and Mozart as rivals, he was born in Legnano, Italy (then part of the empire of Venice), and studied in Vienna. In 1774, he became court composer and made his reputation as a stage composer and writer for the Vienna and Italian opera houses and in Paris, where he was hailed for three works, including his greatest success, *Tarare* (1787). On October 14, 1790, Mozart told his wife, Constanze, in a letter that from "the overture to the last chorus" there had not been "a single number that did not call forth from [Salieri] a bravo! or bello!"

When Mozart sent the letter, he had a commission from Count von Walsegg to write a Requiem. The work had been ordered through an anonymous intermediary who had appeared at Mozart's home wearing a hooded gray cloak. Mozart biographers speculate that composing a funeral work and the mysterious figure caused him to brood about death. This foreboding mood deepened with the sudden appearance "like a ghost" of the man in gray on the eve of a journey by Mozart to Geneva. According to Franz Niemetschek, Mozart's first biographer, he became ill in Prague and required continuous medical attention. He wrote that while Mozart "was pale and his expression was sad," his good humor was "often shown in merry jest with his friends."

Returning to Vienna, Mozart began work on the Requiem with "energy and interest," but his family and friends observed that his illness was becoming worse and that he was depressed. To cheer him up, Constanze went on a drive with him. According to her account as reported by Niemetschek, "Mozart began to speak of death, and declared that he was writing the Requiem for himself." With tears in his eyes, he said to Constanze, "I feel definitely that I will not last much longer. I am sure I have been poisoned. I cannot rid myself of this idea."

Nearly forty years later, Constanze told two visiting friends, Vincent and Mary Novello, that Mozart had believed that the poison was "aqua toffana." A substance whose principal active ingredient was probably arsenic, it was named after a seventeenth-century Neapolitan woman called Toffana who had employed it, as one historian notes, "with startling effect on the statistics of sudden death."

An account of Mozart's illness was given by Constanze's sister, Sophie Haibel, in 1825 to a Mozart biographer. She reported that as he worked on the Requiem, he had a high fever and painful swelling of his body, which made it difficult for him to move in bed. He spoke of "the taste of death" on his tongue. The illness began with swellings of his hands and feet and an almost complete immobility, followed by sudden attacks of vomiting. On the last day of his life, Sophie went to see him and found him giving instructions to his pupil, Franz Xaver Sussmayr, on how to finish the Requiem.

When Mozart's life appeared to be fading fast, Dr. Nikolaus Closset was summoned. According to Sophie, when he arrived he ordered cold compresses to be put on Mozart's forehead, but these "provided such a shock" that Mozart did not regain consciousness. The last thing Mozart did, according to Sophie, was imitate the kettledrums in the Requiem. He died around midnight on December 5, 1791.

Neither Dr. Closset nor the other attending physicians provided a death certificate stating the cause of death. No autopsy was performed. Within a week, the publication *Musikalisches Wochenblatt* carried a report from Prague that mentioned rumors of poisoning because of the swollen condition of his body. Based on public knowledge that for a decade Salieri had been an implacable rival of Mozart in Vienna, suspicion turned to him. Prior to Salieri's death in 1825, the rumors that he had poisoned Mozart were fueled by a report that when Salieri was in failing health, he confessed his guilt and attempted suicide.

An alternative theory placed the guilt on Freemasons. It was based on conjecture that in *The Magic Flute* Mozart had offended Masons by his excessive attachment to the figure of the Queen of the Night and his use of Christian music in the chorale of the "Men of Armor," who were believed to have been patterned on Masons. It was also said that the murder had thwarted a plan by Mozart to establish his own secret lodge to be called "The Grotto."

In later speculation about Freemasonry as the culprit, Mozart had hidden under the pro-Masonic surface of the opera a secret counterplot in which Tamino was Mozart, Pamina was Marie Antoinette, and Pamina's captors were Freemasons. In this scenario, Mozart's murder was part of a Masonic conspiracy to assassinate Leopold II, as well as Gustav III of Sweden, who was actually murdered at a masked ball a few months after Mozart's death. This fantastic plot originated seventy years later (in 1861) in the imagination of Georg Friedrich Daumer, a researcher of antiquities, a religious fanatic, and an anti-Semite. His work would be seized by a Nazi leader in the 1930s. General Erich Ludendorff, along with his wife, Mathilde, asserted that the secret of Masonry was "the Jew" and that Freemasonry's goal was to "rob the Germans of their national pride and to assure the glorious future of the Jewish people."

A Masonic explanation for Mozart's death was proposed in 1958 by Dr. Gunther Duda in *Gewiss, man hat mir Gift gegeben*. Presented as a comprehensive study of Mozart's death, it notes that Mozart was a Mason, that Masonic lodges claimed the right to sentence disobedient members to death, that Mozart was a disobedient member, and that the manner in which he died proved the culpability of Freemasonry. The book also suggests that Masons caused the death of Mozart's librettist, Johann Emanuel Schikaneder (1812), and that of Carl Ludwig Gieseke (1833), who may have had a role in shaping *The Magic Flute*.

In one construction of Mozart's death as a conspiracy, the spooky messenger in gray was not an agent of Count von Walsegg, but had been sent by Masons to announce a death sentence. Mozart's death was either a ritual murder in which he was offered as a sacrifice to Masonic deities or a punishment for the crime of having revealed Masonic secrets in *The Magic Flute*. Nearly two centuries after Mozart's demise, novelist David Weiss in *The Assassination of Mozart* has a reactionary Austrian regime give tacit approval to Salieri to kill him and thwart an investigation of the crime. In the 1984 film *Amadeus*, based on the play by Peter Schaffer, the murder is the work of Salieri, without a governmental or Masonic link.

Conspiracy theories about the death of Mozart that thrived for two centuries were laid to rest in February 2000 by a panel of physicians and a Mozart scholar. At the sixth annual Clinical Pathological Conference, dedicated to notorious case histories, at the University of Maryland School of Medicine, the panel concluded from the symptoms of Mozart's illness that it was not poisoning by Salieri or Masons that killed him, but rheumatic fever.

"While conspiracy theories make good fiction," said Mozart scholar Neal Zaslaw, "there is no historical evidence that Mozart was murdered."

Although homicide has been ruled out in the demise of one of the world's most beloved composers, in a mystery that unfolded in the United States thirty-five years later the finger of guilt was pointed directly at Freemasonry.

CHAPTER 10

WHATEVER HAPPENED TO WILLIAM MORGAN?

A FTER CLEMENT XII ISSUED HIS BULL *IN EMINENTI* IN 1738 condemning Freemasonry on the grounds of its naturalism, demand for oaths, religious indifference, and the possible threat to church and state, other popes specifically proscribed Freemasonry. Benedict XIV did so in *Providias* (1751), Pius VII in *Ecclesiam* (1821), and Leo XIII in *Quo graviora* (1825). By church law, no Catholic was permitted to join a Masonic lodge or an affiliated organization without incurring excommunication. Any Mason who wished to enter the Catholic Church was required to sever all ties with Freemasonry. The church of Pope John Paul II still condemns Masonry.

The first Protestant country to enact restrictive measures against Masonry was Holland in 1735. It was followed in 1738 by Sweden and the cities of Geneva (1738), Zurich (1740), and Berne (1745). After the papal bull of 1738, Spain, Portugal, and Italy attempted to suppress Masonry. Bavaria followed in 1784, Austria in 1795, and Russia in 1822. These restrictions were based more on political considerations and a fear of revolutions than on religious grounds. This was not the case in the British Isles, where Freemasonry flourished with royal approval. Between 1725 and 1733, the number of lodges rose from 63 to 126. As English Masonry turned away from Deism and incorporated elements of Christian orthodoxy, lodge chaplains were appointed and the support of members of the Protestant clergy was enlisted. Prior to the papal bull of 1738, several Roman Catholics served as grand masters. The Catholic duke of Norfolk became grand master in 1730. Another prominent Catholic Freemason was Viscount Montagu, Robert Edward, the ninth Lord Petre. Considered the head of the Catholic community in England, he became a grand master in 1772 and held the office for five years.

When the Grand Lodge of Ireland, the second oldest in the world, was formed in 1725, it preserved some Christian elements, such as the Lord's Prayer, in its ritual. Catholic laymen and priests participated in Irish lodges because the bull of 1738 was not promulgated in Ireland until later in the century. The Irish patriot Daniel O'Connell was initiated in 1799 and served as master of Lodge No. 189 in Dublin. He later renounced his Masonic ties when the attitude of the Church was made known. Today the Irish lodges are patronized by a Protestant minority.

The Grand Lodge of Scotland, from which many American lodges would receive their charters, was organized in 1736. One of its most famous members was poet Robert Burns.

After the first German lodge formed in Hamburg in 1737, Frederick the Great dabbled in the Craft and members of the Hohenzollern family and Prussian officers took Masonic degrees. In Scandinavia, monarchs became hereditary grand masters and patrons of Masonry. The first Belgian lodge opened in 1765. In the Netherlands, the first lodge met at the Hague in 1734. Although it was initially proscribed by the government, the fraternity survived and gained a measure of respectability.

In Spain, lodges existed under English warrants till 1769, when its independent grand lodge changed the name to "grand orient of Spain." Portugese lodges have existed since 1735. Italian Freemasonry began with a lodge in Naples (1764). In Russia. Emperor Peter III served as grand master of the Russian Grand Lodge, organized in St. Petersburg in 1771. Attacked by the Russian Orthodox Church, it was finally banned by Alexander I in 1822.

Two years after Wolfgang Amadeus Mozart "passed to the Grand Lodge above" (in the language of Masonry), a royal edict dissolved all secret societies in the Austrian dominions. As suspicions of secret societies erupted and spread among the rulers of the continent, they also gripped Britain. An act of Parliament in 1799 declared that all groups "exacting an oath" from its members should be deemed unlawful. The exception in the law were lodges of Freemasons, "in so far as they complied" with the law's

provisions. That Masonry was given this distinction was most likely because so many members of the Houses of Commons and Lords and numerous royalty and nobility belonged.

Because American Freemasonry existed in a predominately Protestant
nation and was therefore unhampered by the will of a pope and in a
democracy with freedom of association and speech protected by the Bill
of Rights, membership and the number of lodges flourished. Between the
inauguration of George Washington and the start of the Civil War,
Grand Lodges opened in twenty-five states, from Maine to Washington.
But this proliferation was dealt a severe setback in 1826.

In what has been described as "the most romantic story of Freemasonry,"
the mysterious disappearance and suspected murder of the author of a book
that would reveal "secrets" of Freemasonry generated a wave of anti-
Masonic hysteria that threatened the existence of the "Ancient Craft" and
caused an historic upheaval in American politics.

The chain of events that culminated in this crisis for Masonry began
with the arrival of William Morgan in 1824 in the town of Batavia, New
York, close to the Canadian border. A native of Culpepper County,
Virginia, he had worked at various jobs in Canada and now called himself
"Captain" on a claim to have served in the War of 1812 "with distinction." Regarding Morgan's past, a historian of American Masonry writes,
"Accounts of him differ widely, as they do of any notorious person. Few
are so wicked as to be without friends; few are so good they have not their
detractors. From the estimates of both enemies and friends, the years
have brought an evaluation of Morgan which shows him as a shiftless
rolling stone; uneducated but shrewd; careless of financial obligations:
often arrested for debt; idle and improvident; frequently the beneficiary
of Masonic charity."

The historical record shows that Morgan had received the royal arch
degree in the Western Star Chapter No. 33 of Le Roy, New York, on May
31, 1825. Masonic legend supposes that he "lied his way into a Lodge in
Rochester by imposing on a friend and employer, who was led to vouch
for him." What is known is that he visited lodges, was willing to assist in
their work, made Masonic speeches, and took part in degrees. When
companions of Batavia asked for a royal arch chapter, he was among those

signing the petition. But apparently suspicion of his "regularity began to grow." When the charter was granted, he was omitted as a member.

Taking this as an affront, Morgan retaliated by asserting that he had written a book that would reveal Masonic secrets. He stated that he had entered into a contract (March 13, 1826) with three men for its publication. They were David C. Miller, an entered apprentice of twenty years' standing who had been stopped from advancement "for cause" and appears to have nursed a grudge against the fraternity; John Davids, Morgan's landlord; and Russel Dyer, of whom little is known. The agreement reportedly guaranteed Morgan a half-million dollars. According to a chronicler of the event, "Morgan boasted in bars and on the street of his progress in writing this book. The more he bragged, the higher the feeling against him ran, and the greater the determination engendered that the exposé should never appear. Brethren were deeply angered. Fearful that were the 'secrets' of Freemasonry 'exposed,' the Order would die out, feelings ran high."

Matters came to a head in September 1826. Morgan was arrested for the theft of a shirt and tie (probably a trumped-up charge). He was acquitted, but immediately rearrested and jailed for failure to pay a debt of $2.68. After one day behind bars, someone paid the debt. When he was released, he left in a coach with several men, apparently not of his own free will. He was taken to an abandoned fort (Niagara) and confined in an unused ammunition magazine.

When he disappeared from Batavia, a rumor spread that Freemasons had kidnaped and murdered him in order to prevent the publication of his exposé. Freemasons indignantly denied the charge. As time passed with no sign of Morgan, New York governor DeWitt Clinton, a past grand master, issued a proclamation offering a $300 reward "that, if living, Morgan might be returned to his family; if murdered, that the perpetrators might be brought to punishment."

A few weeks later, a body floated to the shore of the Niagara River, about forty miles from the fort. It was identified by Morgan's widow from the clothing. But the mystery deepened when doubts were voiced concerning known markings on Morgan's body that were not on the corpse. Three inquests were held. The third decided, on the evidence of Sara

Munro, who minutely described the body, its marks, and the clothes it wore, that the corpse was not Morgan, but her husband Timothy Munro, of Clark, Canada. There was no doubt that Morgan had been kidnaped. As he was being shoved into a carriage outside the jail, he had been heard to shout, "Murder!" The lingering question was: What had happened to him?

The answer came with the arrest of prime suspects in the abduction. All Masons, they were Lotan Lawson; three men named Chesbro, Sawyer, and Shelton; and Eli Bruce, high sheriff of Niagara County. Because kidnaping was only a misdemeanor at that time, no one was sentenced to more than two years and four months.

Without a body, no one was charged with murder.

One story that gained currency, if not credence, was that a Mason named John Whitney had consulted with Governor Clinton in Albany about what could be done to prevent Morgan from executing his plan to print the exposé. The governor ruled out anything illegal. He suggested that Morgan's manuscript be purchased for enough money to enable Morgan to move beyond the reach of the influence and probable enmity of his associates in the publishing enterprise. Whitney met with Morgan and made an offer of $500 for Morgan to go to Canada and "disappear." His family would be provided for and later sent to him. To make the story plausible, Morgan would be "arrested" and "kidnaped." In this account, Morgan and his "abductors" traveled to a spot near Hamilton, Ontario, where they paid him $500 and got a receipt and a signed agreement from Mason that he would never return to New York.

The more credible explanation is that Morgan was kidnaped and taken to Fort Niagara for a time in the expectation of his captors that he would give up the location of the manuscript. Why the gang decided to kill him, how, and what they did with the body is not known, nor has there been any evidence that he was murdered, except that he was never seen again. But the fact that he had vanished after being abducted by Freemasons, combined with the publication of the book that they had sought to suppress, triggered an explosion of anti-Masonic sentiment across the United States. The "fame and infamy of the Morgan affair," as one historian puts it, "grew and spread like wild fire." Anti-Masonic meetings were held. The order was denounced by press and pulpit. An anti-Masonic newspaper, *The Anti-Masonic Review*, was published in New York. Groups in Pennsylvania, already opposed to any oath-bound society (Quakers, Lutherans, Mennonites, Dunkards, Moravians, Schwenkfelders, and German Reformed Church), were aroused to "a high pitch of feeling" against Morgan's "murderers" and "kidnappers."

In 1903, Robert Freke Gould writes in *History of Freemasonry:*

> This country has seen fierce and bitter political contests, but no other has approached the bitterness of this campaign against the Masons. No society, civil, military or religious, escaped its influence. No relation of family or friends was a barrier to it. The hatred of Masonry was carried everywhere, and there was no retreat so sacred that it did not enter. Not only were teachers and pastors driven from their stations, but the children of Masons were excluded from the schools, and members from their churches. The Sacrament was refused to Masons by formal vote of the Church, for no other offense than their Masonic connection. Families were divided. Brother was arrayed against brother, father against son, and even wives against their husbands. Desperate efforts were made to take away chartered rights from Masonic Corporations and to pass laws that would prevent Masons from holding their meetings and performing their ceremonies.

John C. Palmer, grand chaplain of the Grand Lodge of the District of Columbia, writes in *Craft, Morgan and Anti-Masonry:*

> The pressure was so strong that withdrawals by individuals and bodies were numerous. In 1827, two hundred and twenty-seven lodges were represented in the Grand Lodge of New York. In 1835, the number had dwindled to forty-one. Every Lodge in the State of Vermont surrendered its Charter or became dormant; and the Grand Lodge, for several years, ceased to hold its sessions. As in Vermont, so also in Pennsylvania, Rhode Island, Massachusetts, Connecticut; and in lesser degrees in several other states. The Masonic Temple was cleft in twain; its brotherhood scattered, its working tools shattered.

Typical of this anti-Masonic fever was *An Account of the Savage Treatment of Captain William Morgan, in Fort Niagara, Who Was Subsequently Murdered by the Masons, and Sunk in Lake Ontario, for Publishing the Secrets of Masonry*, by former royal arch Mason Edward Giddins. At the time of Morgan's kidnaping, Giddins had been the "keeper" of Fort Niagara and, therefore, an accomplice in imprisoning Morgan. The introduction to his book reads:

CAPTAIN WILLIAM MORGAN, of New York, an intelligent man, and an inflexible republican, convinced of the dangers of Secret Societies, in a free Government, resolved to use his best endeavors for their suppression. Being a Royal Arch Mason, he had witnessed the corruption of the Institution. He saw it was an engine of personal advantage and political aggrandizement; that it gave to its members unfair advantages and extra privileges over the unsuspecting community; that its insidious influence extended to every transaction in society, raising as it were the Masonic combination unto a PRIVILEGED ORDER, who, under the Royal Names of GRAND KINGS, Grand Sovereigns, and Grand High Priests, in darkness and secrecy, ruled and plundered the people. CAPTAIN MORGAN was a soldier and a brave man. He saw this detestable conspiracy and he dared to risk his life by bursting its shackles and warning an injured people! He was seized by a gang of Masonic desperadoes, who came 60 miles after him, in the morning about sunrise, Sept. 11, 1826, under a pretended process of law, (in the manner Mr. Jacob Allen was taken by Masons at Reading) and carried 60 miles, and placed for safe keeping in a county jail, in the care of a masonic jailer. Thence he was taken in stillness of the night, crying murder! murder! and transported one hundred miles further, and placed in a U.S. fortress, also in the keeping of a Mason.

Thus it appears that our county jails and our national fortresses are all at the service of the Masons, to carry their bloody schemes of kidnaping and murder into execution. Will a free and patriotic people submit to these things in silence! Fellow citizens! Read this pamphlet, and answer the question, ought a secret society to exist amongst us whose members can commit murder and yet escape punishment? MASONS HAVE done this, and their brethren, as may be seen by the oaths on our last page, are sworn to protect them.

Fellow citizens, are men bound by such Obligations and possessing such principals, FIT to be rulers of a FREE PEOPLE?

As to his part in the Morgan affair, Gibbins was remorseful:

I beg leave to observe that I have no other excuse to make for the part I took in this foul transaction, than that I was a Royal Arch Mason, and did at that time consider my masonic obligations binding upon my conscience; and now, since these obligations are before the public, I am willing to abide by their decision, how much I was actuated by principles and how much by fear; one thing, however, is certain, that although nothing could have been more repugnant to my natural feelings, yet a sense of duty, and the horrid consequences of refusal, outweighed every other consideration.

In justice to those who took part in this transaction, I would observe, that as far as I am acquainted with them, I feel warranted in saying, that they were urged to those excesses by a strong sense of duty, they blindly thought themselves bound by the most horrid penalties, to perform; and it is to be hoped that the world will be charitable to them by commiserating their misfortunes and extenuating their faults, should they renounce this iniquitous combination, and honestly and fearlessly disclose the parts they acted in this conspiracy, and the causes which urged them to it; but, should they still persist in their obstinate silence, they must not expect that lenity which they otherwise might be entitled to from an indulgent public.

It is to be hoped that an institution whose very principles lead directly to such horrid outrages, and which is entirely made up of dissimulation and fraud, will be completely suppressed in this country and throughout the world, and that a barrier be instituted to prevent it from ever again polluting the earth with its insidious influence. But the public must not expect to accomplish this desirable object without unwanted pains and incessant vigilance; their task is but commencing, and, should they lack in circumspection or perseverance, the monster will yet flourish with more power and commit greater enormities than ever.

The popular feeling that Masons held themselves above the law and had formed a secret government combined to produce a public campaign against Freemasonry. It was said that the secrecy hid illegal and immoral activities, that Masonic oaths were unlawful and "bloody," and that Masons sought to subvert American political and religious institutions. Women joined the anti-Masonic movement by demanding that their husbands resign because of the exclusion of women from Masonry. Many Americans joined what they called the "Blessed Spirit" of fighting to abolish Freemasonry.

This rising animosity soon extended into politics, giving birth to the first "third party" in U.S. history. Leaving no room for doubt as to its purpose, it was called the Anti-Mason Party. It grew so quickly and became powerful enough that its candidates were elected governor in Vermont and Pennsylvania, to the U.S. Senate and House of Representatives, and to legislatures in several states. In 1832, it invented the national nominating convention and chose William Wirt as its standard bearer for president in a three-way contest against incumbent Andrew Jackson and Henry Clay. Wirt carried only Vermont. By 1835, the Anti-Mason Party constituted a force only in Pennsylvania, but it quickly faded away there. Among prominent politicians, including some Masons, who supported the Anti-Mason Party were former president John Quincy Adams, William A. Seward (later a founder of the Republican Party and secretary of state during the Civil War), Daniel Webster, and former grand master of Kentucky Henry Clay.

As a direct result of the anti-Masonic movement of the 1800s, Masons ceased the types of public ceremonies in which they had previously engaged. Ambitious and socially conscious men no longer joined the Craft. It became more of a social group than an intellectual society. The number of U.S. Masons declined from about 100,000 to 40,000 in ten years. New York went from 20,000 to 3,000 and from 480 to 82 lodges. Freemasonry was devastated in Vermont, Pennsylvania, Massachusetts, Rhode Island,

Connecticut, and Ohio. In several states, Grand Lodges ceased to meet. Officers resigned and no new ones could be found. For many years, there were no initiations. Yet, ironically, the country that turned against Free-masonry in the first half of the nineteenth century would experience births of new "secret societies"during the second half that would be mod-eled on Freemasonry and its degree systems. These groups included the Order of Odd Fellows, Knights of Pythias, and the Sons of Temperance.

But enemies of Masonry who found reason to congratulate themselves on the success of their efforts to eradicate it were premature. In 1859, after three decades of decline almost to extinction, a fresh voice sum-moned remnants of the brotherhood in the United States to a new life. In doing so, he would become enshrined in American Masonry with the words: "No purer, nobler man has stood at the Altar of Freemasonry."

CHAPTER 11

FROM LOG CABIN TO TEMPLE

FREEMASONRY IN THE UNITED STATES IN THE EARLY 1800s had grown rapidly. As the century wore on, one branch, the Ancient and Accepted Scottish Rite, was undergoing turmoil that would eventually provide vigorous reinforcement for the fraternity. As noted earlier, the Scottish Rite had been brought to America by Stephen Morin in 1761. By 1763, he had organized his own Rite of Perfection of twenty-five degrees in the British West Indies. By 1767, this was taken to North America by an associate, Henry Francken, who established a Lodge of Perfection at Albany, New York. He continued to propagate the rite after Morin's death in 1771 and was succeeded by the Comte de Grasse-Tilly, who had been involved in the creation of the Grand Constitutions of 1786 that formed the basis of the "Mother Supreme Council 33°, Ancient and Accepted Scottish Rite," formed in 1801 by the Reverend Frederick Dalcho.

Born in October 1770 in the Borough of Holborn, London, in the parish St. Giles-in-the-Fields, Dalcho arrived in Baltimore on a sailing vessel on May 23, 1787, at the age of fifteen "after a boisterous passage of eight weeks on the sea from London." He went to live with his father's sister, who was married to Dr. Charles Frederick Wiesenthal, a Mason. The boy received a classical education, learning about botany and commencing his medical studies under his uncle's guidance. Appointed a lieutenant of artillery in the army, Dalcho was transferred to Fort Fidius in Georgia on the Oconee River. After receiving his medical degree, he was appointed a surgeon's mate in the army in 1792 and stationed in Savannah,

Georgia. It was there that he joined a Masonic lodge, believed to be Hyram Lodge No. 2, Ancient York Mason. Transferred from Savannah's Fort Johnson, located in the Charleston harbor in 1796, he was promoted into the corps of artillerists and engineers, but a commission to become a ship's surgeon to the factoring firm of McClure and Company took him on several trips to Africa. After returning to the army for an additional fifteen months' service, he settled down to practice medicine with a friend, Dr. Isaac Auld. On May 31, 1801, with John Mitchell, he opened the first Supreme Council of the Scottish Rite in America at Shepheard's Tavern in Charleston, South Carolina. He was elected to the office of lieutenant grand commander.

The group's manifesto gave it the name "Supreme Council of the Thirty-third Degree for the United States of America." It retained jurisdiction over all other states and U.S. territories (at home and abroad). Yet, for almost seventy years the Scottish Rite in America followed a convoluted course marked by chaos, divisions, rivalries, schisms, and even spurious Supreme Councils.

All that would change in 1859 with the election of a poet, lawyer, Civil War general, mystic, and Masonic ritualist of genius named Albert Pike as the new sovereign grand commander of the Supreme Council (Southern Jurisdiction).

As noted in chapter 1, Pike was born in Boston on December 29, 1809, to poor parents. He was educated in the public schools in Boston. Although he passed examinations for admission to Harvard College, he was unable to enter because of a requirement that two years' tuition be paid in advance or secured by bond. He became a schoolteacher and taught in country schools in Massachusetts from 1825 to 1831. Venturing west, he joined a trading party from St. Louis to Santa Fe, then in Mexico. On his return, he traveled the "Staked Plains" and "Indian Territory" and settled at Van Buren, Arkansas, where he opened a school.

At that time, the territory was divided between the Conway party (Democrats) and the Crittenden party (Whigs). Because Pike was a Whig, he published articles in the Whig newspaper at Little Rock that attracted John Crittenden's attention. He sought out Pike in his country schoolroom and persuaded him to go to Little Rock as one of the editors of the party paper. While working on it, he studied law. Admitted to the bar in 1834, he rose rapidly in the esteem of Arkansas lawyers. Among his earlier achievements was preparation of the first revision of the statutes of that state.

At the outbreak of the Mexican War, Pike entered the army and was in action at Buena Vista. For criticizing the military conduct of the state governor, he was challenged to a duel that ended bloodlessly. At the conclusion of the Mexican War, he returned to Arkansas (he eventually sat on the state's supreme court) and entered Masonry. Made a master Mason in Western Star Lodge No. 1 in Little Rock, he became fascinated with its symbolism. When he heard of the Scottish Rite in 1852, he believed that it had no relation to the Masonry he knew. He recalled that he felt as a Puritan would if a Buddhist ceremony were performed in a Calvinistic church. To learn about the Sottish Rite, he went to Charleston and embraced it. He received the degrees from fourth to thirty-second in 1843 and the thirty-third in 1857 at New Orleans. The following year he gave the lecture on the evil consequences of schisms and disputes in Masonry.

Elected sovereign grand commander of the Supreme Council (Southern Jurisdiction) in 1859, Pike examined the rites and rituals that were being followed and found "a chaotic mass" of "incoherent nonsense and jargon." So many pains had been taken to conceal the meaning of the symbols, he said, that their true meaning was for the most part lost, and "ignorance or dullness had supplied others, invented by themselves." He found that the jargon of some of the degrees was as "unintelligible as that of the Alchemists convincing me that their real meaning had been communicated orally and that the rituals were purposely framed to mislead those into whose hands they might unlawfully Fall."

Copying all the rituals "so as to have them in uniform and available shape," Pike produced "a memorandum book of 400 pages." (It is preserved in the archives of the Supreme Council, Washington, D.C.) Of this monumental task, he wrote, "After accumulating a good quantity of material, by reading and copying, I commenced on the Scottish Rite. I found it almost equivalent, as to the degrees I selected, to making something out of nothing. I first endeavored to find, in the degree I had under consideration, a leading idea: and then to carry that out and give the degree as high a character as I could."

He later recalled:

> I satisfied myself that many of the degrees were purposely constructed to conceal their meaning and the objects of those who used them as the means of union and organization. Such, I believed, were the Fifteenth and Sixteenth [degrees], of the Knight of the East and princes of Jerusalem, but I could not fathom their meaning or detect the concealed allegory. They seemed to teach nothing and almost to be nothing. After I had collected and read a hundred rare volumes upon religious antiquity, symbolism, the mysteries, the doctrines of the Gnostics, and the Hebrew and Alexandrian philosophy...and many others of our Rite still remained as impenetrable enigmas to me as at first. The monuments of Egypt with their hieroglyphics gave me no assistance. The fruits of the study and reflection of twelve years are embodied in our degrees. Hundreds of volumes have been explored for the purpose of developing and illustrating them, and the mere labor bestowed on them has been more than many a professional man expends in attaining eminence and amassing a fortune.

The study of the rite left him feeling that its rituals were "for the most part a lot of worthless trash." In the 1887 pamphlet *Beauties of Cerneauism,* he said that the rituals of the degrees of the Ancient and Accepted Scottish Rite that he found "were not impressive in any way." He wrote that no man of intellect and knowledge could regard them "with any respect." Trivial, insipid, and without originality, as "literary productions" they were "contemptible" collections "of flat, dull, common place."

Taking the material home to Arkansas, he "copied the whole of them." The result of Pike's work was *Morals and Dogmas of the Ancient and Accepted Scottish Rite of Freemasonry,* which was published in 1859. A philosophical work rather than a manifesto, it was an attempt to provide a framework for understanding the religions and philosophies of the ancient past. He felt that without understanding the history of a concept, one could not grasp the concept itself. Every edition of *Morals and Dogmas* since its first publication has been prefaced with, "Everyone is free to reject and dissent from whatsoever herein may seem to him to be untrue or unsound. It is only required of him that he shall weigh what is taught, and give it a fair hearing and unprejudiced judgment."

Pike did not assert that *Morals and Dogmas* contained the beliefs of Masonry, but only information about ancient cultures, religions, beliefs, and customs in a single book. He did not claim that they were his personal beliefs, or imply that they were the basis of Freemasonry. He reported what he found, and left the reader to form conclusions. As a consequence, said Philip Elam, grand orator of Masons in Missouri, at a Scottish Rite Men's Luncheon Club in May 2000, "Today, some Masons attempt to diminish Pike's importance in order to deflect the charges of the anti-Masonic contingent. Other Masons, particularly those who may not be very familiar with the genius and accomplishments of this man, will dismiss him as being a meaningless figure in the role of Freemasonry."

A man who symbolized many of the looming national issues of his era, Pike was also an emblematic figure in a time when most Americans were self-educated. But Americans of his generation were a people who valued refinement. The concert hall and the lecture platform were popular. To be able to sing, to play, and to write were regarded as highly desirable accomplishments. Pike sang, played the violin, and wrote poetry that was highly praised. Many of his orations were reprinted in newspapers and books. The best-known Freemason in the United States, as well as its most prolific writer and philosopher, he lived at a time of colorful personalities, including Davy Crockett, Sam Houston, Harriet Beecher Stowe, Stephen Crane, Henry Wadsworth Longfellow, and Abraham Lincoln. Knowing many of them, and counting most of them among his friends, he became a familiar figure in the nation's capital as a larger-than-life man on the social scene, an outstanding dancer, a host without parallel, and a man of action with unshakable confidence that the best was yet to come for America and for humanity.

An avowed Whig and antisecessionist, he was a prominent lawyer and a large landowner in Little Rock until 1861. Against his better judgment, he was appointed Confederate commissioner to the tribes of Indian Territory.

In that capacity, he brought the Creek, Seminole, Choctaw, Chickasaw, and Cherokee Nations into alliance with the Confederacy. Because of his appointment as Indian commissioner, he was also commissioned a brigadier general in the Confederate army. At the Battle of Pea Ridge, he commanded a brigade of Indians, making him the only Confederate commander to lead Indian troops into battle. When they refused to pursue Union forces beyond their territories, Pike was accused of failing to rally or reorganize his troops. After considerable hostility, he resigned his Confederate commission in 1862. Like most other Rebel officers, he was indicted for treason by the United States, but was subsequently restored to his civil rights.

After the war, he resided in Memphis and edited the *Memphis Appeal* until 1867. The following year he moved to Washington, D.C., and practiced law in the federal courts until 1880. During the remainder of his life, he devoted his attention to writing legal treatises and promoting the Masonic order. On April 2, 1891, he died at his desk in his office at the Scottish Rite Temple in Washington, D.C. He was buried in Oak Hill Cemetery.

Among his memorable quotations are:

"Human Thought is an actual EXISTENCE, and a Force and Power, capable of acting upon and controlling matter as well as mind."

"A man should live with his superiors as he does with his fire: not too near, lest he burn; nor too far off, lest he freeze."

"A war for a great principle ennobles a nation."

The only Confederate soldier to be honored in Washington, D.C. (a statue of him stands in Judiciary Square), he is also memorialized in the Albert Pike Highway, running from Hot Springs, Arkansas, to Colorado Springs, Colorado, while a national park and several schools are named for him. The Grand Lodge of Arkansas currently presents the Albert Pike Award for excellence in Masonic Internet Web site design and content.

American Freemasonry remembers him as a towering leader who "found the Scottish Rite in a log cabin and left it in a Temple."

CHAPTER 12

BATTLEFIELD BROTHERS

B Y THE TIME OF THE CIVIL WAR, THIRTY-EIGHT INDE-
pendent Grand Lodges existed in the United States. Each was independent and absolutely sovereign within its own jurisdictional
boundaries. This lack of a national leadership is a major reason why
Freemasonry as a whole did not fracture along geographical boundaries,
as did many of the other organizations on the eve of war. In those cases,
groups like the Baptist churches, the Presbyterian churches, and others all
had some sort of national leadership council, comprised of representatives
of all of the various regions of the country. As war fractured the country, it
splintered the national committees of many groups.

Because there was no "Grand Lodge of America," there existed no national committee. Individual lodges were on their own. But this did not
mean that Masons did not feel the pain of division. In a letter drafted in
June 1861, the Grand Lodge of Pennsylvania replied to a letter from the
Grand Lodge of Tennessee:

> As to the present deplorable state of this country, Masons cannot fail
> to have opinions as to the cause that produced it. It is to be feared that
> some of our brethren are in arms against the union of the States; oth-
> ers are in the ranks of its defenders. Taught by the history of the
> Order...they have carried these principles into the formation of
> opinions on the present crisis in our national history. But while
> Masons, as individuals, have been thus influenced and are acting in

harmony with such views, Freemasonry is a silent, unimpassioned, abstracted observer of events.

Brethren, we, with you, deplore the present unnatural and deeply distressing condition of our national affairs.... But if this whirlwind threatens to overwhelm us, yet in this last extremity, the still small voice of Masonic faith will be uttered and heard, saying, "Brethren, there is help at hand in this time of need. Surely your God is our God; your faith our faith; your landmarks our landmarks; your joy our joy; your prosperity our satisfaction." Then let us unitedly work together for the preservation and perpetuity of a common inheritance.... We will aid in maintaining unity, peace and concord, among the brethren and citizens of united sovereign States in our glorious Union. If all bonds should be broken, all ties rent asunder; if discord, dissension, and disruption, shall mark the decline and fall of the most wise and wonderful of the governments of mankind, let the Masonic temple, in all States, kingdoms, lands, peoples or confederacies, be common refuge of an indestructible Masonic fraternity.

Allen E. Roberts notes in *House Undivided: The Story of Freemasonry and the Civil War* that while the war raged around them, Freemasons held on to "the ties and the idealism that brought them together in the first place." Thousands of Masons fought in the war. Many died, but the tenets of the Craft were able to overcome the animosity the war generated.

Masonry historians cite a number of reasons for this, beginning with beliefs and tenets of the lodge that predated not only the Civil War, but also the Constitution, the discovery of the New World, and, according to some, even the birth of Christ. A second reason given to explain why Masonry held together is that membership in a Masonic lodge was by choice. No man had ever been recruited into joining a lodge. Rules prohibited Masons from recruiting. A man who was interested in becoming a Mason must "of his own free will and accord" actively seek out a member of the lodge that he wished to join and ask for a petition for membership. The third reason lay in the structure of the Craft. Internal rules and customs helped the lodge as a whole avoid the turbulent politics and divisiveness of the war, allowing the lodge to continue to function as a place a man could go when he needed help, or a quiet haven from the storms that raged outside the Craft.

The most famous example of these ties of brotherhood occurred at Gettysburg. A turning point of the war, this battle resulted in more than 35,000 killed or wounded in the three days of fighting from July 1–3, 1863. Of those who fought, 17,930 were Freemasons, with roughly 5,600 becoming casualties. On the final day, in a Confederate infantry attack known as Pickett's Charge, the leader, Major General George Pickett, a member of Dove Lodge No. 51, Richmond, Virginia, led nearly 12,000 men on a long rush across open fields toward the center of the Union line on Cemetery Ridge. One of the leaders of the charge, Brigadier General Lewis Addison Armistead, belonged to Alexandria-Washington Masonic Lodge No. 22 in Alexandria.

Originally from North Carolina, Armistead had attended West Point and fought with the U.S. Army for a number of years before resigning his commission to fight for the Confederacy. During that time, he had occasion to serve with Winfield Scott Hancock of the Charity Lodge No. 190, Norristown, Pennsylvania, while both men were in the West. The two had become good friends. After Armistead's resignation, it had been nearly two and a half years since the two men had any contact.

At Gettysburg, Hancock, now a major general, had taken command of the fragmented Union troops on Cemetery Ridge on July 1. He organized them into a strong front that withstood three days of pounding from the Confederate guns. On July 3, his troops were in the center of the Union line and the focus of Pickett's Charge. During the action, Armistead was shot from his horse and mortally wounded. Hancock's saddle was struck, driving nails and pieces of wood into his thigh. Armistead exhibited the Masonic sign of distress. It was recognized by Captain Henry Harrison Bingham, the judge-advocate of Hancock's Second Corps and member of Chartiers Lodge No. 297, Canonsburg, Pennsylvania. Rushing to Armistead, he declared he was a Mason.

As the two men spoke, Armistead realized that Bingham had direct access to Hancock. He gave him personal effects, including his Masonic watch and the Bible on which he had taken his Masonic obligations.

Bingham said farewells and returned to the Union camp to deliver the items to Hancock. Armistead died two days later.

There were numerous documented stories of warfare being put aside for the purposes of Masonic funerals. In Galveston, a Confederate major named Tucker performed Masonic funeral services for a Union captain named Wainwright who had died in Tucker's prison. In a public procession consisting of friends and foe wearing the insignia of the order, and accompanied by a proper military escort, Wainwright's body was carried to the Episcopal cemetery. In another case, a Masonic Union naval commander named Hart was killed on board his vessel during a long bombardment. A small craft sailed into that Louisiana port under a truce flag and asked for a Mason. W. W. Leake responded by immediately opening a lodge to give Hart full Masonic rites.

Some Masons wore signs and symbols of the Craft on their uniforms, hoping a Mason on the other side would recognize him as a brother and spare him harm. Masons were also active in hospitals and care units at the sites of major battles. Hospitals were located on the farms or in the buildings owned by Masons. The Masonic Temple in Vicksburg was used as a hospital first by the Confederates, and later by the Union after the fall of Vicksburg.

Other Freemasons who played significant roles at the Battle of Gettysburg include:

- Colonel Joshua Lawrence Chamberlain, United Lodge No. 8, Brunswick, Maine, was awarded the Congressional Medal of Honor for heroics on Little Round Top.

- Captain Henry H. Bingham, Chartiers Lodge No. 297, Canonsburg, Pennsylvania, a life member of Union Lodge No. 121 in Philadelphia. He received the Medal of Honor and was elected to Congress in 1878 and served thirty-three years.

- Major General Henry Heth, senior warden of Rocky Mountain Lodge No. 205, Utah Territory. A close friend of Robert E. Lee, he was severely wounded at Gettysburg but survived.

- Brigadier General Solomon Meredith, commander of the Iron Brigade, also called the Black Hat Brigade, had three sons in the Union Army, two of whom were killed. He was a member of Cambridge Lodge No. 105, Indianapolis, Indiana.

- Brigadier General Alfred Iverson, Columbian Lodge No. 108, Columbus, Georgia. His father was a U.S. senator from Georgia before the war.

- Major General Carl Schurz, born in Cologne, Prussia, left Europe after supporting failed revolutions. A prominent politician, he backed Lincoln in the 1860 election. Given a generalship to command the large number of Germans in the Union Army, he did not enjoy a distinguished career in the Civil War. After the conflict, he served as ambassador to Spain, U.S. senator from Missouri, and secretary of the interior. He died in 1906 in New York City, where a park is now named for him. He was a member of Herman Lodge No. 125 in Philadelphia.

- Brigadier General John B. Gordon of Upson County, Georgia, attended the University of Georgia and trained in law. At the Battle of Antietam, he was wounded so severely in the head that only a bullet hole in his hat prevented him from drowning in his own blood. He was wounded eight times. After the war, he was elected U.S. senator from Georgia three times, and later governor of Georgia. Some publications listed him a member of Gate City Lodge No. 2 in Atlanta, but members of that lodge said there are no records to support that claim.

- Brigadier General George T. "Tige" Anderson left college in Georgia to enter the Mexican War. Severely wounded in Gettysburg, he was a Freemason, but details of his membership are not known.

- Brigadier General John H. H. Ward of New York City fought in many Civil War battles, but was removed from the army in 1864 for misbehavior and intoxication in the face of the enemy. This was disputed for thirty years and never settled. After the war, he served as clerk of courts in New York. In 1903 while vacationing in Monroe, New York, he was run over by a train and killed. He was a Mason in the Metropolitan Lodge No. 273, New York City.

Other Masons at Gettysburg were:

Brigadier General Rufus Ingalls, Williamette Lodge No. 2, Oregon

Brigadier General Joseph B. Kershaw, Kershaw Lodge No. 29, South Carolina

Brigadier General Alfred T. A. Torbert, Temple Chapter No. 2, Delaware

Brigadier General William Barksdale, Columbus Lodge No. 5, Columbus, Mississippi

Major General David B. Birney, Franklin Lodge No.134, Pennsylvania

Brigadier General Harry T. Hays, Louisiana Lodge No. 102, Louisiana

Major General Daniel Butterfield, Metropolitan Lodge No. 273, New York

Brigadier General John W. Geary, Philanthropy Lodge No. 255, Pennsylvania

Major General Alfred Pleasonton, Franklin Lodge No. 134, Pennsylvania

Brigadier General George J. Stannard, Franklin Lodge No. 4, Vermont

Brigadier General James L. Kemper, Linn Banks Lodge No. 126 (PM), Virginia

Major General George E. Pickett, Dove Lodge No. 51, Virginia

Brigadier General John D. Imboden, Staunton Lodge No. 13, Virginia

In 1993, the Grand Lodge of Pennsylvania completed and dedicated a monument on the Gettysburg National Cemetery, with cooperation and support of the U.S. government. It depicts "Brother Bingham, a Union officer, assisting Brother Armistead." The statue is called "Masonic Friend to Friend Masonic Memorial." In the words of Sheldon A. Munn, one of the Freemasons who helped bring about its construction, it is meant to "demonstrate to the world that Freemasonry is, indeed, a unique fraternity; that its bonds of friendship, compassion and brotherly love withstood the ultimate test during the most tragic and decisive period of our nation's history; it stood then as it stands now, as 'A Brotherhood Undivided!'"

Abraham Lincoln was not a Mason, but Masonic historian Paul M. Bessel notes that "he possessed and displayed all the important qualities of Freemasonry: faith, hope, and charity, belief in God, the equality of all people, and the ability of each person to improve." He also "came into contact with many Masons." When the Grand Lodge of Illinois recessed a meeting being held during the 1860 presidential campaign, it called on Lincoln. He was reported to have said, "Gentlemen, I have always entertained a profound respect for the Masonic fraternity and have long cherished a desire to become a member." When a Mason told Lincoln during that campaign that all his opponents were Freemasons, especially noting that Stephen A. Douglas was an early member of the Masonic lodge in Springfield, Lincoln's home town, and he was not, Lincoln was reported to have replied, "I am not a Freemason, Dr. Morris, though I have great respect for the institution."

After Lincoln's death, the grand master of Masons in the District of Columbia, Benjamin B. French, who had been a friend of Lincoln's, wrote to the editor of *The Masonic Trowel*, who was also the grand secretary of the Grand Lodge of Illinois, "[Lincoln] once told me how highly he respected our Order and that he at one time had fully made up his mind to apply for admission into it." French also wrote to the deputy grand master of the Grand Lodge of New York, in response to a similar inquiry, that Lincoln once told him, in the presence of Mason J. W. Simons, that "he had at one time made up his mind to apply for admission to our Fraternity but feared he was too lazy to attend to his duty as a Mason, as he should like to do, and that he had not carried out his intentions."

Lincoln biographer Carl Sandburg states, "Though not a Mason, he had at hand a personal copy of the bound 'Proceedings of the Grand

Royal Arch Chapter of the State of Illinois,' being reports of conventions of the Masonic order for the years 1851–1857."

Succeeding to the presidency when Lincoln was assassinated on April 14,1865, Andrew Johnson of Tennessee had been a Freemason since 1851. He was probably a member of the Greeneville Chapter No. 82, Royal Arch Masons. He joined Nashville Commandery of Knights Templar No. 1 in 1859. As president, he received the Scottish Rite degrees in the White House in 1867. Because Radical Republicans in the Senate perceived him as weak and too soft in his policy toward the South, the pretext of the dismissal from the cabinet by Johnson of the anti-South Secretary of War Edwin M. Stanton (a Mason) was employed in an effort to remove Johnson from office through impeachment. Led by anti-Mason Charles Sumner, freshman congressman and Freemason General Benjamin F. Butler, and former Anti-Mason Party leader Thaddeus Stevens, who had participated in the anti-Mason fervor in the Morgan affair, the effort failed by one vote in the Senate.

Outside the corridors of government, societies formed to promote white supremacy in the South, including the Men of Justice, the Pale Faces, the Constitutional Union Guards, the White Brotherhood, and the Order of the White Rose. But it was the Ku Klux Klan that would move to the fore. Begun by former Confederate soldiers in Pulaski, Tennessee, in May 1866, the Klan was a disorganized group until 1867. In April of that year in Nashville, Tennessee, General Nathan Bedford Forrest, a heroic cavalry leader of the Confederacy, was chosen "Grand Wizard of the Empire." Each state constituted a "Realm" under a "Grand Dragon," each with a staff of eight "Hydras." Several counties formed a "Dominion" controlled by a "Grand Titan." A "Province" was ruled by a "Grand Giant" and four "Night Hawks." A local "Den" was governed by a "Grand Cyclops" with two night hawks as aides. Members were "Ghouls."

As a historian of the Klan writes, "Its strange disguises, its silent parades, its midnight rides, its mysterious language and commands, were found to be most effective in playing upon fears and superstitions. The riders muffled their horses' feet and covered the horses with white robes. They themselves, dressed in flowing white sheets, their faces covered with white masks, and with skulls at their saddle horns, posed as spirits of the

Confederate dead returned from the battlefields." Although the Klan was often able to achieve its aims by terror alone, lynching and whippings were used not only against blacks, but also against so-called carpetbaggers and scalawags.

Concerned about reckless and lawless local leaders, Forrest ordered the disbandment of the Klan and resigned as grand wizard in January 1869. The next year, Congress passed a law to combat the Klan that effectively put it out of business until it was revived in the years before World War I. Led by William J. Simmons, a former minister and a promoter of fraternal orders, the Klan held its first meeting at Stone Mountain, Georgia. In one form or another, the Klan has existed ever since.

While there is no question that Masonry was an influence in the Klan's structure after the Civil War, a controversy continues to this day over whether Pike held the office of chief justice at a time when he was the sovereign grand commander of the Scottish Rite (Southern Jurisdiction). Those who assert this as a fact cite Pike's declaration that he had an "obligation to white men, not to Negroes." He had vowed, "When I have to accept Negroes as brothers or leave Masonry, I shall leave it."

Pike's Masonic defenders assert that the claim that he was a Klansman is impossible to either substantiate or disprove because there is no primary source material on the subject. They state that "the only writings that would come close to qualifying as a primary source" was a booklet written by Captain John C. Lester, one of the Klan founders, in 1884, fifteen years after the fact, in which the only name noted is one reference to "Gen. Forrest."

This argument further notes:

> It was not until Dr. Walter L. Fleming republished Lester's booklet in 1905 that a list of names of key Klansmen was included in a preface. In 1924, Ms. Susan L. Davis published her Authentic History, in which she contradicts a number of points made by Lester, denigrates Fleming for his superficial knowledge of the Klan and condemns Lester's co-author, David L. Wilson, for suggesting the Klan had failed. Any other book or article promoting Albert Pike's association with the Klan will either cite Fleming or Davis, cite other authors

who cite Fleming or Davis, or not cite anyone. Both Fleming and
Davis accepted, unquestioningly, the fifty year old reminiscences of
several of the founding members of the Klan. There is no source doc-
umentation, corroborating evidence or other testimony to implicate
Albert Pike with the Klan. Pike had been dead fourteen years when
Fleming first published, and was in no position to address the issue.

This defense of Pike attributes claims that he had a Klan leadership
role or membership to "hearsay" and that his "racism, while nothing to be
proud of, was mild by his contemporaries' standards." The assertion that
there are no records from the late 1860s to the early 1870s that connect
Pike with the Klan was bolstered by Dr. Walter Lee Brown's Ph.D. dis-
sertation on Pike. Considered a leading authority on the subject, Brown
states that there are "no primary sources which provide evidence that Pike
was involved with the Klan." Pike defenders also note that a congressional
investigation in 1872 into the "Condition of Affairs in the Late In-
surrectionary States" found that there were "references to alleged Klan
leaders in several states, but no mention of Pike."

Had there been such evidence, it would have been unlikely that
Congress would have authorized the placement of a statue to Pike on federal land in Washington, D.C., as it did on April 9, 1898, in Joint Resolution 20. The monument was erected by the Supreme Council of the
Scottish Rite (Southern Jurisdiction) in front of what was then the Scottish Rite House of the Temple. The enabling legislation omitted reference
to Pike's service in the Confederate Army

This congressional recognition of Pike's contribution to American
Masonry, and the lack of proof that he had been a Klansman, made no difference to groups of protesters that gathered around the statue in September
1992 to denounce him as "the chief founder" of the Ku Klux Klan in Arkansas.
The protesters were led and organized by and consisted mainly of supporters of Lyndon LaRouche, a controversial political figure. According
to the Masons, the protesters' chief organizer was Anton Chaitkin, affiliated with the Shiller Institute, a LaRouche entity.

The Masons maintained that "Messrs. LaRouche, Chaitkin, and their
supporters contend that the Klan was founded as the terrorist arm of the

Scottish Rite as part of a wide Masonic conspiracy to keep the South in Confederate hands," and that Chaitkin appeared to believe "that Masonic historians have been actively rewriting American history as part of a Masonic conspiracy. He believes that the Scottish Rite is a British Imperial plot, hatched in Charleston, South Carolina, to perpetuate slavery, [and] failing that, to perpetuate the Ku Klux Klan; and that the whole American legal system is largely controlled by the Scottish Rite."

During the period of weekly rallies, the statue was painted, chipped, and decorated with a Klan costume. On April 20, 1993, Chaitkin and an associate, Reverend James Bevel, were convicted of climbing on the statue after a police official had asked them to step down. At the trial, the two defendants attacked the sitting judge for having reputedly been a member of an Albert Pike DeMolay Chapter in San Antonio, Texas, while outside the courtroom LaRouche followers carried large banners stating, "Down with Pike!"

While Freemasonry's connection to the Ku Klux Klan remains a topic of debate, there is no doubt that the revival of Masonry in the second half of the nineteenth century reflected shifts in American customs and attitudes. Historians cite the influence of the Temperance movement to explain Freemasonry taking on aspects of "an 18th-century men's club that carefully separated its ritual meeting from banquets and social functions." Still sensitive to the criticism of clergymen that surfaced during the anti-Masonic period, Freemasonry's teachings moved further from eighteenth-century Enlightenment philosophy and Deism to more closely parallel nineteenth-century religion.

It was a time when other organizations grew directly out of the divisiveness of the Civil War experience. In 1864, the Knights of Pythias was organized by a group of federal clerks in Washington, D.C., who felt that the nation urgently needed to rekindle a brotherly spirit. A ritual designed by Justus H. Rathbone was based on the fourth-century B.C. story of the friendship of Damon and Pythias. A Mason, Rathbone incorporated aspects of Freemasonry. Although the society's motto, "Friendship, Charity, and Benevolence," echoed Freemasonry, a Pythian writer, James R. Carnahan, said in *Pythian Knighthood*, "We do not, as does Masonry, have clustering about our shrine the clinging ivy of centuries' growth, nor is it yet wreathed about our altars the mysterious legends reaching back into the dim and musty ages of the long ago. We come with present relief for man's present necessities."

After a tour of the post–Civil War South for the Bureau of Agriculture, Oliver Hudson Kelly (a Freemason) helped found the Order of the Patrons of Husbandry. Commonly called the Grange, it was a fraternal organization to promote agriculture through "cooperation, mutual benefit, and improvement." At the urging of Kelly's niece, Caroline Hall, the Grange was one of the first fraternal organizations to admit women.

The Benevolent and Protective Order of Elks originally began as a group of actors in New York City. Meeting for lunch and refreshments and at first calling themselves the "Jolly Corks," they soon organized as a secret, social, and benevolent fraternity with the elk as their symbol. Broadening membership beyond entertainers, the "Elks" incorporated many Masonic influences and eventually instituted benefit programs to "spread the antlers of protection."

In 1888, the Loyal Order of Moose was organized in Louisville, Kentucky. Although it did not prosper at first, in 1906 under the direction of John Henry Wilson, a politician and labor activist, the group began to expand. In 1911, it acquired property for a school by purchasing a dairy farm in Illinois to support children who had lost one or both parents. Incorporated as the village of Mooseheart, it became the organization's headquarters.

The Order of Knights of Labor, founded by Uriah Stevens and other garment workers in Philadelphia in 1869, became the first mass organization representing the American working class. A Freemason, Stevens included many features of Masonry in the ritual. The organization was able to attract large numbers of workers among Philadelphia artisans in the 1860s, adding miners in the 1870s and skilled urban tradesmen in the 1880s. The Knights of Labor was one of the few post–Civil War labor organizations that welcomed black members.

Freemasonry historians find a connection between the ideals of Masonry and social groups formed by European immigrants that flooded into the United States in the late nineteenth and early twentieth centuries. They included the Workmen's Circle (1894) that worked to assimilate Jewish Americans by providing insurance and English lessons and Union St. Jean

Baptiste. It formed in 1900 at Woonsocket, Rhode Island, "to unite in a common spirit of brotherhood persons of French origin living in the United States and to promote their collective individual welfare." Of many small societies providing social activities and benefits, the Sons of Italy (1905) became the largest and most influential and soon had 125,000 members nationally.

Organized in 1882, the Knights of Columbus offered Roman Catholic men of varying backgrounds an acceptable fraternal organization. American Catholics found themselves unable to participate in the many fraternal organizations that offered insurance benefits because the church had condemned secret societies. Founded by Michael J. McGivney, a New Haven, Connecticut, parish priest, the Knights of Columbus paralleled the structure of Freemasonry with ritual, degrees, passwords, and the motto "Charity, Unity, Fraternity, and Patriotism."

While the Knights of Columbus enjoyed the approval of the Roman Catholic Church in 1884, the position of the Vatican regarding Masonry that had been stated by Pope Clement XII in 1739 had not changed. An encyclical by Leo XIII in 1884 called on each member of the clergy to help defeat Catholicism's old enemy with the words:

> We pray and beseech you, venerable brethren, to join your efforts with Ours, and earnestly to strive for the extirpation of this foul plague, which is creeping through the veins of the body politic. ...We wish it to be your rule first of all to tear away the mask from Freemasonry, and to let it be seen as it really is; and by sermons and pastoral letters to instruct the people as to the artifices used by societies of this kind in seducing men and enticing them into their ranks, and as to the depravity of their opinions and the wickedness of their acts.

As the latest papal bull was being read by the Catholic hierarchy in American cities, the number of Grand Lodges that had been established in states since the close of the Civil War stood at ten (counting the "Indian Territory" that would become Oklahoma). By the end of the nineteenth century, the Scottish Rite would predominate, with thirty-six Southern Jurisdiction states and fourteen Northern. Comparing the democracy of

Masonry in the "great Land of the West" with English High Masonry's social class "exclusivity" and a tradition of ties to royalty and the aristocracy, Arthur Edwin Waite in *A New Encyclopedia of Freemasonry* sees the American way as the wiser course. If a time should come for something "great and vital to arise in the World of Ritual," it would be in the United States. The "generous Brotherhood of America" would reap its reward, and "Masonry will receive its crown."

Because of the Grand Lodge of London's coveted and symbiotic relationship with the British monarchy, Freemasonry would find itself tangled in a web of mystery surrounding the identity and motivation of the world's first and most famous serial murderer.

CHAPTER 13

WAS JACK THE RIPPER A MASON?

O N FRIDAY, AUGUST 31, 1888, PROSTITUTE MARY ANN Nichols was found murdered in Buck's Row in the Whitechapel district of East London. Eights days later (Saturday, September 8) in a rear yard at 29 Hanbury Street in the Spitalfields section, prostitute Annie Chapman's body was discovered. On Sunday, September 30, Elizabeth Stride was found in a side yard at 40 Berner Street. On the same day, Catherine Eddowes was murdered in Mitre Square, Aldgate. All had been slashed across the throat and mutilated in the abdomen. Chapman's uterus was taken away by the killer. Eddowes's uterus and left kidney had also been removed. The following Friday in a room of a boarding house at 13 Miller's Court, 26 Dorset Street, Spitalfields, Mary Kelly was discovered slaughtered in her bed.

Deeming the investigation "too extensive" for Detective Inspector Edmund Reid of the Whitechapel Division of the Criminal Investigation Division (CID) of the Metropolitan Police, known as Scotland Yard, to handle alone, the Central Office assigned Detective Inspectors Frederick Abberline, Walter Andrews, and James McWilliam and a team of subordinate officers. They had no suspects. But on September 29, they learned the killer's name. In a letter dated four days earlier that was signed "Jack the Ripper," the writer declared, "I am down on whores and I shant quit ripping them till I do get buckled [caught]."

After the two murders on September 30, another letter arrived. Referring to the "double event," it was written in red ink. Signed "Jack the Ripper," it referred to himself as "saucy Jack" The authenticity of this letter is still debated by "Ripperologists."

Witnesses had described the elusive killer as a "shabby genteel" man in dark clothing and a slouch hat and carrying a shiny black bag. Dozens of men were questioned "on suspicion," but quickly released. The police went house to house looking for leads, handbills were circulated, and private detectives and members of the "Whitchapel Vigilance Committee" joined the hunt. On October 16, its chairman, George Lusk, received a cardboard box containing half of a human kidney and a letter. Scrawled in a spidery hand was "from Hell" and a claim that the writer had fried and eaten the other half of the "kidne," which was "very nise." At the end was written "Catch me when you can Mishter Lusk." Detectives and a police surgeon felt it was probably a hoax by a medical student.

Investigators had few clues, but immediately after the Eddowes murder, a piece of her bloodstained apron had been found in a doorway in Goulston Street, Whitechapel. Written in chalk on the brick wall above the piece of apron was the message: "The Juwes are The men that Will not be Blamed for nothing."

Summoned to the scene, the head of the Metropolitan Police, Sir Charles Warren, had the message erased. He explained that he did so out of fear that "Juwes" would be taken by the public to mean "Jews" and lead to anti-Jewish rioting. Because the order to obliterate the words was given by one of England's most prominent Freemasons, the erasure would become the basis of a contention, voiced nearly a hundred years later in a book and later in two films that Jack the Ripper was a fiction created by Freemasons to conceal a conspiracy to preserve the British monarchy and that all the murders were committed according to Masonic ritual.

A soldier, explorer, and archaeologist, Warren had been educated at Sandhurst (England's military academy). As an agent of the Palestine Exploration Fund in 1867, he surveyed Herod's Temple on the site of Solomon's Temple, made significant excavations in Jerusalem, and wrote of them in two books, *The Temple or the Tomb* and *Under Jerusalem*. Initiated into Freemasonry on December 30, 1859, he became past master in 1863 and belonged to the Royal Lodge of Friendship No. 278 at Gibralter and was past grand deacon of the United Grand Lodge of England (1887). At the time of the Ripper murders, he was worshipful master of the Quatuor Coronati Lodge No. 2076. Its meetings were held not far from the Kelly murder scene. Warren had been elected its founding master in 1884. The lodge warrant had been granted on November 28, 1884. Because of Warren's departure to Buchuana, Africa, the lodge did not meet until after his return at the end of 1885. He was installed at a meeting on January 12, 1886. When the lodge was consecrated, he attended three of the seven meetings called during his almost three-year term of office.

On November 7, 1888, ostensibly because of a conflict with Henry Mathews, the home secretary, he resigned as head of Scotland Yard. Earlier that day, Mary Kelly had become the last Whitechapel murder victim ascribed to Jack the Ripper.

In *Jack the Ripper: The Final Solution*, Stephen Knight asks, "What possible reason could [Warren] have had for so blatantly destroying evidence?" He continues, "The whole episode remains incongruous until we realize there is only one reason why a senior police officer would go to great lengths to defeat the ends of justice. That is when the officer owes allegiance to a master higher even than justice.... But what was it in that scrawled message that pointed the finger at a Freemason? The answer lies in the word 'Juwes.'"

It was not a misspelling of the word Jews, Knight proposes, but a reference to the three apprentices to Hiram Abiff (Jubela, Jubelo, and Jubelum, or "Juwes") and possibly a signal that the murder was the work of Masons. Recognizing it as such, Warren was obligated as a royal arch Mason to "aid and assist a companion Royal Arch Mason, when engaged in any difficulty, and espouse his cause, so far as to extricate him from the same, if in my power, whether he be right or wrong." This included "murder and treason."

Among the suspects who emerged during the investigation were a poor Polish Jew named Kosminski, of Whitechapel; Montague John Druitt, a thirty-one-year-old lawyer and school teacher who committed suicide in December 1888; Michael Ostrog, a Russian-born thief and confidence man who had been detained in asylums on several occasions; and Dr. Francis J. Tumblety, a fifty-six-year-old American quack physician who was arrested in November 1888 for gross indecency and fled the country later that same month. The first three of these suspects were cited by Sir Melville Macnaghten, who joined the Metropolitan Police as assistant chief constable, and second in command of the CID in June 1889. He based his assertion on a February 23, 1894, report in which Kosminski was favored by Dr. Robert Anderson, the head of the CID at the time, and Chief Inspector Donald Swanson, the officer in charge of the case. Druitt appears to have been Sir Melville's preferred candidate. Why Ostrog was named by Macnaghten is a puzzle. The fourth suspect, Tumblety, was stated by John George Littlechild, the former head of the Special Branch at Scotland Yard in 1888 and former detective chief inspector to have been "amongst the suspects" at the time of the murders and "to my mind a very likely one."

Regardless, no one was charged with the Ripper murders.

Nearly a century after Jack's rampage, Knight claims to have solved the case. He writes that the twenty-four-year-old grandson of Queen Victoria, Prince Albert, also known as Eddy, had secretly fathered a baby and married the mother, an illiterate Catholic "shop-girl" named Annie Crook. A friend of Prince Eddy hired a nanny who was a witness at the secret marriage, to care for the illegitimate royal baby. Because Britain was in political turmoil, it was feared that if word got out that the second in line to the throne had married and had a child with a low-class, illiterate, Catholic commoner, the people might have toppled the monarchy, taking with it all those in power, including Masons holding influential government posts.

According to this theory, the nanny turned to prostitution and shared her information about Prince Eddy's marriage and child with three other prostitutes. They threatened to go public with the story. The British prime minister or the queen herself turned to the queen's doctor to eliminate the threat. Sir William Gull, a Freemason, decided to kill them and called on his Masonic brethren to assist. Confident that they would feel bound by their Masonic oath of fraternity to protect each other, Gull learned the names of the women who knew Prince Eddy's secret, offered them carriage rides as though he were hiring them for prostitution services, murdered them, mutilated their bodies in ritualistic ways, and left their bodies in easy view.

The basis of Knight's story was a confession by artist Walter Sickert (Prince Eddy's friend and witness to the marriage) to his son Joseph, who repeated it to Knight. In the 1976 film *Murder by Decree*, the same conspiracy was discovered by Sherlock Holmes. In its climactic scene, the prime minister had summoned the sleuth of Baker Street to demand that he desist in his investigation. Holmes silences him by making a Masonic signal. He recites the "Jubela, Jubelo, Jubelum" murder of Hiram Abiff as the basis of the ritualistic murders of the prostitutes that prove a Masonic conspiracy involving the highest officials of the government. In the 2001 film *From Hell*, the Masonic connection is discerned by Inspector Fred Abberline (Johnny Depp).

With Knight's readers and millions of moviegoers believing this solution to the Ripper murders, Freemasons have attempted to refute the story by explaining "the real facts." Mason historian Paul M. Bessel points out that every allegation of Masonic involvement in the Ripper murders is based entirely on a story that Knight claims had been told to him by Joseph Sickert. Yet, as Bessel points out in an article in the *Sunday Times* of London (June 18, 1978), Sickert is quoted as having said about his father's confession, "It was a hoax; I made it all up."

The Sickert story was also challenged by Jack the Ripper expert Donald Rumbelow. In his authoritative *Jack the Ripper: The Complete Casebook*, he declares, "Those parts of Mr. Sickert's story which can be tested have been shown...to be untrue." Commenting on Knight's book, he asks, " 'Where's the evidence?' The answer, of course, is that there isn't any.... The book becomes more and more frustrating as one searches for hard facts.... Whichever way you look, there is not a shred of evidence to back up Knight's theory."

Concerning Knight's "the Masons did it" explanation, Bessel notes:

> Those who are familiar with Masonic ritual know that the mutilations of the Ripper murder victims' bodies do not reflect any Masonic practices, rules, ritual, or ceremonies. Any seeming similarity is only slight, inaccurate, and circumstantial.... Knight said that Masonic penalties (which in any case are purely symbolic, not actual) mention having the heart removed and thrown over the *left* shoulder. But he admits

it was the intestines, not heart, that were placed over some of the Ripper's victims' *right* shoulders."

Whatever was meant by the "Juwes" message found on a wall near one of the murder scenes, continues Bessel, that term

> has never been used in Masonic ritual or ceremonies, and the story of the three ruffians [who killed Hiram Abiff: Jubela, Jubelo, and Jubelum] had been removed from Masonic ritual in England (but not in the United States) 70 years before Jack the Ripper's murders took place. The erasure of the "Juwes" message near a murder site could have been a well-meaning attempt to prevent anti-Semitic mob violence against innocent people, since some were already thinking of blaming Jewish immigrants for these murders.

Even more significantly, the baby girl said to have been the child of Prince Eddy was born on April 18, 1885, which means she was conceived while Prince Eddy was in Germany. Knight also states that Eddy and Annie Crook met in 1888 in Sickert's studio. This was impossible. The building had been demolished in 1886 and a hospital was built on the site in 1887. As to Dr. Gull having been the key man in the Ripper murders, he was seventy-two years old at the time and had already suffered one heart attack and possibly a stroke. "Yet he is alleged," observes Bessell, "to have brutally murdered five young and reasonably strong women in a carriage on public streets and discarded and mutilated their bodies in public areas, all without anything being seen or heard by the large number of Londoners who were looking and hoping to catch 'Jack the Ripper.'"

Finally, under British law, then and now, any marriage of a member of the royal family can be set aside by the monarch, and any royal who marries a Catholic cannot inherit the Crown. Therefore, no murders were necessary even if the story of Prince Eddy's marriage to Annie Crook were true. (Also, research by so-called Ripperologists finds that Annie was not a Catholic.)

Knight's story is based on the theory that the British public would have been so scandalized by the story concerning Prince Eddy that it would have rebelled against the royal family and the British governing class. Bessel surmises that the "supposed police cover-up was probably simply due to lack of experience with murders such as these, as well as some degree of police and government incompetence. Most likely, these factors, not a Masonic conspiracy, prevented the capture of 'Jack the Ripper.' "

In 2003, celebrated crime novelist Patricia Cornwall published *Portrait of a Killer: Jack the Ripper—Case Solved*, claiming that her investigation of the Ripper case had proved that "Saucy Jack" was none other than Walter Sickert.

That Masons could be suspected of serial murders, even today, is because of suspicions about what transpires behind the locked doors of the Masonic lodge.

A LODGE IS BOTH A GROUP OF MASONS AND THE ROOM
or building in which they meet. Some Masonic buildings are also
sometimes called temples. As previously noted, the term "lodge"
was given to structures built by stonemasons in the Middle Ages adjacent
to cathedrals that were under construction. One of the earliest known descriptions of a lodge describes it as "an assemblage of brothers and fellows
met together for the purpose of expiating on the mysteries of the Craft
with the Bible, square and compass, the Book of Constitutions, and the
warrant empowering them to act." A lodge was later depicted as "an assembly of Masons, just, perfect and regular who are met together to expa-
tiate on the mysteries of the Order just, because it contains the volume of
the Sacred Law unfolded; perfect, from its numbers, every order of Masonry
being virtually present by its representatives, to ratify and confirm its proceedings; and regular, from its warrant of constitution, which implies the
sanction of the Grand Master, for the country where the lodge is held."

Robert Macoy's *A Dictionary of Freemasonry* notes that a lodge "is an
oblong square" that is formed by three "well-informed brethren from a
legal lodge" and that "five improve it, and seven make it perfect." Their
meeting place, called a Masonic hall,

should be isolated, and, if possible, surrounded by lofty walls so as to
be included in a court, and apart from any other buildings, to pre-
clude the possibility of being overlooked by cowans [non-Masons] or
eavesdroppers; for Freemasonry being a secret society, the curiosity

of mankind is ever on the alert to pry into its mysteries, and to obtain by illicit means, that knowledge which is freely communicated to all worthy applicants. As, however, such a situation in large towns, where Masonry is usually practiced can seldom be obtained with convenience to the brethren, the lodge should be formed in an upper story; and if there be any contiguous buildings, the windows should be either in the roof, or very high from the floor.

The lodge extends from east to west (horizon to horizon) and between north and south. The covering of the lodge is the "canopy of heaven." East in a lodge does not necessarily mean the point of the compass. It is the station of the worshipful master, from which is dispensed "light and instruction." The "supports" of the lodge are three pillars (wisdom, strength, and beauty) and relate to three "immovable" jewels of the lodge: the square, plumb, and level.

Other features of the lodge are called "Ornaments of the Lodge." They consist of the "Mosaic Pavement," the "Indented Tessel," and the "Blazing Star." They represent opposites: good and evil, night and day, hot and cold, love and hate.

Open only to members, a lodge conducts two kinds of meetings. In business sessions, there will be a reading of the minutes of the previous meeting, a vote on petitions from men who wish to join the fraternity, planning of charitable events, and sharing information about other members (brothers) who are ill or have some sort of need. The second type of lodge conducts rituals of initiation into levels of membership called "degrees."

Lodges in the United States are called "blue" because of the color of the ceiling of the meeting room. Every blue lodge must be chartered by the Grand Lodge of the state or region. Otherwise, a lodge is considered irregular or clandestine. The head of a grand lodge is called "Grand Master" and is elected to a one-year term. He may attend any meeting anywhere at any time and may conduct the business of that lodge. Because a blue lodge may define Masonry any way it wishes, descriptions have varied widely. It has been interpreted as the spreading of knowledge through studying and learning more about all subjects. Another view is that the purpose of

Freemasonry is the perfection of humanity by organizing the moral sentiments of mankind and improving law and government. Freemasonry has been called an examination of the traditions of philosophy and religion as a means to know God and His works. Albert Pike said that Freemasonry is a method of studying basic principles with the goal of revealing the "universal principle." To master the universe ("the Absolute"), Freemasons are required to study the allegories and symbols of the Craft until they reveal "the light."

In the early eighteenth century, a "modern" purpose of Freemasonry was to preserve, develop, and transmit to posterity an insistence on "the universality of mankind and the transmission of an immemorial tradition of human solidarity." Masonic theorist William E. Hammond talks of "moral discipline" by which Masonry "produces the finest type of character and culture through fellowship and mutual helpfulness." Another Masonic leader, Joseph Fort Newton, defines it as "a form of public service and public mindedness imposing a social duty to help one's neighbors by working in communities to promote freedom of the mind and education to maintain democracy, and to unite people in common service for mankind." Allen E. Roberts and Albert G. Mackey say that Masonry is "a system of ethics and brotherhood, making men better not just to themselves but to each other by teaching the meaning of life and death," with the search for the "lost word" in an attempt to find "God's truth in our lives."

Arthur Edward Waite and W. L. Wilmshurst write about Masonry as spiritual activity. Waite describes it as the mysticism of "a first-hand experience with God, with symbols for those who are not yet capable of understanding." Wilmshurst talks of spiritual life as "the meaning of the Masonic ritual and symbols, all leading toward a path of life higher than we normally tread, an inner world where the ancient mysteries of our being are to be learned." J. S. M. Ward sees in Freemasonry a combining of political, social, ritualistic, archeological (historical), and mystical thought into the "great idea." W. Kirk MacNulty describes Freemasonry as a method to learn more about our own minds and to transform our being to a higher plane where we are reborn in a higher state. To H. L. Haywood, Freemasonry is a system of ethics, showing each man the way toward a new birth of his nature (symbolized in the Hiram Abiff drama) to bring divine power to the individual. In all of these men, Freemasonry means the equal right of all people to use their mind, abilities, and liberty and to govern themselves, even if they sometimes make mistakes.

Freemasonry is described as "an oath-bound fraternal order of men, derived from the medieval fraternity of operative Freemasons, adhering to many of their Ancient Charges, laws, customs, and legends." Loyal to the civil government under which it exists, it inculcates moral and social virtues by symbolic application of the working tools of the old stone-masons through allegories, lectures, and "charges." Members are obligated to observe principles of brotherly love, equality, mutual aid and assistance, secrecy, and confidence. Masons have secret ways of recognizing one another, whether in public or in lodges.

Today, the fraternity is spread around the globe and has experienced mutations in its organization, doctrine, and practices. Lodges have become subordinate to Grand Lodges that are presided over by grand masters, each sovereign within a given nation, state, or other political subdivision. They commonly demand that a candidate for membership seek admission of his own free will and express a belief in a "Supreme Being" and immortality of the soul. A Holy Bible or other volume of "Sacred Law" is displayed in the lodge and used at each step (degree) of initiation (entered apprentice, fellowcraft, and master Mason).

One historian writes:

> In its broadest and most comprehensive sense Freemasonry is a system of morality and social ethics, and a philosophy of life, all of simple and fundamental character, incorporating a broad humanitarianism and, though treating life as a practical experience, subordinates the material to the spiritual; it is of no sect but finding truth in all; it is moral but not pharisaic; it demands sanity rather than sanctity; it is tolerant but not supine; it seeks truth but does not define truth; it urges its votaries to think but does not tell them what to think; it despises ignorance but does not proscribe the ignorant; it fosters education but proposes no curriculum; it espouses political liberty and the dignity of man but has no platform or propaganda; it believes in the nobility and usefulness of life; it is modest and not militant; it is mod-

erate, universal, and so liberal as to permit each individual to form
and express his own opinion, even as to what Freemasonry is or ought
to be, and invites him to improve it if he can.

Freemasonry is a Fraternity composed of moral men of legal age
who believe in God and, of their own free will, receive in lodges degrees which depict a system of morality that, as they grow in maturity,
teaches them to be tolerant of the beliefs of others, to be patriotic,
law-abiding, temperate in all things, to aid the unfortunate, to practice Brotherly Love, and to faithfully accept and discharge solemn
obligations.

American Freemasonry resembles two sets of stairs that begin and end
together. The first step is entered apprentice. A member than climbs to
fellowcraft and ultimately reaches the third degree of master Mason. If he
desires to go higher, he enters either the Scottish or York Rites. In the
Scottish Rite, he climbs thirty-two degrees. Each has a name (King Solomon,
King Cyrus, George Washington, and so on) and teaches a moral. The
thirty-third degree is awarded by the Supreme Council. A Mason in York
Rite advances ten degrees, also known by name and not by number: temple workman, past master (virtual), Israel tribesman, high priest of Jews,
King Hiram of Tyre, a knight of Malta, and knight of Templar, which is
equal in prestige to the thirty-third degree in the Scottish Rite.

In the United States, all Masons did business in lodges open on the first
degree until the mid-1840s. For the next half-century, all U.S. lodges
were required to conduct business only on the third degree, with entered
apprentices and fellowcrafts excluded. In recent years, some U.S. Grand
Lodges have changed their rules to allow lodges to open and conduct
business on any degree, but with voting restricted to master Masons. (As
of January 2000, there were twelve [24 percent] where this was permitted.)

A lodge must be governed by a master. Titled "Worshipful Master" or
"Right Worshipful Master," the post is equivalent to a group's president.
The senior warden and junior warden function are the vice presidents.
There is a secretary and a treasurer. Deacons serve as messengers.
Stewards are in charge of refreshments. All lodges when "at work" must

be "tiled." This means that the door is guarded (by a "tyler") to ensure that no non-Mason (a cowan) may enter and that no one is able to over-hear the proceedings ("eavesdroppers").

Rituals of degrees have been called plays that teach the importance of integrity and honor, reliance, self-control, trustworthiness, the realization that humans have a spiritual nature as well as a physical or animal nature, knowing how to love and be loved, and the importance of keeping confi-dences. Because the Masonic teaching method is ritual, Freemasons are unwilling to reveal the contents of ritual to non-Masons. The words in Masonic ritual are controlled by the Grand Lodge in whose jurisdiction the ritual is performed. This is why Masonic ritual is always performed behind closed doors. Only those who have proven themselves to be Masons and those who are being initiated into the degrees of Freemasonry are al-lowed entrance.

Authoritative Masonic teaching is conducted through small books that are given to men when they are "raised" to the degree of master Mason. Known as "monitors," these books are authorized by the Grand Lodges for distribution in their jurisdiction. They contain explanations of the meaning of the major symbols used in Masonic ritual and explain mean-ings of important portions of the ritual. A widely used text was derived from the 1862 writings of Albert G. Mackey. In *Manual of the Lodge*, he writes:

> It was the single object of all the ancient rites and mysteries practiced
> in the very bosom of pagan darkness to teach the immortality of the
> Soul. This is still the great design of the third degree of Masonry.
> This is the scope and aim of its ritual. The Master Mason represents
> man, when youth, manhood, old age, and life itself have passed away
> as fleeting shadows, yet raised from the grave of iniquity, and quick-
> ened into another and better existence. By its legend and all its ritual,
> it is implied that we have been redeemed from the death of sin and
> the sepulchre of pollution . . . and the conclusion we arrive at is, that
> youth, properly directed, leads [us to the honorable and virtuous ma-
> turity, and that] the life of man, regulated by morality, faith, and jus-

tice, will be rewarded at its closing hour by the prospect of eternal bliss.

The design of the degree, Mackey continues, "is to symbolize the great doctrines of the resurrection of the body and the immortality of the soul; and hence it has been remarked by a learned writer of our order, that the Master Mason represents a man saved from the grave."

This journey begins as an entered apprentice.

CHAPTER 15

ENTERING THE BROTHERHOOD

"THE WORD DEGREE, IN ITS PRIMITIVE MEANING, SIGNI-fies a step," writes Albert G. Mackey in *An Encyclopedia of Freemasonry*. "The degrees of Freemasonry are, then, the steps by which the candidate ascends from a lower to a higher condition of knowl-edge."

Each of the degrees requires the candidate to participate in a drama that is found in what has been called a Masonic catechism. It consists of a series of memorized questions and answers pertaining to a specific degree. To prepare for membership, a candidate meets with a member of the lodge who knows the catechism well and helps him to memorize the work. The first degree is "Entered Apprentice." To qualify, an applicant must be of legal age (eighteen or twenty-one), have no record of criminal convictions (felonies), be of good moral character, and assert belief in a Supreme Being and the immortality of the soul.

After a candidate has applied for membership and his background has been thoroughly investigated, lodge members vote by secret ballot to ac-cept or reject him. One of the Craft's ancient customs, the secret ballot has been called the "Ordeal." Election requires affirmative votes from every member at the meeting. The ballots are white and black cubes or balls, hence the term "black balling." If one member casts a black cube or ball, membership is denied. Many more applicants are approved than re-jected.

Freemasonry insists it is not a religion, but ceremonies have similarities to the Christian rites and rituals of baptism, confirmation, and other sacraments. Like converts to religions, the aspiring Mason must be "duly and truly prepared" by learning the catechism. For the ceremony of the first degree called the Rite of Destitution, he is provided special garments by the lodge that emphasize concern with his internal qualifications, rather than worldly attainments. He is not to bring into the lodge room his worldly clothing and "his passions or prejudices, lest that harmony, which is one of the chief concerns of Masonry, be destroyed."

Suitably attired, the candidate is blindfolded or hooded ("hoodwinked"). The symbolism emphasizes the veil of secrecy and silence surrounding the mysteries of Freemasonry and represents the mystical darkness, or ignorance, of the uninitiated. When the "hoodwink" is removed at a specified time, it means that he is deemed in the proper attitude to receive "Light."

The hoodwinked candidate is led by a rope. Called a "cable tow,"it symbolizes the voluntary and complete acceptance of, and pledged compliance with, whatever Masonry may demand. With his first step into the lodge room, the entered apprentice begins to leave "the darkness, destitution and helplessness of the world for the light and warmth of a new existence."

A Freemason attests that this is "not an idle formality, but a genuine experience, the beginning of a new career in which duties, rights and privileges are real." If a candidate is not to be an apprentice in name only, he "must stand ready to do the work upon his own nature that will make him a different man." They are "workmen" and lodges are "quarries" and "scenes of toil." Freemasonry offers "no privileges or rewards except to those who earn them." To become a Mason is "a solemn and serious undertaking" that may change the course of a man's life.

The reception of the candidate into the lodge room is intended to symbolize the fact that the rituals are serious and confidential, with consequences for violating this confidence. It also reminds a man that his "every act has a consequence," either as a reward or a penalty. It also points out the "virtue needed to gain admission into the mysteries of Masonry." In a rite known as "Circumambulation," performed in a clockwise manner and patterned after the movement of the sun as it is seen from the earth (moving from east to west by way of the south), the hooded and leashed candidate makes a journey around an altar that enables the brethren to observe that he is properly prepared.

The central piece of furniture in the lodge is the altar. Its location in the center of the lodge symbolizes the place that God has in Masonry. The candidate approaches the altar in search of light and to assume his "obligation." Before "God and his Brethren," he offers himself to the service of the Supreme Architect of the Universe and to mankind. The "Obligation" is the heart of the degree. When it is assumed by the candidate, he binds himself to Freemasonry and accepts certain duties for the rest of his life, among them protecting the fraternity's secrets of recognition and symbolic instruction.

At the center of the ritual of entered apprentice, the "Three Great Lights of Masonry" are a "volume of sacred law" (in the United States, the Bible), a square, and a compass (used in architecture and drawing, not for geographical direction). The Bible (opened) signifies that Masons should regulate their conduct according to its teachings. The square is a symbol of morality, truthfulness, and honesty (to act "on the square"). The compass signifies the use of action and is a symbol of restraint, skill, and knowledge. The Square and Compass (capitalized in Masonry) have become the symbol of Freemasonry.

The Three Great Lights are consistent with the three-tier system of blue lodge Masonry, in which human nature is divided into body (square), mind (compass), and soul (volume of sacred law). The tools of the entered apprentice recall those used by the ancient operative craftsmen. To the speculative Mason, they represent moral habits and forces by which man has shaped and reshaped the essence of his human nature.

Because the northeast corner of a building is traditionally where a cornerstone is laid, the apprentice is placed in the northeast corner of the lodge, from which he will "erect his own temple by the principles of Freemasonry." The northeast corner also reflects that in Masonry the north is "darkness," the east "light," and the northeast, being midway, "equilibrium."

A lecture given to the candidate by the worshipful master elaborates phases of the ritual and provides a broader explanation of the ceremonies and the cardinal virtues of temperance, fortitude, prudence, and justice.

At the close of the ceremony, the candidate is "charged" to do his Masonic duties. The candidate is then required to memorize the "Proficiency." It teaches each candidate the language of Freemasonry, fixes in his memory the teachings and structure of the degree, impresses on his consciousness the different points of the Obligation, and instills in him an "ancient method" to contemplate the meanings behind the degree.

The language of Freemasonry is a product of the early decades of the eighteenth century and contains much of the language of that time period. The belief is that if time and effort are spent studying the words of the ritual, the candidate will discover that the thoughts and teachings imparted cannot be put in fewer words and still retain their meaning.

Masonic tradition forbids discussion in the lodge of religion and politics. Once a matter is put to vote and a decision is made, the outcome must be accepted by all members.

The term "worshipful master" is an Old English phrase meaning "worthy of respect." He is regarded as the source of Masonic knowledge as the brethren "approach the East in search of light." He wears a hat as a symbol of superior rank.

In recognition of completing the ritual of the first degree, the entered apprentice is given a white lambskin apron. In Masonic ritual, the apron symbolizes the condition of the soul. As a Mason rises in degrees of spiritual development, alterations in the appearance of the apron show the progress that has been made. The entered apprentice's plain white indicates innocence. In Masonic terms, this means clean thinking and living, a loyal obedience to the laws of the Craft, and sincere good will to one's brethren. The apron also recalls that Masons are workers and builders. A Masonic historian notes that the lamb has always been a symbol of innocence and sacrifice (Abraham sacrificing a lamb to God instead of his son and Jesus as the "lamb of God"). An apron was also a mark of distinction found in ancient organizations that featured rites of initiations, including the Essenes, the Mythraic Mysteries, Egyptians, Greeks, and Romans. The Masonic apron consists of a square and a triangle that represent the numbers four and three (adding up to the other meaningful Masonic number, seven).

Rights of an entitled entered apprentice are limited. He cannot vote or hold office, but he is entitled to a Masonic funeral. He is not entitled to organize Masonic charity, but is not barred from receiving assistance from a Mason. His responsibility is to keep secret everything entrusted to him, conduct himself with proper decorum, and work to learn his Proficiency and prepare himself to advance to the next degree.

CHAPTER 16

FELLOWCRAFT

THE SECOND DEGREE OF MASONRY IS "FELLOWCRAFT." IT symbolizes the stage of adulthood and responsibility during a man's life on Earth. A fellowcraft is expected to acquire knowledge and apply it to the building of his character and improving the society in which he lives. Masonic leader and theorist William Preston sees Masonry as "a means to educate men in the liberal arts and sciences." A fellowcraft Mason is urged to advance his education in these fields during the ritual of the degree. The symbolism of the entered apprentice degree dealt with beginnings, spiritual birth, and orientation to the Light. Fellowcraft symbolizes methods of developing and progressing in the Craft and emergence into spiritual manhood. "The man who enters the Fellowcraft degree," explains one writer, "is invested with the ability to hear the teachings of the Fraternity and keep them close to his heart."

In the second degree, symbols of advancement, passage, instruction, and elevation in approaching "the East" deepen the connection with the fraternity and add new commitments. The central symbol is the "winding staircase." Its steps ascend to the "Middle Chamber of the Temple." Staircases, ladders, extended vertical ropes, and mountains are seen as symbols of ascending to new heights. Attaining this level provides access to certain benefits to which an entered apprentice is not entitled. These "wages" are symbolized by corn, wine, and oil.

The lodge of initiation to the second degree is open only to members admitted to the fellowcraft degree. The ritual followed proceeds almost identically with that of the entered apprentice (hoodwink, cable tow, and circumambulation of the lodge).

"At the outset of this Degree," writes another expert on fellowcraft, "it should be clear to the candidate that although much of it seems familiar, it is also very different, and some aspects even seem to be in opposition to the previous degree. There are certain avenues of further exploration that should be brought out here. We are usually given an explanation for most parts of the ritual in the various lectures."

The tools of fellowcraft are the square (symbol of morality, truthfulness, and honesty), the level (symbol of equality), and plumb (uprightness of conduct). Other important symbols are the "Pillars on the Porch." They represent strength and establishment and, by implication, power and control. They recall the pair of pillars in the Hiram Abiff story and signify guardianship of the temple and a connection between heaven and earth. Some researchers speculate that the two pillars before Solomon's Temple represented the Pillar of Cloud and the Pillar of Fire, which led the Israelites through the desert to the Promised Land. The two pillars correspond to the Three Great Supports of Masonry: wisdom, strength, and beauty/balance.

The number three is of great significance in Masonry. There are three degrees, the Three Great Lights, the three columns, three officers, three grand masters, and three Principle Tenets of Freemasonry. The number also refers to three theological virtues: faith, hope, and charity. The number seven is also central to Masonry. Seven steps of the winding staircase symbolize the seven liberal arts and sciences. Formulated as early as A.D. 330 and adopted by Christian scholars, they were considered a means to the knowledge of God. This principle was expressed in the construction of the Gothic Cathedral of Chartres that for the first time included sculpted representations of the seven liberal arts (on the cathedral's west door). A Masonic historian writes, "The Masters of Chartres taught that the proper study of the Seven Liberal Arts guided the intellect to approach the hidden light behind the world. The invisible underlying structure of Reality, the Truth, could be apprehended in this way."

In the mid-thirteenth century, the humble mason who had mastered the seven liberal arts was entitled to the designation of "architect" and "master of arts." This is why the fellowcraft must become proficient in the seven liberal arts. A study of these subjects is demanded to gain admission to the "Middle Chamber." In this process, the fellowcraft receives the corn, wine, and oil. They symbolize wealth in the mental and spiritual worlds. Corn represents nourishment and the sustenance of life. Wine means refreshment, health, spirituality, and peace. Oil stands for joy, gladness, and happiness. Together, corn, wine, and oil represent the temporal rewards of living a good life and are, as one Mason notes, "the intangible but no less real compensation for a faithful and intelligent use of the Working Tools," fidelity to Masonic obligations, and "unflagging interest in and study of the structure, purpose and possibilities of the Fraternity."

Corn or grain (wheat is sometimes used) also represent the concept of resurrection. Wine symbolizes mystical attainments, divine intoxication, and ecstasy. Oil has always been one of the elements of religious consecration or anointment.

The fellowcraft candidate also receives enlightenment on the subject of the display in the lodge of the letter G.

A scholar of Masonry explains:

> Like the sphinx before the pyramids, [the letter G] stands before us in silence and mystery. It is not consistently displayed throughout the Masonic world and there are Masonic scholars who feel it should be removed. The reason that it is so displayed is plainly given to the candidate in this Degree. We are told that it is the initial of Geometry as well as the initial of the name of the Supreme Being. From the time of the "Old Charges" and manuscripts up to the present, the synonymous nature of Geometry and Masonry is clearly stated. It is also obvious that "G" is the initial of God. This alone may be sufficient reason for its presence.
>
> There are other considerations that the Masonic student might want to take into account. The immediate question for some may be why is Geometry given such exalted status? One might also observe that the word "God" is not a name per se, but is a category of being,

like "human being." The name of the Supreme Being depends on what tradition a person follows, and it would not be incorrect to say that the True Name of the Supreme Being cannot be known.

A fellowcraft candidate also learns the importance of geometry to a full understanding of Freemasonry. He is informed that geometry is the basis of masonry. This connection is traced to ancient Egyptians who developed surveying because annual floods of the Nile River obliterated boundary markers of fields. They had to set out and calculate new ones each year. The Greeks named this earth measurement "geometry" and extended it into a theoretical science known as deductive reasoning. Credit for this goes to Pythagoras. Later, Plato lifted geometry to a sacred science of discovering the nature of reality and through it the Deity. Geometry rightly treated, he said, is the knowledge of the eternal and that geometry "must ever tend to draw the soul towards the truth." Euclid in *Elements of Geometry*, beginning with five unproved principles about lines, angles, and figures, which he called postulates, used only the compass and straight edge for all his drawings, proofs, and solutions.

Because the ancient philosophers believed geometry had the power to lead the mind from the world of appearances to the contemplation of the Divine Order, the teachings of the fellowcraft degree stress the importance of the study of number, order, symmetry, and proportion. These laws are discovered in the practice of the seven liberal arts, so-called because their practice liberated the mind.

Presented to the worshipful master by a senior deacon, the candidate is told to kneel on his right knee with his left foot in the form of a square, body erect, right hand on the sacred volume, and left hand supported by the compass to form a square. He is led in this oath:

> I_____, in the presence of the Grand Geometrician of the Universe, and in this worshipful and warranted Lodge of Fellowcraft Masons, duly constituted, regularly assembled, and properly dedicated, of my own free will and accord, do hereby and hereon most solemnly promise and swear that I will always hail, conceal, and never reveal

any or either of the secrets or mysteries of, or belonging to, the second degree of Freemasonry, known by the name of Fellowcrafts; to him who is but an Entered Apprentice, no more than I would either of them to the uninitiated or the popular world who are not Masons. I further solemnly pledge myself to act as a true and faithful craftsman, obey signs and maintain the principles inculcated in the first degree. All these points I most solemnly swear to obey without evasion, equivocation of mental reservation of any kind, under no less a penalty, on violation of any of them, in addition to my former obligation, than to have my left breast cut open, my heart torn therefrom, and given to the ravenous birds of the air, or the devouring beasts of the field, as prey: So help me Almighty God, and keep me steadfast in this my great and solemn obligation as a Fellowcraft Mason.

The fellowcraft is then charged to not only conform to the principles of the order and "steadily persevere in the practice of every commendable virtue," but also to the "study of the liberal arts, that valuable branch of education, which tends so effectually to polish and adorn the mind; especially the science of geometry, or masonry, originally synonymous terms [which] is of a divine and moral nature, and enriches the most useful knowledge ... proves the wonderful properties of nature [and] demonstrates the truth of morality." As in the first degree, a lecture tells the story of Solomon's Temple, the murder of Hiram Abiff, and the fate of the three "ruffians." The lecture includes questions from the worshipful master that the fellowcraft must answer. Among them is the query, "By what means was the system of Masonry extended?"

The fellowcraft replies, "Our Grand Master Solomon, observing the effects produced by the strict order adopted by the Masons employed in his work, conceived the great idea of uniting the wise and good in every nation, in the bond of brotherly love and in the pursuit of scientific acquirements."

In a colloquy that traces Masonry to Pythagoras, the worshipful master asks, "What Masonic observations do we find in his instructions?"

The fellowcraft answers, "He enjoined his disciples a long probation of

secrecy and a strict love for, and fidelity towards, each other. He distinguished them by secret signs, and divided them into classes, according to
their abilities and knowledge."

Completion of the second-degree initiation is marked by the addition
of blue rosettes to the Masonic apron. They convey that progress is being
made in the "science of regeneration" and that the candidate's spirituality
is developing. Blue (the sky) is associated with devotion to spiritual concerns.

The lodge closes with the worshipful master exhorting the brethren to
remember that "whereever we are and whatever we do," the "all-seeing
eye" of the Grand Geometrician of the Universe "beholds us, and while
we continue to act as Fellowcraft Masons, let us never fail to discharge
our duties towards him [God] with fervency and zeal."

This draws a reply in a traditional Masonic expression (similar to "Amen")
marking an ending and agreement: "So mote it be." ("Mote" is Old English
for "might.")

In contemplating the symbolism of the winding staircase in the ritual
of the fellowcraft degree, W. M. Wilmshurst finds a comparison in the
parable told by Jesus of the prodigal son who had wandered away into a
far country. He writes, "You have come down and down, as by a spiral
motion on a winding staircase, into this lower world and imperfect form
of existence. Now the time and the impulse have at last come for you to
turn back to that inward world [of your real nature and the nature of true
life]. Therefore reverse your steps. Look no longer outward, but inwards.
Go back up that winding staircase. It will bring you to that Center of Life
and *Sanctum Sanctorum* from which you have wandered."

Having progressed from entered apprentice to fellowcraft, the Freemason
next faces what Wilmshurst calls "the last and greatest trial of his fortitude and fidelity."

CHAPTER 17

MASTER MASON

REGARDED AS THE "CROWN OF THE BLUE LODGE," THE third degree is the culmination of all that the candidate did in the two preceding ceremonies. As entered apprentice, he had symbolically balanced his inner natures and shaped them into the proper relationship with his more spiritual parts. Physical nature had been purified and developed to a high degree. Mental faculties were sharpened and horizons expanded. In Masonic terms, the next degree "delves into the deepest recesses of man's nature and leads the initiate into the *Sanctum Sanctorum* of the Temple and a probing into the Holy of Holies in his heart." The master Mason degree is "symbolic of old age and by the wisdom of which a man may enjoy the happy reflections consequent on a well-spent and properly directed life, and die in the sure knowledge of a glorious immortality."

In the drama that is enacted, the candidate assumes the role of the "Grand Master Hiram Abiff" and symbolically experiences death, burial, and resurrection The ritual is meant to forge a link with the "inner soul" of the fraternity and a legend (Hiram Abiff) that is "completely and absolutely consistent" with the Mystery schools of antiquity. One Masonic scholar sees it as "communing with the archetypal forces that are the foundation of our tradition." Hiram Abiff is in essence "identical with many Mystery School heroes." As in his story, there was the drama of the Egyptian god Osiris. It begins with his tragic death. There is a search for his body by Isis. It is discovered and resurrected. Similarly, the Greek god

Dionysus was attacked by the Titans and ultimately overcome. The Titans dismembered him, but the goddess Rhea came to his aid and he rose glorious and entire. These ancient tales present a sacred king who is destined to be sacrificed so that the earth can become regenerated and uplifted by the divine power.

In the building of Solomon's Temple, there were three grand masters: Solomon, king of Israel; Hiram, king of Tyre; and Hiram Abiff. Secrets known only to them typify a Divine Truth that was not to be communicated to man until he had completed his own spiritual temple. Once these secrets were attained, a man could reap the rewards of a well-spent life and travel to the "unknown country." In Freemasonry, this does not mean going to a geographical location, but to a spiritual place in immortality. The journey is taken through the "inner recesses of the Craft" that is accompanied by the use of passwords, grips, signs, names, and secret words.

The three ruffians of the Hiram Abiff ritual, with their attempt to obtain the secrets not rightfully theirs, and the consequences of their actions, signify that trying to gain knowledge of Divine Truth by means other than a reward for faithfulness makes the culprit both a thief and a murderer. The ruffians are symbols of ignorance, passions, and wrong attitudes that must be controlled and subdued.

Because the death of Hiram Abiff resulted in a great loss of a knowledge of the "Divine Word," the Masonic ritual built on the story represents a feeling of "loss and exile" from the "Source of Life." Masons believe they are searching for "Divine Truth" that Masons connect with the "Light" of "Divine Power and Truth."

Progressing through the three degrees is the Mason's way of attaining it. The lesson of the final step is that every man must die, but if he has reached the Light, he overcomes death and achieves immortality. In *Freemasonry: A Journey through Ritual and Symbol*, W. Kirk MacNulty explains, "The 'death' which faces the Candidate in the Third Degree will cause him to recognize that he is no more a psychological being than he is a physical one; but, rather, that he is a *spiritual* being who has both a soul and a body.... Since that requires the death of the Candidate's Self (his psychological essence); and since his Self is his concept of his existence, that 'death' can be a very difficult and frightening process."

The candidate takes an oath:

I, _____, of my own free will and accord, in the presence of Almighty God, and this Worshipful Lodge, erected to Him and dedicated to the holy St. John, do hereby and hereon most solemnly and sincerely promise and swear, that I will hail, ever conceal, and never reveal any of the secrets, arts, parts, point or points, of the Master Mason's Degree, to any person or persons whomsoever, except that it be a true and lawful brother of this Degree, or in a regularly constituted Lodge of Master Masons, nor unto him, or them, until by strict trial, due examination, or lawful information, I shall have found him, or them, as lawfully entitled to the same as I am myself. I furthermore promise and swear, that I will stand to and abide by all laws, rules, and regulations of the Master Masons Degree, and of the Lodge of which I may hereafter become a member, as far as the same shall come to my knowledge; and that I will ever maintain and support the Constitution, laws, and edicts of the Grand Lodge under which the same shall be holden. Further, that I will acknowledge and obey all due signs and summons sent to me from a Master Masons' Lodge, or given me by a brother of that Degree, if within the length of my cable tow. Further, that I will always aid and assist all poor, distressed, worthy Master Masons, their widows and orphans, knowing them to be such, as far as their necessities may require, and my ability permit, without material injury to myself and family. Further, that I will keep a worthy brother Master Mason's secrets inviolable, when communicated to and received by me as such, murder and treason excepted. Further, that I will not aid, nor be present at, the initiation, passing, or raising of a woman, an old man in his dotage, a young man in his nonage, an atheist, a madman, or fool, knowing them to be such. Further, that I will not sit in a Lodge of Clandestine-made Masons, nor converse on the subject of Masonry with a clandestine-made Mason, nor one who has been expelled or suspended from a Lodge, while under that sentence, knowing him or them to be such. Further, I will not cheat, wrong, nor defraud a Master Masons' Lodge, nor a brother of this Degree, knowingly, nor supplant him in any of his laudable undertakings, but will give him due and timely notice, that he may ward off all danger. Further, that I will not knowingly strike a brother Master Mason, or otherwise do him personal violence in anger, except in the necessary defense of my family or property. Further, that I will not have illegal carnal intercourse with a Master Mason's wife, his mother, sister, or daughter knowing them to be such, nor suffer the same to be done by others, if in my power to prevent. Further, that I will not give the Grand Masonic word, in any other manner or form than that in which I shall receive it, and then in a low breath. Further, that I will not give the Grand Hailing Sign of distress except in case of the most imminent danger, in a just and lawful Lodge, or for the benefit of instruction; and if ever I should see it given, or hear the words accompanying it, by a worthy brother in distress, I will fly to his relief, if there is a greater probability of saving his life than losing my own. All this I most solemnly, sincerely promise and swear, with a firm and steady resolution to perform the same, without any hesitation, myself, under no less penalty than that of having my body severed in two, my bowels taken from thence and burned to ashes, the ashes scattered before the four winds of heaven, that no more remembrance might be had of so vile and wicked a wretch as I would be, should I ever, knowingly, violate this my Master Mason's obligation. So help me God, and keep me steadfast in the due performance of the same.

During the presentation of the master Mason's apron, the presiding worshipful master states:

You have already been informed that at the building of King Solomon's Temple, the different bands of workmen were distinguished by the manner in which they wore their aprons. Master Masons wore theirs turned down in the form of a square to designate them as Master Masons or overseers of the work. As a speculative Master Mason you will therefore wear yours in this manner, to admonish you that your acts toward all mankind should possess the qualities of that perfect

figure, to symbolize the integrity of your service to God, and to remind you of your four-fold duty, to your country, your neighbor, your
family, and yourself.

The working tools of the master Mason degree are specified as the
twenty-four-inch gauge (setting tool) and the common gavel. The ritual
explains, "The Setting Maul is the tool with which our Hiram Abiff was
slain; the Spade that dug his grave; the Coffin that which received his life-
less remains; and the Sprig of Acacia that bloomed at the head of his
grave." In Masonic tradition, the first three are emblematic of mortality
and afford "serious reflection to all thinking men." But they would be
more dark and gloomy, declares the worshipful master, "were it not for
the Sprig of Acacia that bloomed at the head of the grave which serves to
remind us that there is an imperishable part within us which bears the
nearest affinity to the Supreme Intelligence which pervades all nature and
which will never, never, never die."
The ritual also contains and describes these emblems:

- The Pot of Incense, an emblem of a pure heart, which is always an acceptable sacrifice to Deity, and as this glows with fervent heat, so
  should our hearts continually glow with gratitude to the great and
  beneficent Author of our existence for the manifold blessings and
  comforts we enjoy.

- The Beehive is an emblem of industry, and recommends the practice
  of that virtue to all created beings, from the highest seraph in heaven
  to the lowest reptile of the dust. It teaches us that as we came into the
  world rational and intelligent beings, so we should ever be industrious
  ones; never sitting down contented while our fellow creatures around
  us are in want, especially when it is in our power to relieve them without inconvenience to ourselves.

- The Book of Constitutions guarded by the Tyler's Sword reminds us
  that we should be ever watchful and guarded in our thoughts, words

and actions, particularly when before the enemies of Masonry, ever bearing in remembrance those truly Masonic virtues, silence and circumspection.

- The Sword pointing to the Naked Heart demonstrates that justice will sooner or later overtake us; and although our thoughts, words and actions may be hidden from the eyes of men, yet that All-seeing Eye, whom the Sun, Moon and Stars obey, and under whose watchful care even the Comets perform their stupendous revolutions, pervades the inmost recesses of the human Heart, and will reward us according to our merits.

- The Anchor and the Ark are emblems of a well-grounded hope and a well-spent life. They are emblematical of the Divine Ark which safely wafts us over this tempestuous sea of troubles, and that Anchor which shall safely moor us in a peaceful harbor, where the wicked cease from troubling and the weary are at rest.

- The Forty-seventh Problem of Euclid teaches Masons to be general lovers of the arts and sciences.

- The Hour-glass is an emblem of human life. Behold how swiftly the sands run, and how rapidly our lives are drawing to a close. We cannot, without astonishment, behold the little particles which are contained in this machine—how they pass away almost imperceptibly; and yet, to our surprise, in the short space of an hour they are all exhausted. Thus wastes man. Today he puts forth the tender leaves of hope; tomorrow blossoms, and bears his blushing honors thick upon him; the next day comes a frost which nips the shoot; and when he thinks his greatness is still aspiring, he falls, like autumn leaves, to enrich our mother earth.

- The Scythe is an emblem of time, which cuts the brittle thread of life and launches us into eternity. Behold what havoc the Scythe of Time makes among the human race. If by chance we should escape the numerous ills incident to childhood and youth, and with health and vigor arrive at the years of manhood, yet withal we must soon be cut down by the all-devouring Scythe of Time, and be gathered into the land where our fathers have gone before us.

The rights of a master Mason consist of Masonic relief, visitation, and burial. A Masonic writer explains:

> Masonic Relief may be applied for by any Master Mason, either to his own Lodge, or to an individual Master Mason. In every case, the individual asked has the right to determine the worthiness of the request and whether such aid can be granted without material injury to his family. Relief is a voluntary function of both the Lodge and the individual. If the Lodge's financial condition will not allow it to help, he can apply to the Grand Lodge for help. In order to be eligible for Masonic Relief, the Brother must not have been suspended in the past five years, and there can be no charges pending against him at the time of application. The widow and/or orphan of a Master Mason, who had been a member of the Lodge at the time of his death, are entitled to consideration if they apply for assistance.

One of the greatest privileges of being a master Mason is the right to visit other lodges, provided he is a Mason in good standing, no member of the lodge objects, and he is paid up in his dues. The Masonic funeral service is conducted only at the request of a brother or some member of a Mason's immediate family. The service may be held in a church, the lodge room, funeral parlor, or grave site.

The constant responsibility of a master Mason is "to preserve the reputation of the Fraternity unsullied." He also has an obligation to be loyal to the lodge that gave him the "Masonic Light" and the benefits that come with his membership. This means attending the lodge as often as possible.

When a candidate has received the third degree, he is said to have been

"Raised to the Sublime Degree of Master Mason." The pinnacle of symbolic Freemasonry, "the living, dying and raising of a Master" is a drama designed to teach the virtues of "fidelity, faith and fortitude."

Carl H. Claudy, one of the most prolific and authoritative Freemasonry authors, writes in a handbook on Masonry:

> A Master Mason has a public as well as a Masonic character; he must be a citizen before he can be a Freemason. All his reputation as a Master Mason, all the teachings of integrity and fidelity, all the magnificent examples of firmness and fortitude in trial and danger—even in the Valley of the Shadow—which a man has been taught as a Master Mason are concerned in supporting with dignity his character as a citizen.... The newly raised Master Mason is bidden to "support the dignity of your character on every occasion." The Master Mason should be a better citizen than the non-Mason because he has been better taught and has pledged his sacred honor.

Albert G. Mackey's *An Encyclopedia of Freemasonry* states, "The word degree, in its primitive meaning, signifies a step. The degrees of Freemasonry are, then, the steps by which the candidate ascends from a lower to a higher condition of knowledge."

Should a master Mason of the blue lodge wish to expand his brotherhood experience, he may seek "the full light of Ancient Craft Masonry" by ascending to higher degrees.

CHAPTER 18
SCOTTISH AND YORK RITES

The Scottish Rite

Although "pure and ancient Freemasonry" is defined as the three degrees of entered apprentice, fellowcraft, and master Mason, the Scottish and York Rites offer higher degrees. The Scottish Rite was organized in the United States in 1801. Based on the French Scottish Rite of Perfection, it offers thirty-two degrees and an honorary thirty-third degree. It is one of two branches of Freemasonry in which a master Mason may proceed after he has completed the three degrees of symbolic of blue lodge Masonry. Thirty-second-degree Masons meet in centers that are called "Valleys." Founded in the seventeenth century in Bordeaux, France, Sottish Rite membership included both Scottish and English Masons who saw a need for "advanced" degrees that were based on the fundamental principles of the three Masonic symbolic degrees.

Described as "virtually an educational arm of Masonic Fraternity," its degrees take the history and lessons first taught a Mason in the three blue lodge degrees and expand on their history, legends, traditions, and moral lessons. The fourth through fourteenth degrees "take up where the Blue Lodge left off in history, and investigate and contemplate the ineffable name of Deity. The major lesson of the Degrees is that God is not an object of knowledge, but faith." The next four degrees cover the time from the destruction of King Solomon's Temple to the time of the writing of the Book of Revelations and are religious, historical, moral, and philosophical in nature. Nine through twelve cover the time of the Crusades and dramatize the knightly virtues and look at mystical symbolism to teach why morality and the practice of virtue are indispensable to the Mason. The last degrees, the thirty-first and thirty-second, deal with the "ever-changing relationship between human law as a means of achieving justice and divine justice as an ideal in which the path to immortality is more than the mere outward appearance of goodness." The thirty-third degree and the "Knight Commander of the Court of Honor" are honorary and cannot be actively sought.

In the policy of the Scottish Rite, "everyone who wants to participate has a place and there is a place for everyone to participate doing what he does best. The emphasis is on how the individual does, not on what he does. Everyone is equal and every job is important. Whether he is an officer, a ritualist, keeps the door, reads lectures, ushers candidates, helps with costumes, lighting or scenery, fixes the meals, greets new members or candidates, or any of a number of other duties that have to be done to hold a successful Reunion," he "counts just as much as the next guy." Women and families are included in almost all activities, except closed monthly meetings (they may join in refreshments, however).

The degrees consist of:

LODGE OF PERFECTION

4th	Secret Master
5th	Perfect Master
6th	Intimate Secretary
7th	Provost and Judge
8th	Intendant of the Building
9th	Elect of the Nine
10th	Elect of the Fifteen
11th	Elect of the Twelve
12th	Grand Master Architect
13th	Royal Arch of Solomon
14th	Grand Elect Perfect and Sublime

CHAPTER OF ROSE CROIX

15th	Knight of the East or Sword
16th	Prince of Jerusalem
17th	Knight of the East and West
18th	Knight Rose Croix

CONSISTORY

19th	Grand Pontiff
20th	Master ad Vitam
21th	Patriarch Noachite
22th	Prince of Libanus
23rd	Chief of the Tabernacle
24th	Prince of the Tabernacle
25th	Knight of the Brazen Serpent
26th	Prince of Mercy
27th	Commander of the Temple
28th	Knight of the Sun
29th	Knight of St. Andrew
30th	Knight Kadosh
31st	Inspector Inquisitor Commander
32nd	Sublime Prince of the Royal Secret

The modern establishment of the Ancient and Accepted Scottish Rite dates from 1801, when the first Supreme Council was established in Charleston. Under the provisions of the Grand Constitutions, a second Supreme Council was formed and the original council took the name Supreme Council for the Southern Jurisdiction of the United States of America. The oldest existing council, it became the "Mother Council of the World." In 1813, it established the Northern Supreme Council with fourteen original states: Maine, New Hampshire, Vermont, Massachusetts, Connecticut, Rhode Island, New York, New Jersey, Pennsylvania, Delaware, Ohio, Illinois, Indiana, and Michigan. Wisconsin was added in 1818.

The Southern Jurisdiction retained authority in the rest of the United States and in whatever territory became a part of it after 1813, as well as in countries where the Supreme Council had or thereafter established bodies of the rite. There are thirty-four states: Alabama, Arizona, Arkansas, California, Colorado, Florida, Georgia, Idaho, Iowa, Kansas, Kentucky, Louisiana, Maryland, Minnesota, Mississippi, Missouri, Montana, Nebraska, Nevada, New Mexico, North Carolina, North Dakota, Oklahoma, Oregon, South Carolina, South Dakota, Tennessee, Texas, Utah, Virginia, Washington, West Virginia, Wyoming, and Alaska. It also includes the District of Columbia, the army and navy (shared with the Northern Supreme Council), China, Japan, Hawaii, Puerto Rico, the Philippines, and the Panama Canal Zone.

Because the Scottish Rite had its origin from rites practiced on the continent of Europe that later crystallized into the Scottish Rite through the constitutions of 1761, 1762, and 1786, it is sometimes called "Continental Masonry." The form is also known and practiced in South America, Asia, Africa, Australia, and New Zealand.

The Northern Jurisdiction, the Lodge of Perfection, confers the fourth to the fourteenth, inclusive; the Council of Princes of Jerusalem, the fifteenth and sixteenth; the Chapter of Rose Croix, the seventeenth and eighteenth; and the Consistory, the nineteenth to thirty-second, inclusive. In Canada, there are but three bodies: Lodge of Perfection, Chapter of Rose Croix, and Consistory.

Although the Scottish Rite is defined as "nonsectarian," both Northern and Southern Supreme Councils observe the ceremonies of "Extinguishing and Relighting the Symbolic Lights" on the Thursday before Easter and on Easter Sunday. Of the religion in the Scottish Rite, the late Grand Commander James D. Richardson of the Southern Jurisdiction wrote:

> Scottish Rite Masonry has not attempted to propagate any creed, save its own simple and sublime one, of faith in God and good works; no religion, save the universal, eternal and immutable religion, a religion such as God planted in the heart of universal humanity. Its votaries may be sought and found alike in Jewish, Moslem and Christian Temples. It is the teacher of the morals of all religions; it is the teacher of good and not of evil, of truth and not error. As in the days of Dante, its mission is to aid humanity in setting its foot upon despotism, and treading under foot spiritual tyranny and intolerance.

In many states, the Scottish Rite has impressive buildings. In Washington, D.C., the House of the Temple is the home of the Supreme Council Southern Jurisdiction. It contains the Great Library and has a Supreme Council Chamber in which sessions of the Supreme Council are held every two years.

The York Rite

Practitioners of the Ancient York Rite take pride in asserting that "every Grand Lodge of today is a lineal descendant of the 926 York Assembly of Masons" and that every copy of the Ancient Manuscript Constitutions reaffirms that in 1717, when the first organized Speculative Grand Lodge came into existence in London, "the terms of the York Charter were adopted and used as a basis for its Constitution and Declaration of principles."

The reason for the prominence of York in Masonic history is the Regius poem or Halliwell manuscript. Containing regulations for the government of the Craft, it states that Athelstan, the grandson of Alfred the Great, ruled England from 924 to 940. He completed the subjection of the minor kingdoms in England, begun by his grandfather, and has been hailed as the first king of all of England. The Regius poem and other ancient legends relate that Athelstan was a great patron of Masonry and that he constructed many abbeys, monasteries, castles, and fortresses. He studied geometry and imported learned men in these arts. To preserve order in the work and correct transgressors, the king issued a charter to the Masons to hold a yearly assembly at York. He is also reputed to have made many Masons.

The legends proceed to relate that Athelstan appointed his brother, Edwin, as grand master and that the first Grand Lodge was held at York in 926. The accounts state that the constitutions of English Masonry were established there and were based on a number of old documents written in Greek, Latin, and other languages. Aside from direct implications of this legend, scholars speculate that the king and prince were probably "speculative" rather than "operative" members of the Craft and that this makes it easier to account for the fact that so many speculative members of high rank joined the craft in the seventeenth and eighteenth centuries.

Historians of the York Rite note that since the union of the four Grand Lodges in London, seekers of the Craft's origins found them in ancient Egypt, Solomon's Temple, Roman building guilds, and cathedral builders in the Middle Ages. But in the early eighteenth century, a new theory was presented that Freemasonry began in the Holy Land with the Crusaders and Knights Templar. This controversial view was espoused by Andrew Michael Ramsay in Paris in 1737 and became known as the Ramsay Oration. While rejected by some Masons as wrong, the roots of Masonry being attributed to the Knights Templar was introduced into England's American colonies through English military lodges and warmly embraced.

The earliest known record of conferring the York Rite's highest degree (royal arch) in America is found in the records of Fredericksburg Lodge of Fredericksburg, Virginia, dated December 22, 1753. The first templar to be initiated in the United States was William Davis. He received the degrees of excellent, super excellent, royal arch, and knight templar by the St. Andrew's Royal Arch Lodge in Boston on August 28, 1769. An apothecary, he fought in the Battle of Bunker Hill. Paul Revere was initiated on December 11, 1769. Five months later, Dr. Joseph Warren was added to the roster of early American knights templar.

During this period, lodges in the colonies also began conferring the degree of the royal arch. Recording that these degrees resulted in "much turmoil and debate" on how to handle them within the structure of Freemasonry, one historian finds that a

> more reasonable order and structure for all of Freemasonry emerged, bringing with it the establishment of national and state governing bodies, Chapters, Councils and Commanderies that make up today's York Rite, in which a Master Mason may become a member of three York Rite groups: Royal Arch Masons, a Council of Royal and Select Masters, and a Commandery of Knights Templar. None of these requires the memorization of lengthy rituals to advance from one degree to another that is found in the Entered Apprentice, Fellowcraft and Master Mason degrees.

The York Rite has four degrees: mark master, past master, most excellent master, and royal arch Mason. The mark master degree is believed to have originated as a ceremony of registering a craftsman's mark. Some scholars believe it was the earliest degree and may predate all others by many years.

The most excellent master degree is an American innovation. It was conferred in a royal arch chapter as early as 1783 in Middletown, Connecticut. One Masonic scholar calls it "by far the most spectacular degree in all Freemasonry" because "it is the only degree that brings forcibly to our attention the completion and dedication of King Solomon's Temple."

The royal arch degree has been called "the climax of Ancient Craft Masonry" and the "the root and marrow of Freemasonry." Its drama recalls Jewish history from the destruction of Solomon's Temple and the exile of Jews in Babylon to their return with permission from the king to rebuild the temple. During this reconstruction, they discover the long lost Master's Word. For this reason, the royal arch degree is regarded as the completion of Masonic education. It "reveals the full light of Ancient Craft Masonry, presents it as a complete system in accordance with the original plan," and justly entitles its holder to "the noble name of Master Mason."

Other Masonic Groups

Other Masonic groups are known as "fun" orders. The best known to Americans is the Ancient Arabic Order of the Nobles of the Mystic Shrine for North America. Open to thirty-second-degree Masons or knights templar, the "Shriners" was founded in New York City in 1871. It has no official standing in Masonry but has gained great popularity among American Masons. It features "gaudy oriental costumes, grandiose titles, and pranks, and works a ritual that burlesques Islam."

A membership of approximately 800,000 "Nobles" supports orthopedic hospitals for crippled children. The Shrine Auditorium in Los Angeles has frequently been the site of show business ceremonies, including the Academy Awards. While this exposure has made the Shriners famous,

Freemasons in England are forbidden to affiliate with the Shrine on pain of suspension.

Distinguished by an enjoyment of life in the interest of philanthropy, the Shriners believe and practice the philosophy "Pleasure without intemperance, hospitality without rudeness and jollity without coarseness."

The "Short History of the Ancient Arabic Order Nobles of the Mystic Shrine" records that in 1870 there were several thousand Masons living in Manhattan and that since there were "only about 900,000 people in Manhattan at that time, this was a pretty significant number." One of them, William (Billy) Florence, a star of the stage, had often discussed with his brother Masons the idea of another fraternity, where "fun and fellowship" would be stressed more than ritual and elaborate ceremonies.

On one of his tours of Europe, Florence was invited to a party hosted by an Arabian diplomat in which the entertainment was an elaborately staged musical comedy. At the end of the entertainment, the guests were inducted into a fictitious "secret society." Enthralled by this, Florence attended two other parties with the same theme, observed "all of the nuances" of the ceremonies, and wrote them down. Returning to New York, he told a friend, Dr. Walter Fleming, about the "plays" he had witnessed. They reworked the ceremony and the "secret society" into a ritual of the "Ancient Arabic Order of the Nobles of the Mystic Shrine." (Rearranged, its initials spell "A MASON.") On September 26, 1872, the first Shrine temple in the United States was formed and named Mecca Temple. It had few members, but in 1876 a new group was formed, called "The Imperial Grand Council of the Ancient Arabic Order of the Nobles of the Mystic Shrine." In less than two years, the number of Shriners grew from 43 to more than 400 in 13 temples. By 1888, there were 49 temples and more than 7,000 members in the United States and one in Canada. Although it was primarily a social organization in the 1880s, the Nobles came to the aid of the victims of a yellow fever epidemic and the Johnstown flood. By 1898, there were 50,000 men in the order and 71 of 79 temples were engaged in philanthropic work.

This commitment was formalized in June 1920 at a meeting of the Imperial Council in Portland, Oregon. It was proposed that the Shrine open a hospital for crippled children. By June 1922, the cornerstone for the first Shriners Hospital for Crippled Children was laid (Shreveport, Louisiana). Eventually, the Shrine was providing free orthopedic medical care to children of need. In 1962 at the Imperial Session in Toronto, the Shrine resolved to open a burns treatment hospital for children. The next year, an interim seven-bed unit at the John Sealy Hospital of the University of Texas Medical Branch, Galveston, opened. It was followed by units in Cincinnati, Ohio, General Hospital and Massachusetts General Hospital in Boston. Near these interim units, construction of three thirty-bed Shriners burns institutes was begun. They were completed in 1968. The fraternity has also embraced other causes, including the Spinal Cord Rehabilitation Center in Philadelphia, many new orthopedic and burns institutes, special programs for the control and treatment of spina bifida, and the first air ambulance devoted to transporting burns victims.

The most noticeable symbol of Shrinedom is the red fez, worn at official functions, as well as at parades, trips, circuses, dances, dinners, sporting events, and other social occasions. A Shriner can join the Cibara Motor Corps, Drum and Bugle Corps, Oriental bands, motor patrols, horse patrols, and clown units. There are 191 Shrine temples with 750,000 members in the United States, Canada, Mexico, and the Republic of Panama and informal Shrine clubs located all around the world.

The Daughters of the Nile, a benevolent international fraternal organization for women who are related by birth or marriage to Shriners, has 149 constituted temples throughout the United States and Canada. Founded in 1913 by 22 "progressive women with strength of purpose and vision," the group claims 54,000 members throughout North America. Its members assist patients at twenty-two Shriners Hospitals for Children in North America and in Hawaii. Each year, in its Supreme Temple Convalescent Endowment Fund and Convalescent Relief Fund, the Daughters of the Nile contribute more than $1.5 million for prostheses, braces, shoes, and other devices. Temples sew garments and quilts, provide toys, hold parties for the children, and log many hours as volunteers in the hospitals.

Similar charitable and fun organizations are the Grotto and Tall Cedars of Lebanon. Formally known as the Mystic Order of Veiled Prophets of the Enchanted Realm, the Grotto has members who wear a fez identical to that of the Shrine.

The Order of the Eastern Star is described as a quasi-Masonic society. It is open to women who are relatives of master Masons. Each chapter must include a Mason as patron. A five-degree ritual was composed in 1850. Approximately 3 million women belong to the Eastern Star. It is often regarded as a "ladies auxiliary." Similar groups are the White Shrine of Jerusalem and the Order of Amaranth. The Roman Catholic Church prohibits membership.

Boys between the ages of fourteen and twenty-one who are relatives of Masons may join the Order of DeMolay. Named after Jacques de Molay (the last head of the original Knights Templar), it was founded in Kansas City in 1919. Because most "DeMolays" eventually join a Masonic lodge as adults, it serves as a Masonic "novitiate." Another young men's society sponsored by blue lodges is the Order of Builders. Girls have a choice of joining the Order of Job's Daughters or the Order of Rainbow. Among many other special interest groups that demand Masonic membership as a prerequisite are the National Sojourners (active and retired officers of the armed forces), Acacia college fraternity, and the Philalethes (Masonic philosophy). So-called High Twelve clubs, Square and Compass clubs, and similar groups provide social and cultural programs for Masons. The Masonic Service Association of the United States, formed in 1918, coordinates Masonic welfare and public relations activities.

Most higher rites and fun groups are emulated by black Freemasons in the Ancient Egyptian Arabic Order of the Nobles of the Mystic Shrine for North and South America. There are also counterparts of the Scottish and York Rites and the Eastern Star.

The Philalethes Society, an international organization of Masonic research, publishes a magazine that provides Masonic information from around the world. The Societas Rosicruciana in Civitatibus Foederatis (Masonic Rosicrucian Society of the United States) is the most esoteric of all the rites and degrees of Freemasonry and is open to master Masons by invitation only. Other allied Masonic organizations are:

Acasia. A college social fraternity, founded in 1904, composed of Protestant men recommended by two master Masons.

American Lodge of Research Master Masons. It is interested in the study of Masonic history.

Ancient Egyptian Order of Princesses of Sharemkhu. Women relatives of Shriners. It undertakes both charitable and social projects.

Ancient Egyptian Order of Sciots. Masons who pledge to attend their blue lodge meetings monthly. Founded in 1905, its purposes are the promotion of Masonic fellowship and aiding underprivileged and undernourished children.

Ancient Toltec Rite. Members are knights templars, thirty-second-degree Masons, and their women relatives. It confers its own degrees.

Daughters of Mokanna. A fraternal organization for women relatives of the Prophets of the Enchanted Realm.

George Washington Masonic National Memorial Association. Founded in 1912 with membership limited to Grand Lodge members, it maintains the Washington Masonic Memorial in Alexandria, Virginia.

Grand College of Rites of the U.S.A. Studies ancient Masonic rites. Membership is limited to master Masons by invitation only.

Grand Council of Allied Masonic Degrees of the U.S.A. Members are royal arch Masons. It was organized for the practice of old Masonic rituals.

High Twelve International. Founded in 1921, it is composed of master Masons organized to promote inter-Masonic friendships and to support Masonic ideals.

Holy Order of Knights Beneficent of the Holy City. Master Masons organized to strengthen religious devotion. Membership is by invitation only.

Ladies Oriental Shrine of North America. Women relatives of Shriners dedicated to humanitarian work and fellowship.

Legion of Honor. A national Association of Legions of Honor founded in 1931 and open to U.S. servicemen and veterans who are Shriners.

Masonic clubs. Social organizations of master Masons. The Masonic order does not sponsor drinking in its lodges, but Masonic clubs operate barrooms in most lodge halls. A National League of Masonic Clubs was founded in 1905.

Masonic Relief Association of the U.S.A. Founded in 1885 to administer philanthropic aid both within and outside the Masonic order.

Masonic Service Association of the United States. A federation of Grand Lodges that conducts educational and welfare programs, including veterans' hospital visits and disaster relief assistance. While a national organization, it has no authority over state Grand Lodges. Founded in 1919, its headquarters are in Washington, D.C.

Mutual Guild. Promotes the unity of officers of the Grand Jurisdictions of Knights Templar and Royal Arch. Members are specified officers of those jurisdictions.

National Sojourners. Founded in 1900, its members are past or present commissioned officers and warrant officers of the uniformed forces of the United States who are master Masons. The Heroes of the 76 is an affiliated group.

Order of the Amarath. A charitable organization composed primarily of women relatives of master Masons. They are urged to portray, by precept and example, belief in the Golden Rule and by conforming to the virtues inherent in truth, faith, wisdom, and charity they can prove to others the goodness promulgated by the order.

Order of Desoms. Deaf men with close relationship to master Masons. Its purpose is to provide assistance to its members.

Order of Knight Masons (of Ireland). Open to master Masons by invitation only. It awards the green degrees.

Order of the Rainbow for Girls. Founded in 1922, it consists of girls from the ages of twelve to eighteen related to master Masons or Eastern Stars and friends of these girls. Its purpose is "the teaching of right living."

Red Cross of Constantine–United Imperial Council. Its purposes are studying and purifying the science of Masonry. Membership is restricted to royal arch Masons. The group was founded in 1870.

Royal Order of Jesters. It follows the motto "Mirth is King." Its members are Shriners by invitation only.

Royal Order of Scotland. Christian Scottish or York Rite Masons of at least five years' standing. The order confers its own degrees.

Tall Cedars of Lebanon of the United States of America. Master Masons organized primarily for social purposes.

Throughout the history of Freemasonry, whether a man reached the highest degree of the Craft attainable or stood at the lowest degree as entered apprentice, membership in a society that veiled itself in mystery and chose to be shrouded in secrecy not only set a Mason apart, but also stirred fears among outsiders that behind the locked doors and shaded windows of the lodge something sinister was going on.

CHAPTER 19

THE MEN WHO RULE THE WORLD

THROUGHOUT FREEMASONRY'S HISTORY, WARY, SUSPICIOUS, and often frightened outsiders have denounced it as a seed of paganism and/or being anti-Christian, explorers of dark mysteries of the Occult, a web of Satanism, and a revolutionary threat to the established order, whether it be democracy or totalitarianism. In the eighteenth and nineteenth centuries, European monarchs persistently suppressed Masonry in their belief that it fomented revolution. When the Horthy regime took power in Hungary in 1919–1920, it marked the start of raids by army officers on Masonic lodges that included the destruction of libraries, records, archives, paraphernalia, and works of art. Masonic buildings were seized and used for anti-Masonic exhibitions. A decree of 1920 made Masonry unlawful.

In Germany, as noted previously, General Erich von Ludendorff, a hero of World War I, and his wife spread anti-Masonic and anti-Semitic propaganda during the 1920s. They wrote the tract *Annihilation of Freemasonry through Revelation of Its Secrets* and other hate-filled material that explained Germany's defeat in World War I as "a knife in the back by Jews and Masons." Later, in *Mein Kampf* (Adolf Hitler's autobiography written while in prison for attempting to overthrow the democratic government in Germany in the 1920s), Hitler wrote that Masonry had "succumbed" to the Jews and had become an "excellent instrument" to achieve their aims. He said Germany's post–World War I "general pacifistic paralysis of the national instinct of self-preservation" began with Freemasonry.

In 1931, Nazi Party officials were given a "Guide and Instructional

Letter" that said, "The natural hostility of the peasant against the Jews, and his hostility against the Freemason as a servant of the Jew, must be worked up to a frenzy." After Hitler came to power in January 1933, his top deputy, Hermann Goering, informed the grand master of the Grand Lodge of Germany there was "no place for Freemasonry" in Nazi Germany. At that time, there were nine principle German Grand Lodges, with a membership of almost 80,000. The largest were the Grand Lodge of the Three Globes, National Grand Lodge of All German Freemasons, and the Grand Lodge Royal York of Friendship. Their leaders were told that the Nazi government did not intend to prohibit the activities of the lodge, but that the Masonic order must discontinue the use of the words "Freemason" and "lodge," break all international relations, require that its members be of German descent, remove the requirement of secrecy, and discard all parts of the ritual that are of Old Testament origin. Thereafter, the Association of German Freemasons called itself the National Christian Order of Frederick the Great.

Dr. Walter Darre, the German minister of agriculture, told a huge gathering that the Freemasons were "arch enemies of the German peasantry" and "planned to sabotage" Nazi policies. The government of the Saxony province issued an order barring Freemasons from the public services such as teaching, and ordered that they should take heed of the "government's attitude toward Masonry." In 1934, Goering, as premier of Prussia, ordered dissolution of the oldest and most influential Masonic Grand Lodges in Prussia (Christian Grand Lodges, Grand Lodge of the Three Globes, All German Freemasons, and Royal York of Friendship) because they "might be regarded as hostile to the State because of their affiliations with international Masonry." A Nazi Party court in Berlin published a decree barring from membership those who had been Freemasons for a number of years or who had received the higher degrees of the order. Masonic lodges were attacked for having borrowed much of their doctrine and ceremonies from "Semitic sources." The minister of defense in Berlin issued an order forbidding members of the armed forces from belonging to Masonic lodges or similar organizations and requiring those who were members to immediately cancel their membership. Officers in the armed forces reserves were not admitted for training.

When a young Austrian named Adolf Eichmann took a lowly job at the rank of sergeant in the Second Bureau of the Sicherheitsdienst Haptant section of Reinhardt Heydrich's security branch of the Schutzstaffeln (the Nazi storm troops) in 1934, Eichmann's secret job was to type index cards listing prominent German Freemasons. His work on the "international character" of the Freemasons brought him into contact with "the Jewish Question" for which Heydrich and Eichmann devised a "Final Solution." On August 8, 1935, the Nazi newspaper *Voelkischer Beobachter* announced the final dissolution of all Masonic lodges in Germany. Freemasonry was also blamed for the assassination of Archduke Francis Ferdinand in Sarajevo in 1914, which had sparked World War I.

When President von Hindenburg issued a decree charging that Masonic lodges engaged in subversive activities, the minister of the interior ordered their immediate disbandment and confiscation of the property of all lodges. The Nazi inspector of schools in Germany traveled from town to town calling together meetings of citizens to tell them Freemasonry working in the map department of the German army in 1918 had committed treason by passing German military secrets to England. In 1936, the German Ministry of the Interior issued an order stating that those who had been members of Masonic lodges when Hitler came to power in January 1933 were ineligible for appointment or promotion in the public service and that they were also prohibited from holding office in the Nazi Party and the Schutzstaffeln. Nazi propagandists warned of a "Judeo-Masonic world-conspiracy." Joseph Goebbels, the chief of the Nazi information ministry, spoke of democracies being run by "conspirators of Freemasonry."

By 1937, many prominent dignitaries and members of Masonic lodges were sent to concentration camps. The Gestapo (secret police) seized membership rolls. Goebbels set up an "Anti-Masonic Exposition" in Munich. Special sections of the Sicherheitsdienst security service and later the Reichssicherheitshauptamt (Reich Security Main Office) determined that Masonry was not only a part of the "Jewish problem," but also "an autonomous ideology with political power" that ruled the press and public opinion and motivated wars and revolutions.

When the Nazis marched into Austria on March 12, 1938, the Gestapo took possession of the Grand Lodge in Vienna and allowed a mob to break in and plunder records, silverware, paintings, statuary, and furniture. Grand Master Dr. Richard Schlesinger was arrested and died shortly after his release as a result of harsh treatment. In Czechoslovakia before the Germans took over, there were two Grand Lodges. When the Nazis entered the country in March 1939, 4,000 Freemasons were arrested. Many were sent to concentration camps. Less than 5 percent of Czech Freemasons escaped to England and formed a Grand Lodge Comenius in Exile.

In Italy on February 23, 1923, Benito Mussolini's Fascist Grand Council had decreed that any fascists who were Freemasons had to choose between the Craft and fascism. When the Grand Orient replied that fascist Freemasons were at liberty to give up Masonry and that such action would be in accord with the love of country, which is taught in the lodge, many Masons resigned. The dictator then declared (August 1924) that fascists must disclose the names of Masons who were not in sympathy with the fascist government. Committees were appointed to collect data about Freemasonry. In 1925, Mussolini gave an interview in which he said that while Freemasonry in England, America, and Germany was a charitable and philanthropic institution, Italian Masonry was a "political organization" subservient to the Grand Orient of France and that Freemasons were agents of France and England and opponents of Italy's military actions. Prominent Masons were assassinated. In January 1925, Mussolini dissolved all Italian Freemasonry. Comizio Torrigiani, the grand master of the Grande Oriente, was exiled to the Lipari Islands in 1932 and died soon afterward. Hundreds of other prominent Italian Masons were also exiled. Between 1925 and 1927, Mussolini's blackshirts looted homes of well-known Masons in Milan, Florence, and other cities and murdered at least 100 Masons.

In Spain, where there were two Grand Lodges (the Grand Orient with headquarters in Madrid and the Grand Lodge Española [or Grand Lodge Cataluna] in Barcelona), the Grand Orient was closed and many Masons were arrested for allegedly plotting against the government. In 1935, the legislature adopted a law prohibiting any member of the armed forces from being a Mason. When the Spanish civil war began in 1936, the

Grand Orient moved its headquarters to Brussels. In October, six Masons were hanged for being Masons. During the war, General Francisco Franco's troops destroyed Masonic temples, confiscated Masonic property, and executed Masons. In Cordova, all who were thought to be Masons were killed. In Granada, lodge members were forced to dig their own graves and then shot. Throughout Spain, Spanish Morocco, and the Spanish Canary Islands, Masons by the hundreds were killed or imprisoned for being Masons. In Spanish Morocco, all Masons who were found were shot. In Cadiz, Masons were tortured and shot. In Seville, the newspaper published the names of Masons so they could be hunted and killed. In Malaga, eighty Masons were garroted. Franco issued a decree in 1938 ordering all symbols connected with Freemasonry to be obliterated from the gravestones of Masons buried in Spain. In 1939, he outlawed Masonry and made membership a criminal offense. Anyone who did not denounce Masonry and reveal to the police the names of all Masons with whom he had been associated faced imprisonment.

In France in 1935, an organization called the Interparliamentary Group of Action against Free Masonry was formed from members of the Chamber of Deputies and the Senate who were fascist sympathizers. "The hour has come," they declared, "when Free Masonry must be struck down. A struggle to the death has been begun against it and the national forces must now fight without truce or respite." When France capitulated to Germany in June 1940, the puppet Vichy government dissolved the Grand Orient and the Grand Lodge of France and seized and sold their property. Their headquarters were sealed with a death penalty for anyone who entered. Anti-Masonic museums were arranged, as in other countries. Individual Masons had their residences searched and were banned from positions of command and often put out of their businesses and professions. The same occurred in every invaded country.

In 1942, Hitler himself decreed "Freemasons and the ideological enemies of National Socialism who are allied with them are the originators of the present war." Masonic libraries, archives, and lodges were seized for "scientific research work." Much of this material was put on display in museums. One of these anti-Masonic exhibits proclaimed, "The Mystic darkness of Freemasonry has ceased to be a darkness long since. These "secrets" have been brought to light and, since 1933 the intrigues of the lodges have come to an end. It is all the more instructive when the world, and especially we Germans, are not being shown that the entire Free-masonry is an organization created and expanded deliberately by England fostering the ultimate aim of promoting and strengthening British world power."

In 1945, *Newsweek* reported, "European Freemasonry has been perse-cuted more thoroughly in the last twenty years than ever before in its tur-bulent history. Mussolini strangled Freemasonry in Italy in 1925. Hitler annihilated the German lodges when he came to power, and later those in Czechoslovakia, Poland, Norway, Holland, Belgium, and Greece. European Masons died, went underground, or fled."

During the Nuremberg war crimes trials, Robert H. Jackson, the chief prosecutor and a U.S. Supreme Court justice, said, "It is not generally un-derstood that among the earliest and most savage of the many persecu-tions undertaken by every modern dictatorship are those directed against the Free Masons. [The] dictators realize that its membership are not likely to support the police state, which lays so heavy a hand on the free-dom of the individual."

With Nazi Germany defeated and Eastern Europe controlled by the Soviet Union, hopes of Freemasons that the Craft would revive were quickly dashed. Although the Grand Lodge of Czechoslovakia had recov-ered enough to open for work, the communist government that took over after the murder of President Dr. Eduard Benes, a Czech patriot who was a Mason, the Craft was suppressed. In March 1946, the Hungarian gov-ernment annulled the anti-Masonic decree of 1920 and restored Freemasonry to a legal status, but on June 13, 1950, the Soviet-imposed government dissolved the lodges as "meeting places of the enemies of the people's de-mocratic republic, of capitalistic elements, and of the adherents of Western imperialism." This would be the policy in every country behind the Iron Curtain.

The era of the Cold War also brought a widespread belief that power-ful men engaged in a complex conspiracy to take over the world. As in every period of uncertainty and fears in all of history, suspicions stirred and thrived among ordinary people that a small group of men gathered in secret to control events and direct the future. In earliest times, they had been tribal elders and religious figures. With the eighteenth century came the Iluminati, consisting of persons who believed they possessed supranatural intellectual powers that entitled them to tell others how to live.

As a result of the Industrial Revolution and the rise of modern capitalism, proponents of socialism pointed to a concentration of power in a few individuals and families as evidence of conspiracies to oppress "the masses." In the first half of the twentieth century, a plot by Bolsheviks in Russia and a Nazi conspiracy in Germany had demonstrated that small groups of plotters were capable of seizing control of countries and trying to impose a particular ideology on the world.

With the domination of the countries of Eastern Europe by the Red Army following the defeat of Nazi Germany and the beginning of the Cold War between the West and the Soviet Union, investigations of "communist subversion and infiltration" of the U.S. government and American industries, including motion pictures, created an apprehension that the United States had become obsessed with finding "Red conspiracies." Along with the Cold War came the formation of organizations for the purpose of containing the threat posed by "international communism." But in the view of many Americans, these groups went far beyond the stopping of communism. They were seen as groups whose purpose was economic, political, and social domination of the world. Among these "conspiracies" are the Council on Foreign Relations (founded in 1921), the Bilderberg Group (1954), and the Trilateral Commission (1973).

Running through this suspicion of elites is a belief that most of the individuals involved in a plan to control the world are either Masons or sympathetic to Freemasonry. Among the most persistent popular beliefs concerning the power of Freemasonry in the United States is that the Great Seal of the United States and the street plan and designs of federal government buildings in Washington, D.C., were laid out on the basis of Masonic beliefs. One discourse on the subject notes that the symbol of an inverted triangle or pyramid can be seen in the street plan (it's a pyramid) and that sites are "connected to famous Freemasons," such as Marquis de Lafayette, for whom a park opposite the north side of the White House is named. Other Masonic connections include the Washington Monument and the Pentagon building, said to have been designed by Masons to conform to a pentagram (an occult symbol).

The U.S. one-dollar note contains Masonic symbols. The Great Seal pictured on the back of the dollar bill has an eagle with thirty-two feathers (the degrees in Scottish Rite Freemasonry). The eagle is also the symbol of St. John the Evangelist, the great patron of Freemasonry. The arrows in its left talon refer to Israel's King David (father of Solomon). The olive branch in the eagle's right talon is associated with Solomon. The thirteen stars above the eagle's head represent Jacob, his twelve sons, and the tribes of Israel. Thirteen stars, in a double triangular form, are symbolic of the delivery of the children of Israel from their oppressors and their attainment of a glorious freedom. The Latin *"E Pluribus Unum"* (Out of Many, One) indicates the Masonic fraternity.

Those who find Freemasonry on the mighty dollar also note that the largest symbol on the buck is the portrait of George Washington, a Mason. Also cited as evidence of Masonry on the greenback is an unfinished pyramid. At the top, inside a radiant triangle. is the "all-seeing eye," representing "the Grand Architect of the Universe," who is omniscient and watching over the United States.

Suspicious individuals also note that the Latin motto inscribed beneath the pyramid in the Great Seal of America is *"Novus Ordo Seclorum"* (New Order of the Ages) and taken as synonymous with a "new world order." An example of this thinking reads, "The 'new world order' involves the elimination of the sovereignty and independence of nation-states and some form of world government. This means the end of the United States, the Constitution, and the Bill of Rights as we now know them." Most of these new world order proposals involve the conversion of the United Nations and its agencies to a world government, complete with a world army, a world parliament, a world court, global taxation, and numerous other agencies to control every aspect of human life (education, nutrition, health care, population, immigration, communications, transportation, commerce, agriculture, finance, the environment, and so on). The various notions of the new world order differ as to the details and scale, but agree on the basic principle and substance.

One historian sees the Statue of Liberty as a "Masonic goddess from

top to bottom." It was "conceived by Freemasons," built by French Freemason Frederic-Auguste Bartholdi (who had already made a statue of the
Freemason Marquis de Lafayette for the city of New York, for the occasion of the centenary of the signing of the Declaration of Independence),
and "installed by Freemasons in a Freemasonic ceremony."

Those who discern a pattern of Freemasonric influence in American
history point to the fact that one-third of the presidents have been members of the Craft:

George Washington. Initiated: November 4, 1752, by the
Fredericksburg Lodge No. 4, Fredericksburg, Virginia. The first
and only Freemason to serve simultaneously as a lodge master and
president.

James Monroe. (Lodge records lost) Initiated: November 9, 1775, St.
John's Regimental Lodge in the Continental army. Monroe was not
yet eighteen, but "lawful age" had not yet been universally fixed at
twenty-one. Later, took membership in Williamsburg Lodge No.
6, Williamsburg, Virginia.

Andrew Jackson. (Lodge records lost) Initiated: date unknown. He
seems to have been a member of St. Tammany Lodge No. 1,
Nashville, Tennessee, as early as 1800. The first Lodge in
Tennessee was organized in 1789 under a dispensation from the
Grand Lodge of North Carolina. The name was later changed to
Harmony Lodge No. 1 on November 1, 1800. Jackson is listed as a
member in the Lodge Return to the Grand Lodge of North
Carolina and Tennessee for 1805. On December 27, 1813, the
Grand Lodge of Tennessee was granted its own constitution.
Jackson was the sixth grand master of Masons of Tennessee, from
October 7, 1822, until October 4, 1824.

James K. Polk. Initiated: June 5, 1820, Columbia Lodge No. 31,
Columbia, Tennessee. Polk assisted in the cornerstone laying of the
Smithsonian Institution, Washington, D.C., May 1, 1847.

James Buchanan. Initiated: December 11, 1816, Lodge No. 43, Lancaster, Pennsylvania. He was worshipful master of Lodge No. 43 (1822–1823) and in 1824 was appointed district deputy grand master for Lancaster, Lebanon, and York Counties.

Andrew Johnson. (Lodge records lost during the Civil War) Initiated: May 5, 1851, Greenville Lodge No. 119, Greenville, Tennessee.

James A. Garfield. Initiated: November 19, 1861, Magnolia Lodge No. 20, Columbus, Ohio. Because of Civil War duties, Garfield did not receive the third degree until November 22, 1864, in Columbus Lodge No. 30, Columbus, Ohio. On October 10, 1866, he affiliated with Garrettsville Lodge No. 246, Garrettsville, Ohio, and served as its chaplain (1868–1869). He became a charter member of Pentalpha Lodge No. 23, Washington, D.C., on May 4, 1869. He was one of the petitioners for the lodge charter.

William McKinley. Initiated: May 1, 1865, Hiram Lodge No. 21, Winchester, Virginia. Affiliated with Canton Lodge No. 60, Canton, Ohio, on August 21, 1867. Demitted (dropped out) of the same to become a charter member of Eagle Lodge No. 431, also in Canton. After McKinley's death on September 14, 1901 (assassinated), the name was changed to William McKinley Lodge effective October 24, 1901.

Theodore Roosevelt. Initiated: January 2, 1901, Matinecock Lodge No. 806, Oyster Bay, New York. He visited the Grand Lodge of Pennsylvania (in its present home, the Masonic Temple at One North Broad Street) for the celebration of the sesquicentennial of George Washington's initiation.

William Howard Taft. Initiated: February 18, 1909. Taft was made a "Mason at Sight" within the Body of Kilwinning Lodge No. 356, Cincinnati, Ohio, by Grand Master Charles S. Hoskinson. His father and two brothers were also members of this lodge. President

Taft addressed the brethren saying, "I am glad to be here, and to be a Mason. It does me good to feel the thrill that comes from recognizing on all hands the Fatherhood of God and the Brotherhood of Man." He visited the Grand Lodge of Pennsylvania on the occasion of a special communication held in the Masonic Temple (One North Broad Street) on March 12, 1912.

Warren G. Harding. Initiated: June 28, 1901, Marion Lodge No. 70, Marion, Ohio. Because of some "personal antagonism," Harding's advancement was hindered until 1920, by which time he had been nominated for president. Friends persuaded the opposition to withdraw the objection, and on August 27, 1920, nineteen years after his initiation, Harding was given the sublime degree of master Mason, in Marion Lodge. At his request, Harding took the Oath of Office of President of the United States on the same Bible as was used by George Washington (the Altar Bible of St. John's Lodge No. 1, New York City).

Franklin D. Roosevelt. Initiated: October 11, 1911, Holland Lodge No. 8, New York. He participated in the "raising" of his son Elliott (1910–1990) on February 17, 1933, in Architect's Lodge No. 519, also in New York City. He was present, but did not participate in the degrees when two other sons, James (1907–1991) and Franklin Junior (1914–1988), became members of their brother Elliott's lodge on November 7, 1935.

Harry S Truman. Initiated: February 9, 1909, Belton Lodge No. 450, Belton, Missouri. In 1911, when several members of Belton Lodge separated to establish Grandview Lodge No. 618, Grandview, Missouri, Truman served as its first worshipful master. At the annual session of the Grand Lodge of Missouri, September 24–25, 1940, he was elected (by a landslide) the ninety-seventh grand master of Masons of Missouri, and served until October 1, 1941. He was made a sovereign grand inspector general, thirty-third degree, and honorary member, Supreme Council on October 19,1945, at the Supreme Council Southern Jurisdiction Headquarters in Washington, D.C., at which time he served as exemplar (representative) for his class. He was also elected an honorary grand master of the International Supreme Council, Order of DeMolay. On May 18, 1959, former president Truman was presented with a fifty-year award, the only U.S. president to reach that golden anniversary in Freemasonry.

Gerald R. Ford. Initiated: September 30, 1949, Malta Lodge No. 465, Grand Rapids, Michigan, along with his half brothers Thomas, Richard, and James. The fellowcraft and master Mason degrees were conferred by Columbia Lodge No. 3, Washington, D.C., on April 20 and May 18, 1951, as a courtesy to Malta Lodge. Ford was made a sovereign grand inspector general and honorary member, Supreme Council Northern Jurisdiction at the Academy of Music in Philadelphia on September 26, 1962, for which he served as exemplar (representative) for his class. President Ford was unanimously elected an active member of the International Supreme Council, Order of DeMolay, and its honorary grand master at its annual session held at Orlando, Florida, April 6–9, 1975. He held this post until January 1977, at which time he became a past honorary grand master, receiving his Collar and Jewel on October 24, 1978, in Topeka, Kansas, from the Honorable Thomas C. Raum Jr., grand master, Order of DeMolay.

Lyndon B. Johnson. A Freemason in the sense that he became an entered apprentice on October 30, 1937, in Johnson City Lodge No. 561, Johnson City, Texas, but did not continue to the second and third degrees. Some consider him to have been a Freemason, but others do not.

Ronald Reagan. Presented with a "Certificate of Honor," which said that Reagan's life was "a testament to his firm belief in brotherly love, relief, and truth," and that his service to the public "broadened the applications of temperance, fortitude, prudence, and justice to the benefit of all mankind." This certificate further recognized Reagan's efforts to promote "good will and understanding throughout the world." According to a press release issued by the D.C. Grand Lodge, the two Scottish Rite grand commanders jointly gave President Reagan a Scottish Rite Certificate, and the imperial potentate gave him a Shrine certificate. According to the *New Age Magazine* and the *Northern Light Magazine*, the Scottish Rite grand commanders jointly presented President Reagan with a certificate that conferred the title "Honorary Scottish Rite Mason" and the imperial potentate presented him with a certificate with the designation "Honorary Member of the Imperial Council" of the Shrine. In a February 22, 1988, letter, he commended "the outstanding charitable work of the Masons as one of our nation's oldest fraternal organizations," thanked the Scottish Rite for the certificate of membership, and said he was "honored to join the ranks of sixteen former Presidents in their association with Freemasonry."

U.S. vice presidents who were Masons:

No. 6	Daniel Decius Tompkins, 1817–1825
14	John Cabell Breckinridge, 1857–1861
16	Andrew Johnson, 1865 (seventeenth president)
24	Garrett Augustus Hobart, 1897–1899
26	Charles Warren Fairbanks, 1905–1909
28	Thomas Riley Marshall, 1913–1921
33	Henry A. Wallace, 1941–1945
34	Harry S Truman, 1945 (thirty-third president)
40	Gerald R. Ford, 1973–1974 (thirty-eighth president)

U.S. secretaries of state:

John Marshall, 1800–1801
James Monroe, 1811–1817
Edward Livingston, 1831–1833

Louis McLane, 1833–1834
James Buchanan, 1845–1849
Louis Cass, 1857–1860
William H. Seward, 1861–1869
Philander C. Knox, 1909–1913
William C. Bryan, 1913–1915
Bainbridge Colby, 1920–1921
Frank B. Kellogg, 1925–1929
James F. Byrnes, 1945–1947
George C. Marshall, 1947–1949
Christian A. Herter, 1959–1961

Chief justices of the U.S. Supreme Court:

John Jay, 1789–1795
Olliver Ellsworth, 1796–1800
John Marshall, 1801–1835
William Howard Taft, 1921–1930
Frederick M. Vinson, 1946–1953
Earl Warren, 1953–1969

Associate justices of the Supreme Court:

William Cushing, 1790–1810
John Blair Jr., 1790–1795
William Paterson, 1793–1803
Thomas Todd, 1807–1826
Joseph Story, 1812–1845
Robert Trimble, 1826–1828
John McLean, 1830–1861
Henry Baldwin, 1830–1844
John Catron, 1837–1865
Samuel Nelson, 1845–1872
Noah H. Swayne, 1862–1881
David Davis, 1862–1877

Stephen J. Field, 1863–1897
John Marshall Harlan, 1877–1911
William B. Woods, 1881–1887
Stanley Matthews, 1881–1889
Samuel Blatchford, 1882–1893
William H. Moody, 1906–1910
Willis Van Devanter, 1911–1937
Joseph R. Lamar, 1911–1916
John H. Clarke, 1916–1922
Hugo L. Black, 1937–1971
Stanley F. Reed, 1938–1957
William O. Douglas, 1939–1975
James F. Byrnes, 1941–1942
Robert H. Jackson, 1941–1954
Wiley B. Rutledge, 1943–1949
Harold H. Burton, 1945–1958
Thomas C. Clark, 1949–1967
Sherman Minton, 1949–1956
Potter Stewart, 1958–1981
Thurgood Marshall 1967–1991

Masonic influence is also cited in the fact that numerous members of Congress have been and are Freemasons. Among five-stars generals and admirals were:

John J. Pershing
Charles Pelot Summerall
Douglas MacArthur
Omar N. Bradley
Malin Craig
Henry Harley "Hap"Arnold
Ernest J. King (admiral)

Director of the Federal Bureau of Investigation J. Edgar Hoover was raised to master Mason on November 9, 1920, in Federal Lodge No. 1,

Washington, D.C., just two months before his twenty-sixth birthday. During his fifty-two years with the Craft, he received innumerable medals, awards, and decorations. He was "coroneted" a thirty-third degree inspector general honorary (1955) and awarded the Scottish Rite's highest recognition, the Grand Cross of Honor in 1965.

The involvement of Freemasons in the government of the Republic of Texas is found in the fact that all of its presidents were Masons, as were all its vice presidents. The lowest percentage of Masons who held executive positions in any of the four administrations was 85 percent. In the last administration that carried Texas into the Union, all those in executive positions in the government of the republic were Masons.

Freemasonry influence in the Endowment Ceremony of the Mormon Church has also been cited. Historian Bill McKeever notes that although the Doctrine and Covenants 124:41 of the Church of Latter Day Saints says that temple ordinances were kept hidden from "before the foundations of the earth," they are "suspiciously close to those used in Freemasonry. Signs, grips, oaths, and tokens used in Mormonism are so similar that one can't escape the suspicion" that founder Joseph Smith "borrowed" these Masonic practices, especially since he became a Mason on March 15, 1842.

Historian Reed C. Durham Jr. insists that Smith did in fact use the Masonic ceremony as a springboard for the Mormon ceremony. He writes, "There is absolutely no question in my mind that the Mormon ceremony which came to be known as the Endowment, introduced by Joseph Smith to Mormon Masons initially, just a little over one month after he became a Mason, had an immediate inspiration from Masonry."

It has been noted that the outside structure of the Salt Lake City Temple contains many designs peculiar to Masonry. These include the all-seeing eye, the inverted five-pointed star (known as the Eastern Star), and the clasped hands or grip. All of these were part of Freemasonry long before Smith incorporated them. Markings in the "Garments of the Holy Priesthood," worn by temple Mormons, also bear resemblance to the compass, square, and level of Freemasonry.

Prominent leaders in Mormonism who were Masons include Joseph Smith's father, Hyrum and William Smith (Joseph Smith's brothers); Brigham Young (Mormonism's second president); John Taylor (third president); and Presidents Wilford Woodruff (fourth) and Sidney Rigdon (fifth); John C. Bennett, assistant to the first president; Willard Richards, the second counselor to Brigham Young; Newell K. Whitney, presiding bishop; Heber C. Kimball, first counselor to Brigham Young; Orson and Parley P. Pratt, Mormon apostles; Orson Hyde, also a Mormon apostle; Orrin Porter Rockwell, Smith's bodyguard; Lyman Johnson, an apostle; William Law, second counselor to Joseph Smith, and William Clayton, Smith's secretary.

An example of the suspicions surrounding Freemasonry is found in *The Brotherhood and the Manipulation of Society*. Ivan Frazer and Mark Beeston write, "The basic recruitment of members to further the Elite's plans is through the secret society network of Freemasonry...the latest incarnation of the Christian/military order known as the Knights Templars who gained staggering riches and a wealth of esoteric knowledge during the Crusades, in which the 'righteous' Christians were dispatched to the Holy Land with free reign to slaughter the Jews and Moslems in a series of campaigns between the 11th and 13th Centuries."

The authors assert that while the vast majority of members are on the first three rungs of the thirty-three-level hierarchy and have no idea of the hidden agenda, they take a pledge of allegiance "to the society above all else." Most initiates are willing to do this because "the temptation of power, wealth and knowledge [are] hard to refuse, that it is hinted that there are penalties to pay for betraying the society and revealing its secrets," and that it is "impossible to achieve high levels of initiation within Freemasonry unless one is hand picked by those of the higher degrees."

At the "apex of the pyramid of the Brotherhood," these "select few" who know "the full agenda have become known as the Illuminati (Latin for "illuminated ones."). All-powerful, they "occupy all top level members of the police and military forces around the world. They are found in every area of society at all levels, but at the top, in the highest social and monetary bracket, the Brotherhood prevails." Freemasonry has been called "the single largest vehicle for perpetuation of the Luciferic consciousness on Earth." Associated with Freemasonry within the elite's hierarchy are the Grand Orient Lodges (France), the Knights of Malta, and the Knights Templar. The brotherhood "owns the law, they own the military, they own the oil companies, pharmaceutical companies and just about everything which provides fuel for the status quo."

Another view of Freemasonry is that it has joined with "New Agers" in pushing for "collectivist motifs that promote monistic pantheism." The new world order is seen as one and the same as the Masonic/New Age ideal of man's divinity and self-transformation in which one must awaken to the original sin of Lucifer, as opposed to Eve in the Garden of Eden, that "we can be as Gods." It is argued that Freemasonry practices the ancient mysteries of Egypt with the goal of their reinstatement in the new world order. To bolster this argument, a quotation by W. L. Wilmshurst in 1927 is offered. In *The Meaning of Masonry*, he writes:

> In this new Aquarian age, when many individuals and groups are working in various ways for the eventual restoration of the mysteries, an increasing number of aspirants are beginning to recognize that Freemasonry may well be the vehicle for this achievement.... [A Mason begins his career] as the natural man; he ends it by becoming through its discipline, a regenerated man.... This the evolution of man into superman—was always the purpose of the ancient Mysteries, and the real purpose of modern Masonry is, not the social and charitable purposes to which so much attention is paid, but the expediting of the spiritual evolution of those who aspire to perfect their own nature and transform it into a more god-like quality.

In 1991, evangelist Pat Robertson published *The New World Order*. A book that finds a "Masonic connection" to the new world order, it uses such phrases as "Masonic power," "dark side," "international conspiracy," "occult," "wealth," "secret society," and "world power." At the same time, other Christian leaders attacked Masonry for promoting devil worship, leading religious men away from the right way to find God, or being inconsistent with the religious beliefs of certain denominations.

While denying any connection to a conspiracy to establish a new world order, Masons respond that the legacy of Freemasons who endured the persecution of Nazis and fascists, and others throughout history who endured similar persecutions, is that "people of good will must act to stop any form of intolerance against Masons or any other fraternal, racial, or religious group."

Ironically, at a time when Freemasonry is suspected of being a vast secret society with sinister plans for the political and economic domination of the United States and the rest of the world, the ancient Craft is facing an uncertain future.

CHAPTER 20

THE FUTURE OF FREEMASONRY

O F THE WORLD'S ESTIMATED 5.9 MILLION FREEMASONS, the majority live in the United States (4 million). Most of the others can be found in English-speaking nations. Statistics for English Masonry are somewhat unreliable because an individual can belong to more than one lodge. Worldwide estimates place the membership in England and Wales at 550,000; Scotland, 400,000; Ireland, 47,000; Canada and United States, 4.1 million; Europe, 80,000; Australasia, 375,000; Latin America, 50,000; Philippines, 10,000; and other areas (India, Japan, Formosa, Africa, and Israel), 288,000.

Since the mid-1960s, the numbers in the United States have been dwindling. This has been attributed in part to an increasingly secular and materialistic society in which the youth of the "MTV generation" prefer to make their social connections by going to shopping malls, the movies, and rock-and-roll concerts, rather than joining groups that attracted their fathers and grandfathers. They appear to believe that the rituals and rites of such organizations offer no relevance to their lives. Historian John J. Robinson, author of *Born in Blood: The Lost Secrets of Freemasonry*, assigns the cause of "the erosion of recruitment" by Freeasonry to "an increasingly permissive and materialistic society [in which] concepts of personal morality, personal pride, and personal honor may appear antiquated."

This does not mean that Masons are resigned to ultimate extinction. In "Freemasonry and Its Future," David F. Coady writes that while "doomsayers are ready to bury the Craft," the future of Freemasonry "lies with the youth of our nation." If these writers "could leave their marble sanctuaries and come down in the quarries of the workmen who are grooming the young men of today to be the Freemasons of tomorrow," he continues, "they would see the light at the end of the tunnel."

Speaking to the District Grand Lodge of North Queensland, Australia, in 1989, Allan D. Wakeham warned, "If we ourselves cannot see in our organization a purpose in the community which is wider than our internal aims then we will never draw into our ranks the type of men we need, neither will we be able to convince the world outside that it is an organization which has a beneficial influence on the affairs of the community at large."

In an address titled "Masonry in the Modern World," Reverend Dean J. O. Rymer, dean of Auckland, New Zealand, said:

> Because the world is modern, it does not follow that it is the best conceivable world that there could be. To my mind it is not. Nevertheless, we have to recognize that nothing stands still. We live in a world of change. If all aspects of life were altered we would repeat mistakes in every generation. There are some values that will be permanent, whatever changes happen in societies. It is these values that we must preserve, whether we are the Church or civic authorities or Freemasonry. It is for Freemasonry to discover in its own self-understanding that which we must never surrender. Belief in God is necessary for any civilization to continue. High moral standards accepted by a community are necessary if people are to live together. The respect for the value of individual persons is obligatory if individuals are to realize their potential. It is the commitment to these beliefs and values that Freemasonry must always uphold. Freemasonry has a solid foundation in unchanging principles, it can be a marvelous training ground in ethical sensitivity, but its effectiveness and its future, will be hindered if it turns its searchlight exclusively on itself, and neglects a study of that larger society which exists outside the lodge room.

Gary A. Henningsen, past grand master and grand secretary, New York State Grand Lodge of Masons, in an address titled "A Look Ahead...No Secret to Masons, Ours Is a Fraternity That Encourages the Human

Imagination and Will Continue to Do So Even into This New Century and Millennium," said:

> Human imagination has always thrived in Freemasonry. We have enticed to our fraternity artists, poets, warriors, inventors, manufacturers, explorers, pioneers, government leaders business tycoons and gentle everyday family men made better because of their association with and love of our beloved Craft. It has been so from the very beginning. And that holds whether you think our beginnings took root with the formation of the United Grand Lodge of England, the *Illuminati*, Knights Templar of Crusader days, the Druids and/or the Egyptians.
>
> Whenever and wherever a people proclaimed a belief in God, in the immortality of their souls, and in a heartfelt obligation to help and serve their fellow man, that environment fostered the unfoldment of human imagination. Whether these people were bona fide Freemasons complete with dues card or forerunners of what was to become bona fide Freemasonry, we have much for which to be grateful as we advance into the uncertainties of this unfolding 21st Century. We've a wondrous track record to lean on and to emulate. For the first time in history, the consequences of our acts as Masons not only will affect our immediate environment, but also can affect the entire planet. We've never been at this point before. We need to give it serious thought.

Calling Freemasons "Eighteen Million Beacons of Light," he saw 6 million men who

> believe in God (by whatever name), believe in the immortality of our souls, and in the heartfelt obligation to serve our fellow man as we would have our fellow man serve us. What a wonderful opportunity we're being given to become responsible planetary stewards of our human creativity, thus preventing others from wreaking unimaginable horror on our planetary home. Nowhere since entering Masonry

have we sensed the boundless possibilities so available to us individually as Masons, and collectively as a fraternity.

Observing that membership in California Masonic lodges is less than 50 percent of what it was in the 1960s, that there are dire predictions that by 2030 Masonic lodges will cease to exist, and that "the reality exists that the entry of new members into our gentle Craft has receded," Ralph Head, editor of the *California Freemason*, writes:

Despite the changes taking place in our society the need for the adoption and practice of Freemasonry's moral and pragmatic principles and tenets is just as urgent today as it was fifty years ago. Is there an answer to declining membership? I not only believe there is, but that it is at hand. Freemasonry has never solicited members, not because it is an elitist society, but because of its belief that those who knock at its doors should come of their own free will and accord. This doctrine has served well and has resulted in a camaraderie of men who have adopted high moral standards, practice the principles of the Golden Rule, and want to help their fellow man.

Paul M. Bessel in a talk on September 8, 2000, at La France Lodge No. 93, in Washington, D.C., declared:

Freemasonry could be, and could have been in the past, the only institution in the world that at all times in every way promotes tolerance and meeting on the level. We could be the leaders in seeking racial harmony, religious ecumenism, cooperation among men and women, civility between people who believe in different political philosophies, and friendliness among those who choose to live their lives differently from others. We could be better than the United Nations, Amnesty International, and interfaith organizations, all together, because we could be the prime organization supporting tolerance for all, everywhere, in all circumstances. This would be a unique role for Freemasonry.

American Freemasonry has plunged into the universe of the Internet. Numerous Grand Lodges have established Web sites providing information on activities and instructions on how to apply for membership. There are also online magazines ("Grand Lodge E-Zines"), including *California Freemason Online*, *Connecticut Square & Compasses*, *The Florida Mason*, *Illinois Freemasonry*, *Louisiana Freemason Magazine*, *Michigan—From Point to Pointe*, *New Jersey Freemason*, *New York—Empire State Mason Online*, *North Carolina Mason*, *Ohio—The Beacon*, *Pennsylvania Freemason*, and *Texas Mason*. There are also several Web sites devoted to Masonic music.

Looking to the future, American Freemasonry also provides information in Masonic libraries, a book club, and through publishers that specialize in Masonic books. A Masonic authors group, the Society of Blue Friars, started in 1932, is one of the oldest "concordant" bodies in Masonry. According to historian Wallace McLeod, the name was chosen because "friar" is related to the French word for "brother." Regulations state that one new friar shall be appointed each year. Others may be appointed to fill vacancies caused by demise or resignation when the total membership is not over twenty. The society has met once a year (except for 1945), in a session that is open to all Masonic brethren. The Consistory takes place in Washington, D.C., in February, as part of an annual Masonic weekend sponsored by the Allied Masonic Degrees. At the annual meeting, the new friar is proclaimed. He is expected to deliver a research paper. In earlier times, the papers were sometimes printed in the *Miscellanea* of the Allied Masonic Degrees. In recent years, they have appeared in *The Philalethes* magazine. The presiding officer of the Blue Friars is the grand abbot, who retains the office for life or as long as he wishes. He appoints the deputy grand abbot (his designated successor) and the secretary-general. The grand abbot receives nominations for new friars, but the final decision rests with him.

Regarding concerns about the decline in Masonry membership in the United States and whether there could ever be a recurrence of the anti-Masonry of the mid-nineteenth century, historian Jasper Ridley, in *The Freemasons: A History of the World's Most Powerful Society*, writes that American Masons,

with their deep roots in the American way of life and widespread influence among their fellow citizens, need not worry unduly if they
form a smaller percentage of the total population than they did seventy years ago, or if fewer Freemasons have been President of the
United States than in the first half of the twentieth century. . . . Their
position in the United States is much more secure than in any other
country. . . . It is difficult to believe that any federal or state authority
in the United States would issue orders [as they have been in Britain
and France] to declare whether or not he is a Freemason, even without the knowledge that any such action would be banned by the courts
as a violation of the Freemasons' constitutional rights. In America
Freemasons are generally respected, not hated and feared.

Although there have recently been outbursts of alarm, such as those by
Pat Robertson and a handful of other American fundamentalist Christian
leaders, Freemasonry in the United States is more likely to be seen as no
more threatening than any group that establishes requirements of membership, whether it be a private golf club or a fraternal organization with
"secret" rituals. Despite allegations that Freemasonry is at the heart of a
vast conspiracy to impose a new world order, most Americans appear to
view Masons as men engaging in nothing more serious than games of
"I've got a secret" that have been revealed in numerous books and articles,
exposed by former Masons, and examined in television documentaries.

The result is that the world's oldest secret fraternal society is no longer
shrouded in the mystery that for centuries gave it the appearance of a sinister scheme, but an attempt by well-meaning, older, mostly white men to
understand the meaning of life, in the words of W. L. Wilmshurst, through
"a philosophic and religious system expressed in dramatic ceremonial."

Ask any Mason if he agrees with this and he is likely to reply, "So mote
it be."

MASONIC SONGS

"Shawn-boy," or "Over the Water to Charlie" (Robert Burns, 1786)

Ye sons of old Killie, assembled by Willie,
To follow the noble vocation;
Your thrifty old mother has scarce such another
To sit in that honoured station.
I've little to say, but only to pray,
As praying's the ton of your fashion;
A prayer from thee Muse you well may excuse
'Tis seldom her favourite passion.

Ye powers who preside o'er the wind, and the tide,
Who marked each element's border;
Who formed this frame with beneficent aim,
Whose sovereign statute is order:
Within this dear mansion, may wayward Contention
Or withered Envy ne'er enter;
May secrecy round be the mystical bound,
And brotherly Love be the centre!

Song for the "Festive Board"

Eternal father, strong to save
Whose arms hath bound the restless wave,
Who bidd'st the mighty ocean deep
Its own appointed limits keep.

O hear us when we cry to thee
For those in peril on the sea.
O Trinity of love and power
Our Brethren shield in danger's hour,
From rock and tempest, fire and foe
Protect them whereso'er they roam.
Thus evermore shall rise to thee
Glad hymn of praise from land and sea.
So Mote it be.

Absent Brethren

Holy Father, in Thy mercy
Hear our anxious prayer,
Keep our loved ones, now far absent
'Neath Thy care
When in sorrow, when in danger.
When in loneliness
In Thy love look down and comfort
Their distress
Father, in Thy love and power
Architect Divine
Bless them, guide them, save them, keep them,
They are Thine
So mote it be.

Song of Welcome

Brethren from the East and West.
Who have stood the Tyler's Test,
You will find a welcome here,
Bright, Fraternal and sincere.

Chorus:
Warm Masonic hearts to meet you,
Hands of fellowship to greet you,
May our welcome here today
Cheer each Brother on his way.
We salute the man of worth.
Whether high or low his birth,
Whatsoever be his lot
Rich or poor it matters not.
And when we have said adieu,
May our love remain with you,
And may we renew that love,
In a Grander Lodge Above.

The Entered Apprentice's Song

Solo:
Come, let us prepare; We Brothers that are
Met together on merry Occasion;
Let's drink, laugh and sing; Our Wine has a Spring,
Here's a health to an Accepted Mason.
Chorus:
Let's drink, laugh and sing; Our Wine has a Spring,
Here's a health to an Accepted Mason.
Solo:
The world is in pain our secrets to gain,
But still let them wonder and gaze on;
'Til they're shown the Light; They'll ne'er know the Right
Word or Sign of an Accepted Mason.
Chorus:
'Til they're shown the Light; They'll ne'er know the Right
Word or Sign of an Accepted Mason.
Solo:
Tis this and 'tis that, They cannot tell what,
Why so many great Men of the Nation,

Should Aprons put on, To make themselves one.
With a Free or an Accepted Mason.
Chorus:
Should Aprons put on, To make themselves one.
With a Free or an Accepted Mason.
Solo:
Great Kings Dukes and Lords have laid by their swords,
This our Mist'ry to put a good grace on;
And ne'er been ashamed to hear themselves named
With a Free or an Accepted Mason.
Chorus:
And ne'er been ashamed to hear themselves named
With a Free or an Accepted Mason.
Solo:
Antiquity's pride We have on our side,
It makes each man just in his station;
There's nought but what's good to be understood
By a Free or an Accepted Mason.
Chorus:
There's nought but what's good to be understood
By a Free or an Accepted Mason.
Solo:
We're true and sincere, We're just to the Fair;
They'll trust us on any occasion;
No mortal can more The Ladies adore
Than a Free and an Accepted Mason.
Chorus:
No mortal can more The Ladies adore
Than a Free and an Accepted Mason.
(All standing and joining hand, right over left)
Solo:
Then joyn hand in hand, T'each other firm stand;
Let's be merry and put a bright face on:
What mortal can boast so noble a toast
As a Free or an Accepted Mason.

Chorus:
What mortal can boast so noble a toast
As a Free or an Accepted Mason

Master's Song

Solo:
This world is so hard and so stony;
That if a man is to get through,
He'd need have the courage of Nelson,
And plenty of Job's patience too.
But a man who is kind to another
And cheerfully helps him along,
God Bless such a man and a brother,
And here's to his health in a song.
And here's to his health, here's to his health
And here's to his health in a song.
Chorus:
And here's to his health, here's to his health
And here's to his health in a song.
Solo:
This life is as cheerless as Winter,
To those who are cold in the heart;
but a man who is warm in his nature,
Bids Winter for ever depart
The ground that he treads on will blossom,
'Till beauty around him shall throng;
God Bless such a man and a brother,
And here's to his health in a song.
And here's to his health, here's to his health
And here's to his health in a song.
Chorus:
And here's to his health, here's to his health
And here's to his health in a song.

Solo:
As clouds that in sunshine are open,
And silvered by light passing through;
So men who are generous in spirit,
Are blessed by the good deeds they do;
There's nothing like helping another
For getting one's own self along;
Who does this is truly a brother.
And here's to his health in a song.
And here's to his health, here's to his health
And here's to his health in a song.
(All standing sing chorus)

Lodge Opening Ode

Hail! Eternal! by whose aid
All created things were made;
Heaven and earth Thy vast design;
Hear us, Architect Divine!
May our work begun in Thee,
Ever blest with order be;
And may we when labours cease,
Part in harmony and peace.
By Thy Glorious Majesty—
By the trust we place in Thee—
By the badge and mystic sign—
Hear us! Architect Divine!
So mote it be.

Closing Ode

Now the evening shadows closing.
Warn from toil to peaceful rest;
Mystic arts and rights reposing
Sacred in each faithful breast.
God of Light, whose love unceasing
Doth to all Thy works extend,
Crown our Order with Thy blessing,
Build,—sustain us to the end.
Humbly now we bow before Thee,
Grateful for Thy aid divine;
Everlasting power and glory,
Mighty Architect! be Thine.
So mote it be.

Third Degree

Days and moments quickly flying,
Blend the living with the dead;
Soon will you and I be lying
Each within his narrow bed.
Soon our souls to God Who gave them
Will have sped their rapid flight;
Able now by grace to save them,
Oh! that while we can we might.
As the tree falls, so must it lie;
As the man lives, so must he die;
As the man dies, so must he be
All through the days of eternity.
So mote it be.

TABLE LODGES

A T "TABLE LODGES" (WHERE FOOD AND DRINKS WERE served) the tables were arranged in the shape of a horseshoe with a warden seated at each end. Tables were called "tracing boards" (drawings depicting placement of people and objects in rituals), plates became "tiles," spoons became "trowels," glasses were "cannon," and wine became "powder." To fill the glass was "to charge it" and to drink the contents was to "fire it." After the toast, the "cannon: (glass) which had been emptied, simultaneous movements of the hand ("clapping") were made concluding with 'three times three.'" After "firing" (draining of the glass), the brethren were called on to copy the worshipful master in making the following movements:

Holding the "cannon" in the right hand, he jerked his hand forward to the full length of the arm, then swung it to the left and then to the right. This he did three times and counted off "one, two, three." At three, everyone banged the cannon on the tracing board (table). The toast was honored by claps of the hands (three times three).

Movements called the Masonic fire consisted of a downward stroke (laying of a brick), a movement to the left, signifying spreading the cement of human kindness, and movement to the right, meaning building up the lodge with brotherly love.

At the conclusion of the festivities, the tyler offers and leads the toast:

Are your glasses charged in the West and South, the Worshipful Master cries;
They're charged in the West, they're charged in the South, are the Wardens' prompt replies:
Then to our final Toast tonight your glasses fairly drain,

Happy to meet—sorry to part—happy to meet again, again, Oh! happy to meet again.

CHORUS: Happy to meet—sorry to part—happy to meet again, again,

Oh! happy to meet again.

The Mason's social Brotherhood around the Festive Board,

Reveal a wealth more precious far than selfish miser's hoard.

They freely share the priceless stores that generous hearts contain

Happy to meet, sorry to part, happy to meet again!

We work like Masons free and true, and when our Task is done,

A merry song and cheering glass are not unduly won:

And only at our Farewell Pledge is pleasure touched with pain

Happy to meet, sorry to part, happy to meet again!

Amidst our mirth we drink "To all poor Masons o'er the World"

On every shore our Flag of Love is gloriously unfurled,

We prize each Brother, fair or dark, who bears no moral stain—

Happy to meet, sorry to part, happy to meet again!

The Mason feels the truth the Scottish peasant told

That Rank is but the guinea stamp, the man himself's the gold.

With us the rich and poor unite and equal Rights maintain

Happy to meet, sorry to part, happy to meet again!

Dear Brethren of the Mystic Tie, the night is waning fast

Our Duty's done, our feast is o'er, this song must be our last: —

Good Night, Good Night—once more, once more, repeat the farewell strain

Happy to meet, sorry to part, happy to meet again!

RUDYARD KIPLING, POET OF FREEMASONRY

ORN IN BOMBAY, INDIA, ON DECEMBER 30, 1865, JOSEPH
Rudyard Kipling became the most famous Freemason of the late
nineteenth and early twentieth centuries.
Of his Masonic life in "Something of Myself" he wrote:

> In 1885, I was made a Freemason by dispensation (being under age) in
> The Lodge of Hope and Perseverance 782 E.C. because the Lodge
> hoped for a good Secretary. They did not get him, but I helped, and
> got Father to advise me in decorating the bare walls of the Masonic
> Hall with hangings after the prescription of King Solomon's Temple.
> Here I met Muslims, Hindus, Sikhs, members of the Araya and
> Brahmo Samaj, and a Jewish Tyler, who was a priest and butcher to
> his little community in the city. So yet another world was opened to
> me which I needed.

In a letter to the *Times* of London (March 28, 1935), he wrote:

> I was Secretary for some years of the Lodge of Hope and Perseverance
> No. 782, English Constitution which included Brethren of at least
> four different creeds. I was entered by a member of the Brahmo Samaj
> (a Hindu), passed by a Mohammedan, and raised by an Englishman.
> Our Tyler was an Indian Jew. We met, of course, on the level and the
> only difference that anyone would notice was that at our banquets
> some of the Brethren, who were debarred by caste rules from eating
> food not ceremoniously prepared, sat over empty plates.

Kipling received the mark Master degree in a Lahore Mark Lodge and
affiliated with a Craft Lodge in Allahabad, Bengal. Later, in England he

affiliated as an honorary member of the Motherland Lodge No. 3861 in London and was a member of the Authors' Lodge No. 3456 and a founder-member of the Lodge Builders of the Silent Cities No. 4948. Another association was formed when he became poet laureate of the Canongate Kilwinning No. 2 in Edinburgh, a lodge of which Robert Burns is said to have served in the same office. He would later accept a fellowship in the Philalethes Society (an organization of Masonic writers formed in the United States in 1928). Before the original list of forty fellows was closed in 1932, he was proposed as the fortieth. When the secretary wrote to advise him that they wished to honor the author of "My Mother Lodge," "The Man Who Would Be King," and other Masonic stories, Kipling accepted.

A Kipling biographer writes, "Freemasonry, with its cult of common action, its masculine self-sufficiency, its language of symbols, and its hierarchy of secret grades, provided him with a natural setting for his social ideals."

On Kipling's first trip to the United States in 1889, he made use of Masonic letters of introductions, including meeting and becoming a friend of Theodore Roosevelt, then serving on the federal Civil Service Commission.

Kipling's Masonic interest is exhibited in three wholly Masonic poems: "The Mother Lodge," "Banquet Night," and "In the Interests of the Brethren." In the story "The Man Who Would Be King," two vagabonds, Daniel Dravot and Peachy Carnegan, went on an expedition in Afghanistan, where they found Masonic practices among the natives and used Freemasonry to further their designs for power, only to meet ultimate disaster from which only one returned, maimed, disfigured, and demented and carrying the shrunken head of his comrade. He relates having found crude mountain tribesmen knowledgeable of the entered apprentice and fellowcraft degrees but ignorant of the Masonic master degree. Dravot then concocted the devious scheme of using the sublime degree as an instrument for control. He declared himself grand master of all Freemasonry in Karfiristan and king of Karfiristan.

A Masonic student of Kipling observed, "Kipling seems ever-ready to insert, often in an incidental manner, Masonic allusions suggested by the ritual, terminology and symbols with which he was so intimately acquainted, and which had become embedded in his mind. The interested reader, who is persistent, will find more of such." Sir George MacMunn wrote that Kipling "uses Masonry in much the same way he uses the Holy Writ, for the beauty of the story, for the force of the reference, and for the dignity, beauty, and assertiveness of the phrase. There is one more effect that familiarity denies us which is present in the Masonic allusion and that is the almost uncanny hint of something unveiled."

"The Mother Lodge"

There was Rundle, Station Master,
An' Beazeley of the Rail,
An' 'Ackman, Commissariat,
An' Donkin' o' the Jail;
An' Blake, Conductor-Sergeant,
Our Master twice was 'e,
With 'im that kept the Europe-shop,
Old Framjee Eduljee.

Outside—"Sergeant! Sir! Salute! Salaam!"
Inside—"Brother", an' it doesn't do no 'arm.
We met upon the Level an' we parted on the Square,
An' I was Junior Deacon in my Mother-Lodge out there!
We'd Bola Nath, Accountant,
An' Saul the Aden Jew,
An' Din Mohammed, draughtsman
Of the Survey Office too;

There was Babu Chuckerbutty,
An' Amir Singh the Sikh,
An' Castro from the fittin'-sheds,
The Roman Catholick!
We 'adn't good regalia,
An' our Lodge was old an' bare,

But we knew the Ancient Landmarks,
An' we kep' 'em to a hair;

An' lookin' on it backwards
It often strikes me thus,
There ain't such things as infidels,
Excep', per'aps, it's us.
For monthly, after Labour,
We'd all sit down and smoke
(We dursn't give no banquits,
Lest a Brother's caste were broke),

An' man on man got talkin'
Religion an' the rest,
An' every man comparin'
Of the God 'e knew the best.
So man on man got talkin',
An' not a Brother stirred
Till mornin' waked the parrots
An' that dam' brain-fever-bird;

We'd say 'twas 'ighly curious,
An' we'd all ride 'ome to bed,
With Mo'ammed, God, an' Shiva
Changin' pickets in our 'ead.
Full oft on Guv'ment service
This rovin' foot 'ath pressed,
An' bore fraternal greetin's
To the Lodges east an' west,

Accordin' as commanded
From Kohat to Singapore,
But I wish that I might see them
In my Mother-Lodge once more!
I wish that I might see them,

My Brethren black an' brown,
With the trichies smellin' pleasant
An' the hog-darn passin' down; [Cigar-lighter.]

An' the old khansamah snorin' [Butler.]
On the bottle-khana floor, [Pantry.]
Like a Master in good standing
With my Mother-Lodge once more!
Outside—"Sergeant! Sir! Salute! Salaam!"
Inside—"Brother", an' it doesn't do no 'arm.
We met upon the Level an' we parted on the Square,
An' I was Junior Deacon in my Mother-Lodge out there!

L' Envoi to "Life's Handicap"

My new-cut ashlar [stone] takes the light
Where crimson-blank the windows flare;
By my own work, before the night,
Great Overseer I make my prayer.

If there be good in that I wrought,
Thy hand compelled it, Master, Thine;
Where I have failed to meet Thy thought
I know, through Thee, the blame is mine.

One instant's toil to Thee denied
Stands all Eternity's offence,
Of that I did with Thee to guide
To Thee, through Thee, be excellence.

Who, lest all thought of Eden fade,
Bring'st Eden to the craftsman's brain,
Godlike to muse o'er his own trade
And Manlike stand with God again.

The depth and dream of my desire,
The bitter paths wherein I stray,
Thou knowest Who hast made the Fire,
Thou knowest Who hast made the Clay!

One stone the more swings to her place
In that dread Temple of Thy Worth—
It is enough that through Thy grace
I saw naught common on Thy earth.

Take not that vision from my ken;
Oh whatsoe'er may spoil or speed,
Help me to need no aid from men
That I may help such men as need!

"The Palace"

When I was a King and a Mason—a Master proven and skilled—
I cleared me ground for a Palace such as a King should build.
I decreed and dug down to my levels. Presently, under the silt,
I came on the wreck of a Palace such as a King had built.

There was no worth in the fashion—there was no wit in the plan—
Hither and thither, aimless, the ruined footings ran—
Masonry, brute, mishandled, but carven on every stone:
"After me cometh a Builder. Tell him, I too have known."

Swift to my use in my trenches, where my well-planned ground-works grew,
I tumbled his quoins and his ashlars, and cut and reset them anew.
Lime I milled of his marbles; burned it, slacked it, and spread;
Taking and leaving at pleasure the gifts of the humble dead.

Yet I despised not nor gloried; yet, as we wrenched them apart,
I read in the razed foundations the heart of that builder's heart.

As he had risen and pleaded, so did I understand
The form of the dream he had followed in the face of the thing he had
  planned.

When I was a King and a Mason—in the open noon of my pride,
They sent me a Word from the Darkness. They whispered and called me
  aside.
They said—"The end is forbidden." They said—"Thy use is fulfilled,
Thy Palace shall stand as that other's—the spoil of a King who shall build."

I called my men from my trenches, my quarries, my wharves, and my sheers.
All I had wrought I abandoned to the faith of the faithless years.
Only I cut on the timber—only I carved on the stone:
"After me cometh a Builder. Tell him, I too have known!"

"Banquet Night"

"Once in so often," King Solomon said,
Watching his quarrymen drill the stone,
"We will club our garlic and wine and bread
And banquet together beneath my throne.
And all the Brethren shall come to that mess
As Fellow Craftsmen—no more and no less."

"Send a swift shallop to Hiram of Tyre,
Felling and floating our beautiful trees,
Say that the brethren and I desire
Talk with our Brethren who use the seas.
And we shall be happy to meet them at mess
As Fellow Craftsmen—no more and no less."

"Carry this message to Hiram Abiff—
Excellent Master of forge and mine:
I and the Brethren would like it if

He and the Brethren will come to dine
(Garments from Bozrah or morning-dress)
As Fellow Craftsmen—no more and no less."

"God gave the Hyssop and Cedar their place—
Also the Bramble, the Fig and the Thorn—
But that is no reason to black a man's face
Because he is not what he hasn't been born.
And, as touching the Temple, I hold and profess
We are Fellow Craftsmen—no more no less."

So it was ordered and so it was done,
And the hewers of wood and the Masons of Mark
With foc'sle hands of the Sidon run
And Navy Lords from the Royal Ark,
Came and sat down and were merry at mess
As Fellow Craftsmen—no more and no less.

The Quarries are hotter than Hiram's forge,
No one is safe from the dog-whips' reach.
It's mostly snowing up Lebanon gorge,
And it's always blowing off Joppa beach;
But once in so often, the messenger brings
Solomon's mandate: "Forget these things!
Brother to Beggars and Fellow to Kings,
Companion of Princes—forget these things!
Fellow Craftsman, forget these things!"

THE ANDERSON CONSTITUTIONS

THE CONSTITUTIONS OF THE FREEMASONS. CONTAINING the History, Charges, Regulations, etc., of that most Ancient and Right Worshipful Fraternity, for the Use of the Lodges. Dedicated to his Grace the Duke of Montagu the last Grand Master, by Order of his Grace the Duke of Wharton the present Grand Master, authorized by the Grand Lodge of Masters and Wardens at the Quarterly Communication. Order'd to be publish'd and recommended to the Brethren by the Grand Master and his Deputy. Printed in the Year of Masonry 5723; of our Lord 1723. Sold by J. Senex and J. Hooke, both over against S. Dunstan's Church in Fleetstreet. THE ANCIENT CHARGES OF A FREE MASON Extracted from the Ancient Records of Lodges beyond the Sea, and of those in England, Scotland, and Ireland, for the use of the Lodges in London. To be read at the making of New Brethren, or when the Master shall order it.

THE GENERAL HEADS

I. Of God and Religion.

II. Of the Civil Magistrate, supreme and subordinate.

III. Of Lodges.

IV. Of Masters, Wardens, Fellows and Apprentices.

V. Of the Management of the Craft in working.

VI. Of Behaviour, viz.:

1. In the Lodge while constituted.

2. After the Lodge is over and the Brethren not gone.

3. When Brethren meet without Strangers, but not in a Lodge.

4. In Presence of Strangers not Masons.

5. At Home and in the Neighbourhood.

6. Toward a strange Brother.

I. Concerning God and Religion A Mason is oblig'd by his Tenure, to obey the moral law; and if he rightly understands the Art, he will never be a stupid Atheist nor an irreligious Libertine. But though in ancient Times Masons were charg'd in every Country to be of the Religion of that Country or Nation, whatever it was, yet 'tis now thought more expedient only to oblige them to that Religion in which all Men agree, leaving their particular Opinions to themselves; that is, to be good Men and true, or Men of Honour and Honesty, by whatever Denominations or Persuasions they may be distinguish'd; whereby Masonry becomes the Centre of Union, and the Means of conciliating true Friendship among Persons that must have remain'd at a perpetual Distance.

II. Of the Civil Magistrate Supreme and Subordinate A Mason is a peaceable Subject to the Civil Powers, wherever he resides or works, and is never to be concern'd in Plots and Conspiracies against the Peace and Welfare of the Nation, nor to behave himself undutifully to inferior Magistrates; for as Masonry hath been always injured by War, Bloodshed, and Confusion, so ancient Kings and Princes have been much dispos'd to encourage the Craftsmen, because of their Peaceableness and Loyalty, whereby they practically answer'd the Cavils of their Adversaries, and promoted the Honour of the Fraternity, who ever flourish'd in Time of Peace. So that if a Brother should be a Rebel against the State he is not to be countenanced in his Rebellion, however he may be pitied as any unhappy Man; and, if convicted of no other Crime though the Loyal Brotherhood must and ought to disown his Rebellion, and give no Umbrage or Ground of political Jealousy to the Government for the time being, they cannot expel him from the Lodge, and his Relation to it remains indefeasible.

Ill. Of Lodges A Lodge is a place where Masons assemble and work; Hence that Assembly, or duly organized Society of Masons, is call'd a Lodge, and every Brother ought to belong to one, and to be subject to its By-Laws and the General Regulations. It is either particular or general, and will be best understood by attending it, and by the Regulations of the General or Grand Lodge hereunto annex'd. In ancient Times, no Master or Fellow could be absent from it especially when warned to appear at it, without incurring a sever Censure, until it appear'd to the Master and Wardens that pure Necessity hinder'd him. The persons admitted Members of a Lodge must be good and true Men, free-born, and of mature and discreet Age, no Bondmen no Women, no immoral or scandalous men, but of good Report.

IV. Of Masters, Wardens, Follows and Apprentices All preferment among Masons is grounded upon real Worth and personal Merit only; that so the Lords may be well served, the Brethren not put to Shame, nor the Royal Craft despis'd: Therefore no Master or Warden is chosen by Seniority, but for his Merit. It is impossible to describe these things in Writing, and every Brother must attend in his Place, and learn them in a Way peculiar to this Fraternity: Only Candidates may know that no Master should take an Apprentice unless he has Sufficient Imployment for him, and unless he be a perfect Youth having no Maim or Defects in his Body that may render him uncapable of learning the Art of serving his Master's Lord, and of being made a Brother, and then a Fellow-Craft in due Time, even after he has served such a Term of Years as the Custom of the Country directs; and that he should be descended of honest Parents; that so, when otherwise qualifi'd he may arrive to the Honour of being the Warden, and then the Master of the Lodge, the Grand Warden, and at length the Grand Master of all the Lodges, according to his Merit. No Brother can be a Warden until he has pass'd the part of a Fellow-Craft; nor a Master until he has acted as a Warden, nor Grand Warden until he has been Master of a Lodge, nor Grand Master unless he has been a Fellow Craft before his Election, who is also to be nobly born, or a Gentleman of the best Fashion, or some eminent Scholar, or some curious Architect, or other Artist, descended of honest Parents, and who is of similar great Merit in the Opinion of the Lodges. And for the better, and easier, and more honourable Discharge of his Office, the Grand Master has the Power to chuse his own Deputy Grand Master, who must be then, or must have been formerly, the Master of a particular Lodge, and has the Privilege of acting whatever the Grand Master, his Principal should act; unless the said Principal be present, or interpose his Authority by a Letter. These Rulers and Governors, supreme and subordinate, of the ancient Lodge, are to be obey'd in their respective Stations by all the Brethren, according to the old Charges and Regulations, with all Humility, Reverence, Love and Alacrity.

V. Of the Management of the Craft in Working All Masons shall work honestly on Working Days, that they may live creditably on Holy Days; and the time appointed by the Law of the Land or confirm'd by Custom shall be observ'd. The most expert of the Fellow-Craftsmen shall be chosen or appointed the Master or Overseer of the Lord's Work; who is to be call'd Master by those that work under him. The Craftsmen are to avoid all ill Language, and to call each other by no disobliging Name, but Brother or Fellow; and to behave themselves courteously within and without the Lodge. The Master, knowing himself to be able of Cunning, shall undertake the Lord's Work as reasonably as possible, and truly dispend his Goods as if they were his own; nor to give more Wages to any Brother or Apprentice than he really may deserve. Both the Master and the Masons receiving their Wages justly, shall be faithful to the Lord and honestly finish their Work, whether Task or journey; nor put the work to Task that hath been accustomed to Journey. None shall discover Envy at the Prosperity of a Brother, nor supplant him, or put him out of his Work, if he be capable to finish the same; for no man can finish another's Work so much to the Lord's Profit, unless he be thoroughly acquainted with the Designs and Draughts of him that began it. When a Fellow-Craftsman is chosen Warden of the Work under the Master, he shall be true both to Master and Fellows, shall carefully oversee the Work in the Master's Absence to the Lord's profit; and his Brethren shall obey him. All Masons employed shall meekly receive their Wages without Murmuring or Mutiny, and not desert the Master till the Work is finish'd. A younger Brother shall be instructed in working, to prevent spoiling the Materials for want of Judgment, and for increasing and continuing of brotherly love. All the Tools used in working shall be approved by the Grand Lodge. No Labourer shall be employ'd in the proper Work of Masonry; nor shall Free Masons work with those that are not free, without an urgent Necessity; nor shall they teach Labourers and unaccepted Masons as they should teach a Brother or Fellow.

VI. Of Behaviour

1. IN THE LODGE WHILE CONSTITUTED You are not to hold private Committees, or separate Conversation without Leave from the Master, nor to talk of anything impertinent or unseemly, nor interrupt the Master or Wardens, or any Brother speaking to the Master: Nor be-

have yourself ludicrously or jestingly while the Lodge is engaged in what is serious and solemn; nor use any unbecoming Language upon any Pretense whatsoever; but to pay due Reverence to your Master, Wardens, and Fellows, and put them to Worship. If any Complaint be brought, the Brother found guilty shall stand to the Award and Determination of the Lodge, who are the proper and competent Judges of all such Controversies (unless you carry it by Appeal to the Grand Lodge), and to whom they ought to be referr'd, unless a Lord's Work be hinder'd the meanwhile, in which Case a particular Reference may be made; but you must never go to Law about what concerneth Masonry, without an absolute necessity apparent to the Lodge.

2. BEHAVIOUR AFTER THE LODGE IS OVER AND THE BRETHREN NOT GONE You may enjoy yourself with innocent Mirth, treating one another according to Ability, but avoiding all Excess, or forcing any Brother to eat or drink beyond his Inclination, or hindering him from going when his Occasions call him, or doing or saying anything offensive, or that may forbid an easy and free Conversation, for that would blast our Harmony, and defeat our laudable Purposes. Therefore no private Piques or Quarrels must be brought within the Door of the Lodge, far less any Quarrels about Religion, or Nations, or State Policy, we being only, as Masons, of the Catholick Religion above mention'd, we are also of all Nations, Tongues, Kindreds, and Languages, and are resolv'd against all Politics, as what never yet conduct'd to the Welfare of the Lodge, nor ever will. This charge has been strictly enjoin'd and obser'd; but especially ever since the Reformation in Britain, or the Dissent and Secession of these Nations from the Communion of Rome.

3. BEHAVIOUR WHEN BRETHREN MEET WITHOUT STRANGERS, BUT NOT IN A LODGE FORMED You are to salute one another in a courteous Manner, as you will be instructed, calling each other Brother, freely giving mutual instruction as shall be thought expedient, without being ever seen or overheard, and without encroaching upon each other, or derogating from that Respect which is due to any Brother, were he not Mason: For though all Masons are as Brethren upon the same Level, yet Masonry takes no Honour from a man that he had before; nay,

rather it adds to his Honour, especially if he has deserve well of the Brotherhood, who must give Honour to whom it is due, and avoid ill Manners.

4. BEHAVIOUR IN PRESENCE OF STRANGERS NOT MASONS You shall be cautious in your Words and Carriage, that the most penetrating Stranger shall not be able to discover or find out what is not proper to be intimated, and sometimes you shall divert a Discourse, and manage it prudently for the Honour of the worshipful Fraternity.

5. BEHAVIOUR AT HOME, AND IN YOUR NEIGHBOURHOOD You are to act as becomes a moral and wise Man; particularly not to let your Family, Friends and Neighbours know the Concern of the Lodge, &c., but wisely to consult your own Honour, and that of the ancient Brotherhood, for reasons not to be mention'd here You must also consult your Health, by not continuing together too late, or too long from Home, after Lodge Hours are past; and by avoiding of Gluttony or Drunkenness, that your Families be not neglected or injured, nor you disabled from working.

6. BEHAVIOUR TOWARDS A STRANGE BROTHER You are cautiously to examine him, in such a Method as Prudence shall direct you, that you may not be impos'd upon by an ignorant, false Pretender, whom you are to reject with contempt and Derision, and beware of giving him any Hints of Knowledge. But if you discover him to be a true and genuine Brother, you are to respect him accordingly; and if he is in Want, you must relieve him if you can, or else direct him how he may be relieved; you must employ him some days, or else recommend him to be employ'd. But you are not charged to do beyond your ability, only to prefer a poor Brother, that is a good Man and true before any other poor People in the same Circumstance. Finally, All these Charges you are to observe, and also those that shall be recommended to you in another Way; cultivating Brotherly Love, the Foundation and Cap-stone, the Cement and Glory of this Ancient Fraternity, avoiding all wrangling and quarreling, all Slander and Backbiting, nor permitting others to slander any honest Brother, but defending his Character, and doing him all good Offices, as far as is consistent with your Honour and Safety, and no farther. And if any of them do you Injury you must apply to your own or his Lodge, and from thence

you may appeal to the Grand Lodge, at the Quarterly Communication and from thence to the annual Grand Lodge, as has been the ancient laudable Conduct but when the Case cannot be otherwise decided, and patiently listening to the honest and friendly Advice of Master and Fellows when they would prevent your going to Law with Strangers, or would excite you to put a speedy Period to all Lawsuits, so that you may mind the Affair of Masonry with the more Alacrity and Success; but with respect to Brothers or Fellows at Law, the Master and Brethren should kindly offer their Mediation, which ought to be thankfully submitted to by the contending Brethren; and if that submission is impracticable, they must, however, carry on their Process, or Lawsuit, without Wrath and Rancor (not In the common way) saying or doing nothing which may hinder Brotherly Love, and good Offices to be renew'd and continu'd; that all may see the benign Influence of Masonry, as all true Masons have done from the beginning of the World, and will do to the End of Time.

Amen, so mote it be.

MASONIC CHRONOLOGY

970-931 B.C. Building of Solomon's Temple in Jerusalem.

A.D. 936 Traditional date for meeting of Masons at York, England. Presided over by Edwin, mythical son of King Athelstan, it agreed on "certain Charges" for government of the brotherhood.

1095 Pope Urban II calls for liberation of Jerusalem from Muslims; beginning of the Crusades.

1118 Hugues de Payens, a knight of Burgundy, and Godefroid de St. Omer, a knight of southern France, take a vow of poverty and the name "Poor Knights of Christ and of the Temple of Solomon." Given sanction by the church in 1128 at the Council of Troyes, they are known as Knights Templar (Templars).

1147 The Ancient Stirling Lodge claims to represent Masons at work on construction of the Cambies Kenneth Abbey, founded by King David I of Scotland

1244 Birth of Jacques de Molay, Knights Templar martyr.

1307 Execution of de Molay, banning of Templars; they flee to Scotland.

1349-50 Wages of English Masons are regulated.

1356 Regulations of the Craft of Masons are said to have been ordained by the mayor, aldermen, and sheriffs of London.

1375 Masons' Company of London is represented on the Court of Common Council. Masons are known as "Ffreemasons" (double f).

1377 A free master Mason is denominated "Magister Operis" and employed at Merton College, Oxford.

1381 A royal proclamation prohibits chapters and congregations.

1390 Earliest ascribed date of the Regius manuscript (poem) containing Constitutions of Masonry.

1425 Congregations and chapters again prohibited and members are considered
      felons.
1430 Date ascribed to the Cooke manuscript containing Constitutions of
      German Masons.
1472 Grant of Arms to Masons' Company of London under title Whole Craft
      and Fellowship Masons.
1495 The word "Freemasons" first appears in Statutes of the Realm (Henry
      VII).
1537 The Masons' Company of London is described as the Company of Free-
      Masons.
1539 King Francis I of France attempts to ban Craft guilds.
1578 Account records of Corpus Christi College, Oxford, distinguish between
      "rough" and "free masons."
1598 Promulgation of Statutes of William ("Schaw") Shaw, "being Codes and
      Laws" for the Craft in general and in particular the Lodge of Kilwinning
      (called "Head Lodge"), giving it precedence to some Masons over Mary's
      Chapel, Edinburgh, Scotland, known as "Principal Lodge," whose lodge
      records began in 1599.
1600 The word "Freemason" appears in a York roll. A Masonic convention is
      held in Janaury at St. Andrews, Scotland.
1604 Incorporation of the Company of Freemasons, Carpenters, Joiners, and
      Slaters in the City of Oxford, England.
1646 Elias Ashmole and other candidates are initiated in Lancashire, England,
      signifying the opening of Masonry to nonstoneworkers and a shift of em-
      phasis from operative to speculative.
1655–56 The Company of Freemasons becomes the Worshipful Company of
      Masons of London.
1691 Founding of the Goose and Gridiron Lodge, St. Paul's Churchyard,
      London.
1705 Presumed date of earliest Roll of Masons belonging to Ancient York
      Lodge, England.
1717 Combined meeting of London lodges at the Apple Tree tavern creates the
      Grand Lodge of England; considered the beginning of present-day Masonry.
1718 Several ancient constitutions collected and collated (England); introduc-
      tion of Masonry to France.

1720 The "Generals Regulations" compiled by London grand master John
       Payne.

1721 John, duke of Montague, elected grand master of Mason lodges in
       England.

1721 Grand Lodge of London commissions James Anderson to digest and pro-
       duce a new and better constitution; duke of Montagu appoints a commis-
       sion of fourteen brothers to report on what becomes known as the
       "Anderson Constitutions."

1722 The Anderson Constitutions are ordered printed.

1723 Degrees of speculative Masonry (entered apprentice, fellowcraft, and mas-
       ter) are recognized by the Grand Lodge of London.

1714 Publication of *The Secret History of Freemasons*.

1725 Formation of Grand Lodge of All England at York.

1729 An Engraved List enumerates fifty-four lodges (forty-two in London).

1729 First speculative lodge in Scotland (Edinburgh, Kilwinning).

1730 Tract entitled "Masonry Dissected" advertised; refuted in "A Defence of
       Masonry."

1731 Founding of a lodge in Philadelphia, Pennsylvania; Benjamin Franklin
       eventually joins.

1733 Opening of Lodge of St. John, Boston, Massachusetts; warrant granted to
       Henry Price.

1735 Second edition of the Anderson Constitutions; Lodge of Solomon formed
       in Charleston, South Carolina.

1736 Institution of Grand Lodge of Scotland and First Grand Lodge of France.

1737 Chevalier Ramsay delivers historic "Oration" in Paris.

1738 A master's lodge is established in Boston; the second edition of the
       Anderson Constitutions is approved by the Grand Lodge of England;
       Pope Clement XII condemns Freemasonry.

1739 Death of James Anderson.

1740 "Scots Degrees" appear in France; Philip V of Spain issues anti-Masonry
       edict; Royal Order of Scotland instituted.

1741 Earliest lodge in Virginia founded in Norfolk by Cornelius Hartnett.

1743 First military lodge formed under Grand Lodge of Scotland.

1749 Benjamin Franklin appointed provincial grand master, Pennsylvania.

1751 Schismatic Grand Lodge of England formed.

1752 George Washington initiated in Fredericksburg Lodge, Virginia (November 4).

1758 Lodges under the Obedience of the Ancients flourish in Philadelphia, replace "Moderns."

1760 Lodge of St. Andrew (Ancients) receives Scottish Warrant.

1764 A work entitled *Hiram, or the Grand Master-key* published in London.

1766 Thirty English lodges operating in the "Province of America" outside Boston.

1769 Degrees of excellent mason, super excellent mason, and knight templar conferred by Royal Arch Chapter of St. Andrew, Scotland.

1770 Stephen Morin creates Council of Princes of the Royal Secret, Kingston, Jamaica.

1772 Dr. Joseph Warren appointed grand master for the "Continent of America."

1773 Freemasons take part in the Boston Tea Party; Grand Orient of France founded.

1775 Joseph Warren killed at Battle of Bunker Hill.

1776 Fifteen Freemasons sign the Declaration of Independence.

1776–81 American War of Independence; half the generals and numerous soldiers in George Washington's army are Freemasons, including the Marquis de Lafayette and Baron von Steuben.

1780 Freemason Benedict Arnold conspires with the British to surrender West Point.

1781 Foundation of Grand Lodge in New York City.

1790 Grand Lodge of All England (Ancient York Rite) becomes extinct; thirteen lodges operating in the United States.

1789 George Washington takes oath as first president of the United States on a Bible provided by the New York Lodge; death of Benjamin Franklin.

1791 Production of Wolfgang Amadeus Mozart's opera *The Magic Flute*; Freemasons suspected in Mozart's death; founding of African Grand Lodge of North America with former slave Prince Hall as grand master. (Beginning of "Prince Hall Masonry.")

1793 George Washington lays cornerstone of U.S. Capitol in Masonic ceremony.

1799   British Parliament bans secret societies, except Freemasons; George Washington given a Masonic funeral.

1801   Formation of Supreme Council of the Ancient and Accepted Scottish Rite, Charleston, South Carolina.

1809   Birth of Albert Pike.

1813   Establishment of the Supreme Council of the Northern Jurisdiction, USA; English Masons end the schism of Antients and Moderns, form a single body: United Grand Lodge.

1814   Pope Pius VII renews the bull of Pope Clement XII against Freemasonry.

1816   Grand Encampment of Knights Templar established in the United States.

1826   The kidnaping and (supposed) murder of William Morgan in Batavia, New York, by a group of Masons in an attempt to stop Morgan from publishing an exposé of Masonry triggers a wave of anti-Masonry and the formation of the Anti-Mason Party, the first third party in U.S. political history

1843   A National Masonic Convention is held in Baltimore.

1849   Pope Pius IX issues an encyclical against secret societies, including Freemasonry.

1853   A Congress of American Lodges is held in Lexington, Kentucky.

1859   Albert Pike elected sovereign grand commander of the Supreme Council, (Southern Jurisdiction); he revises Old Constitutions and publishes *Morals and Dogmas of the Ancient and Accepted Scottish Rite of Freemasonry.*

1861–65   U.S. Civil War; numerous stories of Freemasons on each side aiding a wounded or dying brother.

1896   Masonic conference held at the Hague, Netherlands; Anti-Masonic Conference, Trent.

1917   Grand Lodge of England marks 200th anniversary of Freemasonry.

1975   Publication of *Jack the Ripper: The Final Solution* by Stephen Knight, alleging that the murder of prostitutes in London in 1888 was a Masonic plot; Knight continued to attack Masonry in 1985 with *The Brotherhood: The Secret World of the Freemasons.*

1991   Television evangelist Pat Robertson and others accuse Freemasons of being anti-Christian and a leading force in seeking to establish a "new world order."

1999 Members of Britain's Parliament call for restrictions on Freemasons in
      government and the police force to reveal their membership.
2004 American Freemasonry expresses concerns about a continuing decline in
      membership. Roman Catholics remain banned by the church from mem-
      bership.

FAMOUS MASONS

Abbott, Sir John J. C.—Prime minister of Canada (1891–1892)
Aldrin, Jr., Edwin E. "Buzz"—Astronaut
Alves, Antônio de Castro—Latin American poet
Amundsen, Roald—Norwegian polar explorer
Armistead, Lewis A.—Confederate General
Armstrong, Louis—Jazz musician
Armstrong, Neil—Astronaut
Arnold, Benedict—American general
Arnold, Henry "Hap"—Commander of the Army Air Force
Astor, John Jacob—German American merchant and financier
Austin, Stephen F.—Father of Texas
Autry, Gene—Actor
Bach, Johann Christian—Musician/composer
Baldwin, Henry—Supreme Court justice
Balfour, Lloyd—Jeweler
Banks, Sir Joseph—English scientist
Bartholdi, Frederic A.—Designed the Statue of Liberty
Bassie, William "Count"—Orchestra leader/composer
Baylor, Robert E. B.—Founder of Baylor University
Beard, Daniel Carter—Founder of the Boy Scouts
Bell, Lawrence—Founder of Bell Aircraft Corporation
Benes, Eduard—President of Czechoslovakia (1935–1938, 1946–1948)
Bennett, Viscount R. B.—Prime Minister of Canada (1930–1935)
Berlin, Irving—Songwriter
Berzelius, Jöns Jakob, Baron—Swedish chemist, considered a founder of modern
    chemistry
Bingham, Henry H.—Union captain
Bishop, Sir Henry—Musician
Black, Hugo L.—Supreme Court justice
Blair John, Jr.—Supreme Court justice
Blatchford, Samuel—Supreme Court justice
Bolívar, Simon—"Liberator" of South America
Borden, Sir Robert L.—Prime minister of Canada (1911–1920)

Bordet, Jules Jean Baptiste Vincent—Belgian bacteriologist and Nobel laureate;
    developed whooping cough vaccine
Borglum, Gutzon (father) and Lincoln (son)—Sculpters who carved Mount
    Rushmore
Borgnine, Ernest—Actor
Boswell, James—Eighteenth-century Scottish writer
Bowell, Sir Mackenzie—Prime minister of Canada (1894–1896)
Bowie, James—American pioneer, killed while defending the Alamo
Bradley, Omar N.—General, commanded troops at Normandy on D day
Brant, Joseph—Chief of the Mohawks (1742–1807)
Buchanan, James—Fifteenth president of the United States (1857–1861)
Burbank, Luther—American horticulturist and botanist
Burke, Edmund—Irish-born British politician and writer
Burnett, David G.—First president of the Republic of Texas
Burns, Robert—The national poet of Scotland
Burr, Aaron—Third vice president of the United States (1801–1805)
Burton, Harold H.—Supreme Court justice
Burton, Sir Richard—English explorer
Byrd, Admiral Richard E.—Explorer, flew over North Pole
Byrnes, James F.—Supreme Court justice
Calvo, Father Francisco—Catholic priest who started Freemasonry in Costa
    Rica (1865)
Canning, George—British prime minister (1827)
Cantor, Eddie—Entertainer
Carson, Christopher "Kit"—Frontiersman, scout, and explorer
Casanova—Italian adventurer, writer, and entertainer
Catron, John—Supreme Court justice
Chrysler, Walter P.—Automobile manufacturer
Churchill, Lord Randolph—British politician and father of Winston
Churchill, Winston—British prime minister (1940–1945 and 1951–1955)
Citroen, Andre—French engineer and motor car manufacturer
Clark, Roy—Country Western star
Clark, Thomas C.—Supreme Court justice
Clark, William—Explorer (Lewis and Clark expedition)
Clarke, John H.—Supreme Court justice
Clemens, Samuel L. (Mark Twain)—writer/humorist
Clinton, DeWitt—Governor of New York
Cobb, Ty—Baseball player
Cody, "Buffalo Bill" William—Indian fighter, Wild West Show
Cohan, George M.—Playwright, composer, producer, and actor
Cole, Nat "King"—Singer
Collodi, Carlo—Creator of "Pinocchio"

Colt, Samuel—Inventor of the revolving pistol
Combs, Earle Bryan—Baseball Hall of Fame
Cooper, Leroy Gordon, Jr.—Astronaut
Craig, Malin—General during World War I
Crockett, Davy—Frontiersman and Alamo hero
Cushing, William—Supreme Court justice
Davis, David—Supreme Court justice
DeMille, Cecil B.—Motion picture producer/director
Dempsey, Jack—Heavyweight champion
Desaguliers, John Theophilus—Inventor of the planetarium
Devanter, Willis Van—Supreme Court justice
Dewey, Thomas Edmund—Governor of New York, defeated by Harry S
    Truman for presidency (1948)
Diefenbaker, John G.—Prime minister of Canada (1957–1963)
Dole, Robert—U.S. senator, vice presidential candidate 1976, presidential can-
    didate, 1996
Doolittle, General James—Aviation hero, led first U.S. air raid on Japan in
    World War II
Douglas, William O.—Supreme Court justice
Dow, William H.—Founder of the Dow Chemical Company
Doyle, Sir Author Conan—Author and creator of "Sherlock Holmes"
Drake, Edwin L—American pioneer of the oil industry
Du Bois, W. E. B.—Educator and scholar
Dunant, Jean Henri—Founder of the Red Cross
Edward VII—King of England (1901–1910)
Edward VIII—King of England (1936), abdicated
Eiffel, Gustave Alexandre—French engineer and builder of the Eiffel Tower
Eisele, Donn Fulton—Astronaut
Ellington, Duke—Jazz pioneer and composer
Ellsworth, Oliver—Supreme Court chief justice
Ervin, Samuel J. Jr.—Headed "Watergate" investigating committee
Faber, Eberhard—Head of the Eberhard Faber Pencil Company
Fairbanks, Douglas—Actor
Feller, Bob—Baseball pitcher famous for his fastball
Field, Stephen J.—Supreme Court justice
Fields, W. C.—Comedian
Fisher, Geoffrey—Archbishop of Canterbury (1945–1961)
Fitch, John—Inventor of the steamboat
Fleming, Sir Alexander—Invented penicillin
Ford, Gerald R.—Thirty-eighth president of the United States (1974–1977)
Ford, Henry—Pioneer automobile manufacturer
Franklin, Benjamin—Inventor and signer of the U.S. Constitution

Gable, Clark—Actor
Garfield, James A.—Twentieth president of the United States (1881)
Garibaldi, Giuseppe—Italian nationalist revolutionary
Gatling, Richard J.—Inventor of the Gatling gun
George VI—King of Great Britain during World War II
Gershwin, George—Composer
Gibbon, Edward—Writer, *Decline and Fall of the Roman Empire*
Gilbert, Sir William S.—Operetta librettist (Gilbert and Sullivan)
Gillette, King C.—Founder of the Gillette Razor Company
Glenn, John H.—First American to orbit Earth
Godfrey, Arthur—Entertainer
Goethe, Johann Wolfgang von—Poet, dramatist, novelist, and scientist
Goldwater, Barry—U.S. senator and Republican presidential candidate, 1964
Gompers, Samuel—Labor leader
Gray, Harold Lincoln—Creator of *Little Orphan Annie*
Grissom, Virgil I.—Astronaut
Guillotin, Joseph Ignace—Inventor of the guillotine
Hancock, John—Signer of the Declaration of Independence
Harding, Warren G.—Twenty-ninth president of the United States (1921–1923)
Harlan, John Marshall—Supreme Court justice
Hardy, Oliver—Actor and Comedian ("Laurel and Hardy")
Harlan, John M.—Supreme Court justice
Haydn, Franz Joseph—Composer
Hedges, Cornelius—"Father" of Yellowstone National Park
Heine, Heinrich—Poet
Henson, Reverend Josiah—Inspired the novel *Uncle Tom's Cabin*
Hilton, Charles C.—American hotelier
Hoban, James—Architect of the U.S. Capitol
Hoe, Richard M.—Invented the rotary press
Hogarth, William—English artist
Hoover, J. Edgar—Director of the Federal Bureau of Investigation
Hope, Bob—Comedian
Hornsby, Rogers—An original member of the Baseball Hall of Fame
Houdini, Harry—Magician
Houston, Sam—Second and fourth president of the Republic of Texas
Humphrey, Hubert Horatio, Jr.—Thirty-eighth vice president of the United
    States (1965–1969)
Irving, Sir Henry—English actor
Irwin, James B.—Astronaut
Ives, Burl—Singer
Jackson, Andrew—Seventh president of the United States (1829–1837)
Jackson, Jesse—Civil rights leader

Jackson, Robert H.—Supreme Court justice
Jay, John—Supreme Court chief justice
Jenner, Edward—Inventor of smallpox vaccine
Johnson, Andrew—Seventeenth president of the United States (1865–1869)
Johnson, Jack—American boxer, "The Great White Hope"
Johnson, Lyndon B.—Thirty-sixth president of the United States (1963–1969)
Jolson, Al—Singer
Jones, Anson—Fifth president of the Republic of Texas
Jones, John Paul—U.S. naval hero during the Revolutionary War
Juarez, Benito—President of Mexico (1861–1863 and 1867–1872)
Kalakaua, David—King of the Hawaiian Islands
Kean, Edmund—English actor
Kefauver, Carey Estes—U.S. senator and presidential candidate, 1952, 1956
Kemp, Jack—Quarterback (Buffalo Bills) and vice presidential candidate, 1996
Key, Francis Scott—Wrote "The Star-Spangled Banner," U.S. National Anthem
King, Ernest J.—Commanded the U.S. naval fleet during World War II
Kipling, Rudyard—Writer
Kossuth, Lajos—Hungarian patriot and statesman
Lafayette, Marquis de—French officer during the American Revolution
LaGuardia, Fiorello—Mayor of New York City (1933–1947)
Lamar, Joseph R.—Supreme Court justice
Lamar, Mirabeau B.—Third president of the Republic of Texas
Land, Frank S.—Founder of the Masonic Order of DeMolay
Landon, Alfred M.—Governor of Kansas and presidential candidate, 1936
Lessing, Gotthold Ephraim—German dramatist
Lewis, John L.—Labor leader
Lewis, Meriwether—Explorer (Lewis and Clark)
Lincoln, Elmo—First actor to play Tarzan of the Apes (1918)
Lindbergh, Charles—Aviator
Lipton, Sir Thomas—Tea merchant
Liszt, Franz—Pianist and composer, inventor of the solo piano recital
Livingston, Robert—Co-negotiator of the purchase of Louisiana Territory
Lloyd, Harold C.—Entertainer
MacArthur, Douglas—Commander of the U.S. Armed Forces in the Pacific in
    World War II and in the Korean War
MacDonald, Sir John A.—Prime minister of Canada (1867–1873 and
    1878–1891)
Marshall, James W.—Discovered gold at Sutter's Mill, California (1848)
Marshall, John—Supreme Court chief justice
Marshall, Thurgood—Supreme Court justice
Martí, José Julian—Cuban writer and patriot
Matthews, Stanley—Supreme Court justice

Mayer, Louis B.—Film producer (Metro-Goldwyn-Mayer)
Mayo, Dr. William (father) and Charles (son)—Began the Mayo Clinic
Mazzini, Giuseppe—Italian revolutionary and political theorist
McGovern, George—U.S. senator and presidential candidate, 1972
McKinley, William—Twenty-fifth president of the United States (1897–1901)
McLean, John—Supreme Court justice
Menninger, Charles F. (father) and Karl A. (son)—Psychiatrists
Mesmer, Franz Anton—Practiced "Mesmerism," which led to hypnotism
Meyerbeer, Giacomo—Composer
Michelson, Albert Abraham—Successfully measured the speed of light
Minton, Sherman—Supreme Court justice
Mitchell, Edgar D.—Astronaut, sixth person to walk on the Moon
Mix, Tom—U.S. Marshal turned actor, starred in 400 Western films
Monckton, Lionel—Musician
Monge, Gaspard, Comte de Péluse—French mathematician
Monroe, James—Fifth president of the United States (1817–1825)
Montgolfier, Jacques Étienne—Codeveloper of the first hot-air balloon
Moody, William H.—Supreme Court justice
Mozart, Leopold—Father of Wolfgang, concertmaster, violinist, and composer
Mozart, Wolfgang Amadeus—Composer
Murphy, Audie—Most decorated U.S. soldier of World War II and movie star
Naismith, James—Inventor of basketball
Nelson, Samuel—Supreme Court justice
New, Harry S.—Postmaster general who established airmail
Nunn, Sam—U.S. senator
O'Higgins, Bernardo—Chilean leader, served as supreme dictator
Olds, Ransom E.—American automobile pioneer
Otis, James—Famous for "Taxation without Representation is Tyranny"
Palmer, Arnold—Golf professional
Papst, Charles F.—Coined the term "athletes foot"
Paterson, William—Supreme Court justice
Peale, Charles Willson—American painter
Peale, Norman Vincent—American clergyman and author
Peary, Robert Edwin—First man to reach the North Pole (1909)
Penny, James C. (J. C. Penny)—Retailer
Pershing, John J.—Commander of U.S. troops in France during World War I
Pike, Albert—Masonic author of *Morals and Dogma*
Pitney, Mahlon—Supreme Court justice
Poinsett, Joel R.—U.S. minister to Mexico; also developed the Poinsettia
Polk, James Knox—Eleventh president of the United States (1845–1849)
Pope, Alexander—Writer

Potter, Stewart—Supreme Court justice
Pullman, George—Built first railroad sleeping car
Pushkin, Aleksandr—Russian poet
Reagan, Ronald—Fortieth president of the United States (1981–1989)
Reed, Stanley F.—Supreme Court justice
Revere, Paul—American revolutionary
Rhodes, Cecil—Prime minister of Cape Colony (1890)
Richardson, Elliot—Attorney general
Rickenbacker, Eddie—U.S. Army Air Corps ace during World War I and aviation pioneer
Ringling Brothers—Circus operators, seven brothers and father were Masons
Rizal, José—Filipino physician, novelist, and nationalist martyr
Robinson, Sugar Ray—Boxing champion
Rogers, Roy—Western movie star
Rogers, Will—Humorist
Romberg, Sigmund—Composer
Roosevelt, Franklin D.—Thirty-second president of the United States (1933–1945)
Roosevelt, Theodore—Twenty-sixth president of the United States (1901–1909)
Rutledge, Wiley B.—Supreme Court justice
Salten, Felix—Author of *Bambi*
San Martín, José de—Liberator of Peru
Sanders, Harland ("Colonel Sanders")—Founder of Kentucky Fried Chicken
Sarnoff, David—Broadcasting pioneer
Sax, Antoine Joseph—Invented the saxophone (1846)
Schiller, (Johann Christoph) Friedrich von—German poet and dramatist
Schirra, Walter (Wally) Marty, Jr.—Astronaut
Scott, Robert Falcon—English explorer
Scott, Sir Walter—Writer
Scott, Winfield—American general during the Mexican War
Sellers, Peter—Actor
Shackleton, Sir Ernest—English explorer
Sibelius, Jean—Composer
Skelton, Red—Entertainer
Sloane, Sir John—English artist
Smithson, James—British mineralogist and chemist, whose legacy provided for the foundation of the Smithsonian Institution
Sousa, John Philip—Composer, "The March King"
Speaker, Tris—Baseball Hall of Fame (1937)
Spilsbury, Sir Bernard—Pioneering English criminal pathologist
Stafford, Thomas Patten—Astronaut

Stanford, Leland—Railroad tycoon and founder of Stanford University
Steuben, Baron von—Prussian American general during the American
  Revolution
Stevenson, Adlai—U.S. vice president (1893–1897)
Stewart, Potter—Supreme Court justice
Still, Andrew T.—American physician who developed osteopathy
Story, Joseph—Supreme Court justice
Stratton, Charles "Tom Thumb"—Entertainer
Sullivan, Sir Arthur—Composer
Summerall, Charles Pelot—General during World War I
Swayne, Noah H.—Supreme Court justice
Swift, Jonathan—Author of *Gulliver's Travels*
Taft, William Howard—Twenty-seventh president of the United States
  (1909–1913)
Thomas, Danny—Entertainer
Thomas, Dave—Founder of Wendy's restaurants
Thomas, Lowell—Journalist who brought Lawrence of Arabia to public notice
Tinker, Joe—Famed for baseball triple plays ("Tinkers to Evers to Chance")
Tirpitz, Alfred von—German naval officer
Todd, Thomas—Supreme Court justice
Travis, William B.—Died at the Alamo
Trimble, Robert—Supreme Court justice
Truman, Harry S—Thirty-third president of the United States (1945–1953)
Vinson, Frederick M.—Supreme Court chief justice
Voltaire (Francois Marie Arouet)—French writer and philosopher
Wadlow, Robert Pershing—Tallest human on record, almost nine feet tall
Wallace, George C.—Alabama governor and presidential candidate, 1964, 1968,
  1972, 1976
Wallace, Lewis—Civil War general and author of *Ben Hur*
Wanamaker, John—Nineteenth-century American merchant
Warner, Jack—Movie producer and head of Warner Brothers Pictures
Warren, Earl—Supreme Court chief justice
Warren, Joseph—Killed in the Battle of Bunker Hill
Washington, Booker T.—Educator and author
Washington, George—First president of United States (1789–1797)
Watson, Thomas John—Founder of the International Business Machines
  Corporation (IBM)
Wayne, John—Actor
Webb, Matthew—First man to swim the English Channel (1875)
Weitz, Paul J.—Astronaut
Wesley, Samuel—Musician
Whiteman, Paul—Orchestra leader, "King of Jazz"

Wilde, Oscar—Playwright and novelist (*The Picture of Dorian Gray*, 1891)
Wolfitt, Sir Donald—English actor
Woodbury, Levi—Supreme Court justice
Woods, William B.—Supreme Court justice
Wyler, William—Film director
Young, Denton True "Cy"—First Baseball Hall of Fame pitcher
Zanuck, Darryl F.—Film producer and cofounder of 20th Century-Fox
Ziegfeld, Florenz—Theatrical producer

FURTHER READING

Ankerberg, John, and John Weldon. *The Facts of the Masonic Lodge*. Eugene, OR: Harvest House, 1958.

Armitage, Frederick. *A Short Masonic History Being an Account of the Growth of Freemasonry and Some of the Earlier Secret Societies*. 1909. Reprint; Whitefish, MT: Kessinger, 2003.

Baigent, Michael, and Richard Leigh. *Holy Blood, Holy Grail*. London: Jonathan Cape, 1982.

———*The Temple and the Lodge*. London: Jonathan Cape, 1989.

Bennett, John. *Origin of Freemasonry and Knight Templar*. 1907. Reprint, Whitefish, MT: Kessinger, 1997.

Bullock, Steven C. *Revolutionary Brotherhood: Freemasonry and the Transformation of the American Social Order, 1730–1840*. Chapel Hill: University of North Carolina Press, 1988.

Cartwright, E. H. *Masonic Ritual: A Commentary of the Freemasonic Ritual*. London: Lewis Masonic, 1947.

Castells, F. De P. *Antiquity of the Holy Royal Arch*. 1927. Reprint, Whitefish, MT: Kessinger, 2003.

Coil, Henry Wilson. *Coil's Masonic Encyclopedia*. New York: Random House, 1995.

Daynes, Gilbert W. *Birth and Growth of the Grand Lodge of England 1717 to 1926*. Reprint, Whitefish, MT: Kessinger, 2003.

Duncan, Malcolm C. *Duncan's Masonic Ritual and Monitor*. 3rd ed. New York: McKay, 1976.

Gould, Robert Freke. *History of Freemasonry: Its Antiquities, Symbols, Constitutions, Customs, etc*. New York: John C. Yorston, 1886.

———*Military Lodges: The Apron and the Sword of Freemasonry under Arms*. 1899. Reprint, Whitefish, MT: Kessinger, 2003.

Hannah, Walton. *Darkness Visible*. Devon, England: Augustine, 1952.

Harris, Jack. *Freemasonry: The Invisible Cult in Our Midst*. Chattanooga, TN: Global, 1987.

Haywood, H. L. *A History of Freemasonry*. 1927. Reprint, Whitefish, MT: Kessinger, 2003.

Higgins, Frank C. *Apron: Its Traditions, History and Secret Significances*. 1914. Reprint, Whitefish, MT: Kessinger, 1997.

Johnson, Melvin M. *Beginnings of Freemasonry in America*. 1924. Reprint, Whitefish, MT: Kessinger, 1999.

Knight, Stephen. *The Brotherhood: The Secret World of the Freemasons*. London: Panther, 1985.

———*Jack the Ripper: The Final Solution*. Chicago: Academy Chicago, 1986.

Leadbeater, C. W. *Freemasonry and Its Ancient Mystic Rites*. New York: Gramercy, 1986.

Lester, Ralph P. *Look to the East!: A Ritual of the First Three Degrees of Freemasonry*. Whitefish, MT: Kessinger, 1998.

Macbride, A. S. *Speculative Masonry*. 1924. Reprint, Whitefish, MT: Kessinger, 2003.

Mackey, Albert G. *An Encyclopedia of Freemasonry*. Chicago: The Masonic History Company, 1966.

MacNulty, W. Kirk. *Freemasonry: A Journey through Ritual and Symbol*. London: Thames and Hudson, 1991.

Macoy, Robert. *A Dictionary of Freemasonry*. New York: Gramercy, 1989.

Morgan, William. *Illustrations of Masonry by One of the Fraternity Who Has Devoted Thirty Years to the Subject*. Batavia, NY: David C. Miller, 1827.

Morse, Sidney. *Freemasonry in the American Revolution*. Reprint, Whitefish, MT: Kessinger, 1992.

Munn, Sheldon A. *Freemasons at Gettysburg*. Gettysburg, PA: Thomas, 1993.

Newton, Joseph F. *The Degrees and Great Symbols of Masonry*. Whitefish, MT: Kessinger, 1992.

Oliver, George. *Discrepancies of Freemasonry*. 1875. Reprint, Whitefish, MT: Kessinger, 2003.

Peake, T. DeWitt. *Symbolism of King Solomon's Temple*. 1895. Reprint, Whitefish, MT: Kessinger, 2003.

Piatigorsky, Alexander. *Freemasonry: The Phenomenon of Fremasonry*. London: Harill, 2000.

Pike, Albert. *Morals and Dogmas of the Ancient and Accepted Scottish Rite of Freemasonry*. Whitefish, MT: Kessinger, 2002.

————*What Masonry Is and Its Objects: Ancient Ideals in Modern Masonry*. 1919. Reprint, Whitefish, MT: Kessinger, 2003.

Read, Piers Paul. *Templars: The Dramatic History of the Knights Templar, the Most Powerful Military Order of the Crusades*. New York: DaCapo, 2001.

Ridley, Jasper. *The Freemasons: A History of the World's Most Powerful Secret Society*. New York: Arcade, 2001.

Roberts, Allen E. *House Undivided: The Story of Freemasonry and the Civil War*. Fulton, MO: Ovid Bell, 1961.

Robinson, John J. *Born in Blood: The Lost Secrets of Freemasonry*. New York: M. Evans, 1989.

Rumbelow, Donald. *The Complete Jack the Ripper*. London: W. H. Allen, 1975.

Scott, Leader. *Cathedral Builders: The Story of a Great Masonic Guild*. 1899. Reprint, Whitefish, MT: Kessinger, 2003.

Tatsch, J. Hugo. *Facts about George Washington As a Freemason*. 1931. Reprint, Whitefish, MT: Kessinger, 1942.

Waite, Arthur Edward. *A New Encyclopedia of Freemasonry*. New Hyde Park, NY: University, 1970.

Wilmshurst, W. L. *The Meaning of Masonry*. London: Rider, 1927.

INDEX

ABOUT THE AUTHOR

A broadcast journalist for more than three decades, H. Paul Jeffers has published sixty books. Among his nonfiction are histories of Jerusalem, the Federal Bureau of Investigation and Scotland Yard, the Great Depression, the San Francisco earthquake of 1906, *The 100 Greatest Heroes*, *The Good Cigar*, *High Spirits*, *The Perfect Pipe*, and biographies of Theodore Roosevelt, Grover Cleveland, Fiorello La Guardia, Diamond Jim Brady, Theodore Roosevelt Jr., Eddie Rickenbacker, General Billy Mitchell, and movie star Sal Mineo. His fiction includes fourteen detective and mystery novels and five historical Westerns. He lives in New York City.